PRAISE FOR
Beyond Band of Brothers

"Stephen Ambrose's *Band of Brothers* and the HBO miniseries based on it made Easy Company . . . well-known to more than military-history buffs. . . . Feeling that much of the material Ambrose didn't use deserved an audience, [Winters] chose to air it and satisfy all those requests in [this] excellent narrative. . . . Praised as an exemplar of leadership, he shows here what he did to earn that praise and how he did it. Very well done, book as well as war service."
—*Booklist*

"Winters tells the tales left untold by Stephen Ambrose, whose *Band of Brothers* was the inspiration for the HBO miniseries. It is in the battles and tactical maneuvers of Easy Company that Winters is most at home. . . . He carefully explicates the reasoning behind his strategy, leading the reader along as the company attacks German machine gun and mortar outposts. The narrative is laced with Winters's soldierly exaltations of pride in his comrades' bravery [and] the intrepidness of this group."
—*Publishers Weekly*

"There is a saying that 'Great leaders are born, not made.' Such a man is Dick Winters. . . . A beautifully written book about a truly giant leader. This riveting read clearly reflects Dick Winters's solid character, great integrity, and unerring judgment in critical background situations."
—Lieutenant General Harold G. Moore, coauthor of
We Were Soldiers Once . . . and Young

"Its modesty, its candor, and its insights into the nature of frontline leadership and the fears and behaviors of men in combat make this memoir a classic, ranking with Charles MacDonald's *Company Commander*."
—Dennis Showalter, author of *Patton and Rommel:*
Men of War in the Twentieth Century

"Winters's leadership inspired his soldiers to fight courageously under the most difficult and challenging conditions of battle. [An] extraordinary memoir."
—H. R. McMaster, author of *Dereliction of Duty*

"Dick Winters epitomizes the finest attributes of American citizen-soldiers. . . . A poignant, riveting story with timeless application to the study of leadership in war.."
—Colonel Lance Betros, Chairman, Department of History,
U.S. Military Academy, and Editor of *West Point:*
Two Centuries and Beyond

BEYOND BAND OF BROTHERS

Major Dick Winters
with Colonel Cole C. Kingseed

BERKLEY CALIBER, NEW YORK

THE BERKLEY PUBLISHING GROUP
Published by the Penguin Group
Penguin Group (USA) Inc.
375 Hudson Street, New York, New York 10014, USA
Penguin Group (Canada), 90 Eglinton Avenue East, Suite 700, Toronto, Ontario M4P 2Y3, Canada
(a division of Pearson Penguin Canada Inc.)
Penguin Books Ltd., 80 Strand, London WC2R 0RL, England
Penguin Group Ireland, 25 St. Stephen's Green, Dublin 2, Ireland (a division of Penguin Books Ltd.)
Penguin Group (Australia), 250 Camberwell Road, Camberwell, Victoria 3124, Australia
(a division of Pearson Australia Group Pty. Ltd.)
Penguin Books India Pvt. Ltd., 11 Community Centre, Panchsheel Park, New Delhi—110 017, India
Penguin Group (NZ), 67 Apollo Drive, Rosedale, North Shore 0632, New Zealand
(a division of Pearson New Zealand Ltd.)
Penguin Books (South Africa) (Pty.) Ltd., 24 Sturdee Avenue, Rosebank, Johannesburg 2196, South Africa

Penguin Books Ltd., Registered Offices: 80 Strand, London WC2R 0RL, England

The publisher does not have control over and does not assume any responsibility for author or third-party websites or their content.

PRINTING HISTORY
Berkley Caliber hardcover edition / February 2006
Berkley Caliber trade paperback edition / May 2008

Berkley Caliber trade paperback ISBN: 978-0-425-21375-9

The Library of Congress has catalogued the Berkley Caliber hardcover edition as follows:

Winters, Richard D.
    Beyond band of brothers : the war memoirs of Major Dick Winters / by Dick Winters with Cole
C. Kingseed.
        p. cm.
    ISBN 0-425-20813-3
    1. Winters, Richard D. 2. United States. Army. Parachute Infantry Regiment, 506th. Company E—
History. 3. World War, 1939–1945—Personal narratives, American. 4. World War, 1939–1945—
Campaigns—Western Front. 5. World War, 1939–1945—Aerial operations, American. 6. United
States. Army—Biography. 7. Soldiers—United States—Biography. I. Kingseed, Cole C. (Cole
Christian), 1949– II. Title.

D769.348506th.W56 2005
940.54'21'092—dc22   2005048302
[B]

PRINTED IN THE UNITED STATES OF AMERICA

20   19   18   17   16   15   14   13   12

CONTENTS

For
Ethel

Author's Preface

First, this is not a work of fiction. These are true stories that happened in World War II to real people, men I led, and soldiers I fought beside. Even now, I stay in touch with many who are still living these sixty years later.

Stephen Ambrose, in his book, called us a "band of brothers." Yet in the way we took care of each other, protected each other, and laughed and cried together, we really were even closer than blood brothers. We were like twins—what happened to one of us, happened to us all, and we all shared the consequences and the feelings.

After Ambrose finished the book, he wanted to clear his desk, and his floor, for the next book, the big one, *D-Day: The Climactic Battle of World War II*. His way of clearing was to send me a huge box containing all the memories of the men who had contributed for the writing of *Band of Brothers*. My home den thus became the repository for all these memories. It took me a whole winter to sort all the papers and add them to the records that I already had for the men. Ambrose had roughly put them in piles representing the chapters in which he used them, so I had a lot of sorting and reading to do to gather together the memories of each man.

As I read them, I came across so many good stories that for want of space had not been included in the book. I thought then, as I think now, that it was a shame that so many of them had remained "untold." Since the book publication and especially after the HBO miniseries *Band of Brothers,* produced by Tom Hanks and Steven Spielberg, I have been deluged with letters from people with questions, people begging for more stories—both more from me and from the men.

This book is the only way I know to reach all those many people, from all over the world, who have such a thirst to know more. Whether I read people's letters or go out to speak, the cry is always, "Tell us more! Tell us more!" I cannot possibly write or speak to all these people, but one letter writer succinctly summarized the wide appeal of the men with whom I served and the message I wish to convey: "Generals Eisenhower, Patton, and Montgomery, President Roosevelt, and Prime Minister Churchill were giants on a world stage. You and your men were different to me, though. You came from the cities, backgrounds, and places that I came from. You had some of the same problems and situations. Your triumph was one of character more than ability and talent. I do not mean to imply that you or your men lacked talent and ability, but I could identify with your talents and abilities. I will never be able to speak like Churchill or have the ambition of Patton, but I can have the quiet determination of Easy Company. I can be a leader; I can be loyal; I can be a good comrade. These are qualities that you and your men demonstrated under the harshest of conditions. Surely I can do the same in my normal life."

Another young man wrote from England and mentioned that he had no special links to World War II, "no interesting family war stories, no relatives killed in heroic actions." Indeed his attachment to the conflict, however, was strong enough that one night he sat in tears watching the "Band of Brothers" documentary *We Stand Alone To-gether*. Attempting to express his gratitude to the men of Easy Company, he pondered, "What is my attachment to men such as yourself, whom I have never met? Is it respect because you put your own life on the line to ensure younger people like me have the world we live in today? Is it awe that you could live from day to day watching friends being gunned down or blown apart and still get up the next day prepared to face the same horrors? Or perhaps, fascination at how you and your comrades were able to return to relative normality after the war, with the ghosts of the dead watching what you made of the life they were denied?"

Age is creeping up and taking its toll, and as what war correspondent Ernie Pyle called "the old fraternity of war" enmeshes me one final time, I want to honor the men I served with by telling as best I can the "untold stories." Many of these stories are from men who are no longer with us, and I can think of no better legacy for them and their families. Most important, I want to share my personal memories in the hope that my experience will serve as an example for present leaders and those of future generations who must make difficult decisions and put their lives on the line in the preservation of liberty.

Memoirs, by their very nature, are intensely personal. In combat, a soldier can only relate his memories of his field of fire. Consequently, accounts by the enlisted men and noncommissioned officers in general completely ignore the fact that the army does have a chain of command and that the chain of command usually works. Noncommissioned officers usually ignore the fact that the army has lieutenants. On occasion a company commander might be mentioned; on rare occasions, a battalion commander. But most memoirs never mention the existence of a battalion, regimental, or divisional staff. Usually the men seem to communicate only with the regimental commander.

While assembling my thoughts, I have, at all times, tried to avoid being guilty of the above tendencies. My reminiscences are based on a combat diary I maintained and the letters I sent over the course of the war. I have crosschecked the factual records with contemporary operational reports. Although I shared many of these recollections with Stephen Ambrose, these memoirs contain many unpublished sources. It is my earnest hope that these memoirs will assist each of you to find your personal peace and solitude in a turbulent world.

Foreword to the Paperback Edition

Fifty years after World War II, historian Stephen E. Ambrose told the story of Easy Company, 506th Parachute Infantry Regiment, in *Band of Brothers*. A decade later Steven Spielberg and Tom Hanks produced the HBO Emmy Award–winning miniseries of the same name. *Beyond Band of Brothers* serves as the final chapter on Easy Company and their fellow paratroopers. That war continues to cast its long shadow over the men and women who served so that other men and women could live free.

When my memoirs were finally released, I hoped that they would find a receptive audience, but the public response exceeded my wildest expectations. One of the year's pleasant surprises was the success of the book. That it made the *New York Time*'s bestseller list was something I had never expected. I understand that it is being translated into many languages. That so many readers have welcomed a simple soldier's insights into combat is a direct reflection of the sacrifices of the men of

Easy Company, men who were so brave that I still search my soul to find the proper words to describe their heroism and their willingness to sacrifice everything for each other.

In addition to thousands of letters and best wishes from around the world, the city council of Eindhoven, Holland, conferred the Medal of the City of Eindhoven on me and all Allied troops who risked their lives to liberate their homeland. This unique award is testament to the courage and the sacrifice of the men whom I was honored to command. One of my favorite stories was a phone call from a doctor friend who reported that as he was going through customs in Brussels, the customs official noticed he was from Pennsylvania and asked if he knew how he could get in touch with Dick Winters!

It is within this context that I offer *Beyond Band of Brothers* in its paperback edition. The shadows are lengthening for our band of brothers whose deeds are recorded in these pages. Many have since joined their comrades-in-arms who lie under white crosses on both sides of the Atlantic. I am honored to be a small part of their legacy.

In the twilight of my own memory, my thoughts always return to Easy Company, to happier times when a group of young men joined together to fight for freedom and to liberate a world from tyranny. Especially treasured are memories of experiences we shared with family, friends, and the men of Easy Company. None will ever be forgotten. This is our story.

Hang Tough!
Dick Winters

Prologue

The takeoff occurred on schedule, nice and smooth. Usually on these flights, everybody went to sleep, but tonight I forced myself to stay awake so I'd be able to think and react quickly, but those airsick pills seemed to slow down my emotions. Private Hogan tried to get a song going after a while. A few of us joined in, but our singing was soon lost in the roar of the motors. I fell to saying a last prayer. It was a long, hard, sincere prayer that never really ended, for I continued to think and pray the rest of the ride. When we hit the English Channel, it was really a beautiful sight, but I just couldn't appreciate its full beauty at this time.

"Twenty minutes out," came back from the pilot, and our crew chief took off the door. As jumpmaster for my plane, I stood up and hooked up my static line, went to the door, and had a look. I could see the planes in front and behind us in V of V formation, nine abreast. They seemed to fill the air; their power filled the sky. Then I looked at the

English Channel and I could see this vast magnitude of ships of all sizes, steaming in the same direction that we were going—the Normandy peninsula. The ships were filled with men counting on us to pave the way for them. My mind filled with the realization that we were a vital part of the biggest invasion in history, that I was leading men in actual combat for the first time. I prayed that I was up to the challenge.

We passed those two islands offshore (Channel Islands of Guernsey and Jersey); all water, nice formation, no fire yet. Then we were over land. Standing in the door, I could see the antiaircraft fire, and as we approached what turned out to be Ste. Mere-Eglise, I observed a big barn burning, as well as the landing lights that had been set up by the pathfinders. As the Germans illuminated the night with searchlights and antiaircraft fire, the pilots naturally began taking evasive action. We came in too fast and too low. I did not realize it at the time, but the plane carrying Lieutenant Meehan was hit and plunged toward the earth, killing Easy Company's entire headquarters section save myself.

"OK, boys! Stand up and hook up. Best to be ready to jump at any time now, and if we do get hit, we won't be taking it sitting down."

It was 0110 when the red light went on, ten minutes out, and all was quiet. I saw some antiaircraft fire—blue, green, and red tracers coming up to meet us. My emotions were now accelerating at a rapid rate. Gee, the firing seemed to come slowly, they were pretty wild with it. *Look out, they're after us now. Due to the speed of the aircraft, it is no good shooting straight at us, so the Germans start out right for you, but the antiaircraft fire seems to make a curve and falls to the rear. Now they're leading us, coming so close you can hear them crack as they go by. There, they hit our tail. Straight ahead, I can see the lights set up on the jump field. Jesus Christ, there's the green light. We're holding 150 miles per hour and still eight minutes out. OK, let's go— Bill Lee (former commander of the 101st Airborne Division)! There goes my leg bag and every bit of equipment I have. Watch it, boy! Watch it! Jesus Christ, they're trying to pick me up with those machine guns. Slip, slip, try and keep close to that leg bag. There it lands beside*

*that hedge. Goddamn that machine gun. There's a road, trees—hope I
don't hit them.* Thump. *Well that wasn't too bad. Now let's get out of
this chute.*

So I lay on French soil working free from my chute, machine gun
bullets whistling overhead every few minutes, more machine gun tracers going after planes and chutes still coming in. All of us had lost our
leg bags containing most of our weapons in the initial blast when we
exited the plane. Why we were experimenting with leg bags on this
jump when we had never rehearsed with them during training was beyond me. I later discovered that in our small contingent from Easy
Company, we all lost our leg bags and ended up using whatever
weapons we could scrounge from dead troopers. Unfortunately, we had
no idea if these guns were properly zeroed, but there was little time to
worry about anything except survival.

On the outskirts of town (Ste. Mere-Eglise), I saw a large fire,
which turned out to be a downed plane. In the distance, a church bell
tolled out a warning to the countryside that the airborne infantry was
landing. The sound of the bell sent a tingling sensation down my back.
When I landed, the only weapon I had was a trench knife that I had
placed in my boot. I stuck the knife in the ground before I went to work
on my chute. This was a hell of a way to begin a war.

PART ONE

Band of Brothers

From this day to the ending of the world . . .
We in it shall be remembered . . .
We gallant few, we band of brothers.
For he today that sheds his blood with me
Shall be my brother.

WILLIAM SHAKESPEARE, *Henry V*

1
Beginnings

I am still haunted by the names and faces of young men, young airborne troopers who never had the opportunity to return home after the war and begin their lives anew. Like most veterans who have shared the hardship of combat, I live with flashbacks—distant memories of an attack on a battery of German artillery on D-Day, an assault on Carentan, a bayonet attack on a dike in Holland, the cold of Bastogne. The dark memories do not recede; you live with them and they become a part of you. Each man must conquer fear in himself. I have a way of looking at war that I have stuck with in combat and the six decades since the war. I look at those soldiers who were wounded in action as lucky because they often had a ticket to return home. The war was over for them. The rest of us would have to keep on fighting, day in and day out. And if you had a man who was killed, you looked at him and hoped that he had found peace in death. I'm not sure whether they were fortunate or unfortunate to get out of the war so early. So many men died so that others could live. No one understands why.

To find a quiet peace is the dream of every soldier. For some it takes longer than others. In my own experience I have discovered that it is far easier to find quiet than to find peace. True peace must come from within oneself. As my wartime buddies join their fallen comrades at an alarming rate, distant memories resurface. The hard times fade and the flashbacks go back to friendly times, to buddies with whom I shared a unique bond, to men who are my brothers in every sense of the word. I live with these men every day. The emotions remain intense. Here is my story set against the backdrop of war and among the finest collection of men I've ever had the pleasure to know.

I was born in Lancaster County, Pennsylvania, on January 21, 1918, the son of Richard and Edith Winters. At the time of my birth, my family lived in New Holland, a small town near Lancaster. We moved to Ephrata while I was young and then settled in Lancaster when I was eight years old. What I recall most vividly from my youth was that I was scared to death to go to school and of the strangers around me. By the time I attended junior high school, I had finally adjusted to my changing environment and began to exhibit some leadership talent. The school's principal took a liking to me and I became a school crossing guard. I guess this was the first time that I was in a position to exhibit any leadership. Reading and geography were always my favorite subjects. I was an average student academically and enjoyed high school athletics, particularly football, basketball, and wrestling. My dad worked as a foreman for Edison Electric Company. For forty dollars a week, Dad labored tirelessly to provide for his family and to ensure we had the necessities of life. He was a good father, who frequently took me to baseball games in Philadelphia and in the neighboring communities. I had a wonderful mother—very conservative. She came from a Mennonite family, but never converted to that faith. Honesty and discipline were driven into my head from day one. Not surprisingly, Mother was undoubtedly one of the most influential people in my life. A mother takes a child; she nurtures him, she instills discipline, and she teaches respect. My mother was the first one up every morning; she prepared breakfast for my sister Ann and me; and she was the last one to bed every evening. In many respects she was the ideal company commander, and subconsciously, I'm sure I patterned my own leadership abilities on this remarkable woman. In my early days at home, she had always impressed on me to respect women, and my father had repeatedly told me that if I was going to drink, I should drink at home. I made up my mind, however, that I wasn't going to drink, and I have never lost my respect for women.

My early heroes were Babe Ruth and Milton S. Hershey, who had recently established a chocolate empire near Lancaster, Pennsylvania. Every American boy admired Babe Ruth, the most popular ballplayer of his era. As for Hershey, he was not only a shrewd and determined businessman, he was also a great philanthropist. Born in 1857 on a farm in central Pennsylvania, Hershey believed wealth should be used for the benefit of others. He used his chocolate fortune for two major projects: the development of the town of Hershey, Pennsylvania, in 1903 and the establishment of the Hershey Industrial School for orphaned boys in 1909. Now known as the Milton Hershey School, the school's original deed of trust stipulated that "all orphans admitted to the school shall be fed with plain, wholesome food; plainly, neatly, and comfortably clothed; and fitly lodged. . . . The main object is to train young men to useful trades and occupations, so that they can earn their own livelihood." Any man who would dedicate his life to doing something for orphans had to be a good man. I admired Hershey tremendously.

Growing up during the Great Depression was hard, but Lancaster County provided sufficient jobs for most of the residents. Lancaster lies in the heart of Pennsylvania Dutch country, where the residents developed a work ethic that stemmed from our heritage and our religious affiliation to the Mennonite and the Amish backgrounds. This work ethic rubs off and it accounts for the fact that each day, you strive to do your best.

I graduated from Lancaster Boys High School in 1937 and matriculated to Franklin & Marshall College, where I finally buckled down and studied harder than I had ever studied in high school. While going to school, I naturally did a great deal of reading. The subjects ran from poetry and literature to philosophy, ethics, religion, sociology, psychology, and all the other subjects associated with a liberal education. To defray college expenses, I earned money for tuition by cutting grass, working in a grocery store, and in what might have been prophetic of my future career with the paratroopers, painting high-tension towers for Edison Electric Company. Studies, work, and the ever-present lack of funds did not provide much opportunity for running around, but I did have a great deal of time to spend with my inner thoughts and ideas stimulated by reading. In June 1941, I graduated tops in the business school and earned a bachelor's degree in science and economics.

Rather than having the draft interrupt a promising business career, I immediately volunteered for the U.S. Army. Under the Selective Training and Service Act recently enacted by Congress, each man was required to serve one year of military service. It was my intention to serve my time, and then be free of my commitment to the military. My official entry date was August 25, 1941. Though I felt a strong sense of duty, I had no desire to get into the war currently raging in Europe. I preferred to stay out of it, and I was hoping the United States would remain neutral. Volunteering for military service was merely the quickest way to rid myself of compulsory service. I had already decided not to volunteer for anything, to do the minimum work required, and to return home to Lancaster as soon as my year was up. As the day approached for me to join the army, I expressed my intention to just pass my time to my foreman at Edison Electric, who was a former military man. He jumped on me and told me in no uncertain terms to do my best every day and not to become a slacker. In the years ahead, I sent him a note through my father and thanked him for straightening me out.

September found me at Camp Croft, South Carolina, where I underwent basic training. Pay for a private was $21.00 a month, a far cry from what I had been receiving prior to my enlistment. Military life suited me, but my initial months in the U.S. Army were characterized by long periods of boredom punctuated by brief interruptions of spirited activity. When the majority of the battalion deployed to Panama in early December, I remained at Croft to train incoming draftees and volunteers. I still enjoyed reading, but since I had been in the army, I had not been able to enjoy the luxury of the dreams and aspirations that characterized my youth. The army managed to take up a large portion of the twenty-four-hour day, and by the end of each day, my body was half-dead and my brain stopped functioning about the time that Retreat sounded. If anything, my career was aimlessly drifting.

My world changed dramatically the following Sunday when our unit received news of the Japanese attack on Pearl Harbor. I first heard of the attack while on a weekend furlough at the Biltmore Estate outside Asheville, North Carolina. After the initial shock wore off, my next reaction was somewhat selfish as I realized that I was going to be in the army for more than one year. Everyone clearly understood that he was now in service for the duration of the war and that before too long, each of us would deploy to a combat theater of operations. None of us was exactly sure how each was going to be affected, with the exception that all of us had that empty feeling in the bottom of our stomachs that the country had been attacked without provocation. My duties as a trainer changed dramatically now that the nation was at war. Now that the army had a definite purpose, the cadence around camp quickly accelerated. Officers cracked down on us, proclaiming no Christmas furloughs, censoring mail. Everything now went according to wartime law. The changes gave me an eerie feeling at first, but when I looked at it from a different perspective, I did not feel too badly; the sooner we retaliated against Japan, the quicker the war would be over.

In retrospect, the U.S. Army was totally unprepared for the war in which it was about to embark. Two weeks after the Japanese attack, supply sergeants at Camp Croft collected all our gas masks and shipped them to the Pacific Coast in anticipation of a possible Japanese assault on the California coast. I could not help but think that a few insignificant masks—training masks, no less—would not have much effect on the outcome of the war. Before the reality of war totally transformed the army, I hitchhiked home to Lancaster to enjoy a ten-day furlough with my family.

In mid January, the army picked up its pace and rapidly transitioned from a peacetime establishment to a wartime military force. Six-day weeks gave way to seven-day workweeks. This gave me the opportunity to observe some of the officers more carefully. Most of the officers at Camp Croft had come directly from the Reserve Officer Training Corps (ROTC), including my platoon leader. Neither he nor the other platoon leaders knew their jobs. My frustration reached new heights one rainy day when a lieutenant came to teach our platoon about the new M-1 Garand 30-06 semiautomatic rifle, which the army was just fielding. In giving the nomenclature and the operation of the new weapon, he picked up a 1903 Springfield rifle and spent forty-five minutes talking about the M-1. The lieutenant didn't even realize he wasn't holding an M-1. I thought this was impossible as no leader could be this dense.

I knew that I was a better man than most of the officers whom I had met, so I flirted with joining the commissioned ranks. I was already exploring the possibility of attending Officers Candidate School (OCS), when our commanding officer asked me if I would be interested in becoming an officer. I was very fortunate to be selected since at the time I was only a private and most commanders were picking noncommissioned officers (NCO) who were career soldiers and who had considerably more experience than I had. Things proceeded rapidly from that point. After filling out an application, I breezed through another physical examination and went before a board of officers. I had hoped to have a few hours to prepare for the interview, but I was told to report that afternoon. I tried to be as confident as possible and evidently succeeded because I received orders to attend a three-week preparatory course at Camp Croft for officer candidates.

Competition in the course was stiff and I certainly had to work to make the grade, for just about everybody attending the course was at least a sergeant, while I was a temporary corporal. I felt like an innocent babe in the woods when I compared myself to these seasoned NCOs. What I lacked in experience, however, I compensated for by studying. The one advantage I had over the other officer candidates was a college education, and I clearly understood the importance of study and doing my homework.

The course itself was very broad. The directors of the intelligence, communications, and heavy weapons schools delivered comprehensive lectures to the class during the first few days. By the end of three weeks we received a detailed summary about every aspect of the army. Overall I thoroughly enjoyed the preparatory course and enjoyed the opportunity to acquire additional training before reporting to Fort Benning, Georgia. By keeping my nose to the grindstone, I finished the course with flying colors. The only question remaining was to which OCS class I would be assigned. Until I received definitive orders, I remained at Camp Croft.

As I awaited news of my next assignment, I briefly considered an offer to transfer to Fort Knox, Kentucky, to attend OCS as a member of the Armored Corps. Here was a chance to put an end to all the suspense and to get going quickly so I could leave in a few days. After thinking it over and asking the advice of the other officers, I decided against their common advice and decided to stick with the Infantry. I already had seven months of background in the ground service, and the thirteen weeks at Fort Benning would give me a background sturdy enough to enable me to carry my head high. In the Armored Corps, I'd be taking it cold and I was darned if I wanted to be an officer if I couldn't be a good one. On April 6, I received news that I'd be leaving Camp Croft for the class that started the following day.

Fort Benning, nestled in the red hills outside Columbus, Georgia, is a picturesque military post. Benning was an old army camp with modern facilities. Trees lined the wide streets and brick barracks contained modern furniture and reading rooms. Officer candidates were housed in wooden barracks, like at Croft, but the post was far cleaner than what I had experienced. The food wasn't plentiful, but it had a certain quality; in fact, it was nearly as good as home cooking.

The equipment used in the course was complete and the best possible. Every time I'd turn around there was a tank going by, somebody jumping from an airplane or off the jump tower that had been constructed for parachute troops. I was particularly impressed with the paratroopers who ran around Fort Benning at an airborne shuffle. Their cadence reflected a military unit with a high degree of morale and enthusiasm.

Within a few days of looking things over, I planned to ask my parents if they cared if I joined the paratroopers after I received my commission. When I finally announced my intentions, I received a strong veto, and many more from friends and neighbors. I had usually taken my parents' advice, but this time I was determined to trust my own judgment. The more I looked at the paratroopers, the more I was inclined to join them as soon as I graduated from OCS. Of all the outfits I'd seen at Fort Benning, they were the best looking and most physically fit. After ten months of infantry training, I realized my survival would depend on the men around me. Airborne troopers looked like I had always pictured a group of soldiers: hard, lean, bronzed, and tough. When they walked down the street, they appeared to be a proud and cocky bunch exhibiting a tolerant scorn for anyone who was not airborne. So I took it in my head that I'd like to work with a bunch of men of that caliber. The paratroopers were the best soldiers at the infantry school and I wanted to be with the best, not with the sad sacks that I had frequently seen on post.

In addition, the physical training appealed to me: lots of running—five miles before breakfast, and every place they went during the day. The only thing holding me back was my swimming. I was no flash at that angle and it was a requirement to join the paratroopers. Another selling point was the pay of an airborne 2d lieutenant, $268 a month, which wasn't bad while it lasted. Still, I would have to be accepted, as all the paratroopers were volunteers and they were handpicked to join the elite airborne forces. I reckoned that was why they were so damn good. In the event that I was accepted into the paratroopers, it would mean another month at Fort Benning and then on to an advanced airborne school for parachute officers.

The officer candidate course itself proved physically and mentally demanding, but not as difficult as I had anticipated. Officer candidate school in 1942 was a rudimentary course conceptualized by Army Chief of Staff General George C. Marshall and implemented by Brigadier General Omar N. Bradley, the commandant of the Infantry School. Officer candidates attended classes and conducted field exercises six days a week, being off Saturday afternoon and Sunday. Classes focused on the essentials of combat leadership and familiarity on weapons systems, infantry tactics, and general military subjects. Following the ordinary training day, we studied an average of two hours every night. After a few weeks the cadre conducted an evaluation to determine which candidates would probably be the best officers and surprisingly, this old private won over the more seasoned NCOs.

One of the peculiarities of OCS was that the cadre was so strict. For almost eight months at Camp Croft, I had never been gigged for any infraction during daily inspections. In April, however, I was cited for two minor deficiencies during a barracks inspection. That was good compared to the average candidate, who received one almost daily. We had to have our shoes exactly in position, uniforms spaced equidistant on hangers, and the fold in blankets 7 inches instead of 6 inches. The cadre went around with rulers during every inspection. They ran us ragged daily and we studied like fools each and every night. Missing a formation resulted in dismissal from the course. The transportation to and from Columbus was so inadequate that I resigned myself to remain on post and study for three months, to see an occasional movie, and to eat some ice cream.

Classes covered myriad military topics, ranging from demonstrations on the functions of supply to firepower demonstrations on fortifications with tanks and trucks. Each week the officers and noncommissioned officers told us the next week would be the toughest yet, and they always spoke the truth. Within two weeks we had what was supposed to be the toughest test we would have while we were at Benning. The subject was map reading, but after college, the examination seemed like a true-and-false test. I was not worried in the least about studies, but I studied just for my own satisfaction. Marches increased in length and duration and much more time was spent in the field and on the firing ranges. The range demonstration that perked my interest was one that had been designed to fire machine guns over the heads of our own troops and to hit the enemy. We also learned how to aim at one target and hit another, the idea being that you could still score a hit if a smoke screen had been laid to obscure the principal target. Two weeks prior to graduation we completed the weapons portion of the course and I was not sorry, for all I had been thinking about were lugs, cams, operating rods, and gas-operated and recoil-operated firing mechanisms.

After considerable time on the firing ranges, we began tactical training, which I particularly enjoyed because I could use my head once again. During one field problem, we observed a battalion in the attack at a river line as a company of engineers constructed a footbridge, a vehicle bridge, and a ferry under fire, cover of smoke, and fire from airplanes. In retrospect, I characterized the course as a thirteen-week marathon in the Georgia swamps. As the course neared completion, my ambition remained with joining the airborne troopers and the more I learned about the infantry, the more I was sold on the fact that I wanted no part of it. Stories circulated throughout Fort Benning that 50 percent of the infantry either died from disease resulting from living in the filth or from casualties on the front lines. After observing firsthand the life a doughboy lived, I thought a doughboy had to be crazy.

During my time at OCS one of the officer candidates caught my attention. Lewis Nixon was the son of privilege and wealth. Born September 30, 1918, Nixon was the grandson of the last man to design a battleship as an individual. Educated at Yale and the Massachusetts Institute of Technology, "Nix" was far more educated than most of the members of the class. A world traveler, he returned to the family-run Nixon Nitration Works, a converted industry that manufactured cellulose nitrate to be used in tubing for pens, pencils, sheets for playing cards, and covers for eyeglass frames. Nixon entered military service at Fort Dix, New Jersey, and completed basic training at Camp Croft. Nixon was a hard drinker, a free spirit who enjoyed the wild life and partied with the best of them. On the surface no two individuals were more diametrically opposed in temperament than Nixon and I. I was a confirmed teetotaler and never swore. I preferred a quiet evening in the barracks to the nightlife of Columbus, Georgia, or neighboring Phenix City, Alabama. Despite the differences in lifestyle, I sensed we shared mutual feelings and ways of looking at life. I could understand him and help him understand me, as well as understand himself. Our friendship evolved naturally, and he soon became my closest friend. Lewis Nixon was the finest combat officer with whom I served under fire. He was utterly dependable and totally fearless.

As we neared graduation, I found myself not very excited about the prospect of ending this phase of my career. It was the most despondent that I had felt since my last furlough. This time it was a combination of not knowing where or what my next assignment would be and if I would get my next leave. If I was accepted by the paratroopers, I could be ordered to report the day following graduation. If not, it might be sealed orders, which meant no leave, and then proceed directly to a combat theater. The uncertainty was killing me.

Our OCS class graduated on July 2, 1942. My overall impression of the course was that it had been fairly easy, and while it had not been exactly a vacation, I had enjoyed the experience. We now entered a charmed class, a distinct social class within the army. We now commanded respect and authority. It was the dream of every private from the day he enlisted in the army and we were just about to reach out and grasp it. Minor items now seemed more important, such as the purchase of uniforms. Distinctive officer uniforms had been arriving the past few days and our barracks looked like a fashion show with the men parading around, flashing bars, decorations, and smiles. Even the fact that in three days some of us would be heading for combat made no difference. I determined that was the way to be, to live and let live. At times, however, it was hard to convince myself that I was now a commissioned officer.

With graduation, I was honorably discharged from the United States Army at the convenience of the government in order to accept a formal commission of a second lieutenant. Following lunch at the officers club, we were free to go our own way, though few of us had actual assignments. Nixon was assigned duty at Fort Ord, California, and attached to the military police unit on post. With no immediate openings in the paratroopers, I returned to Camp Croft to train another contingent that had recently arrived. As an officer I didn't last long at Croft: about five weeks to be exact, before receiving orders to report to the 506th Parachute Infantry Regiment, at Camp Toombs, Georgia. At first I hated to leave Camp Croft for I was well acquainted with my old outfit and the new company to which I had been recently assigned. I still had four soldiers from home in my platoon, including one with whom I had gone to college and wrestled while in school. None of us let a little brass come between us. Other officers frowned on my relation with the enlisted men, but it didn't bother me at all. I worked darn hard on that platoon and just before I departed, they all qualified on the firing ranges, with the exception of two soldiers. Before I departed Croft, the platoon gave me a Shaffer pen and pencil set as a token of their esteem. Then I left, leaving a camp that held many fond memories.

There Is Nothing Easy in Easy Company

Toccoa, formerly Camp Toombs, was the birthplace of the 506th Parachute Infantry Regiment (PIR). Cut from the Georgian wilderness, the camp was located in the foothills of the Blue Mountains. Camp Toombs had been an old Georgia National Guard Camp prior to its conversion to an airborne training center. Toccoa was the name of the closest town and it soon became the name of the first Parachute Infantry Training Center. Dominating the camp was 1,740 foot Mount Currahee, a Cherokee word that means "stands alone." The 506th PIR to which I was assigned was officially activated on July 20, 1942. Lieutenant Colonel Robert Sink and Major Robert L. Strayer served as the 506th PIR and the 2d Battalion commanders, respectively. They were the first two officers to arrive at Toccoa. Both would be soon promoted and played important roles in the destiny of Easy Company as well as my own military career.

Sink was a 1927 West Point graduate who would command the

506th through the entire war. A no-nonsense officer, he kept a tight reign on his command and insisted that there would never be a breach of discipline. Strayer was a reserve officer who entered active duty in July 1940. He later commanded a company in the 502d PIR before attending the infantry officer school at Fort Benning in May 1942. As a major, he served as Sink's principal staff officer until he assumed command of 2d Battalion, 506th PIR in September 1942. Major Strayer was promoted to lieutenant colonel in early 1943. His battalion consisted of a Battalion Headquarters Company and Dog, Easy, and Fox Companies. The headquarters company was comprised of a communications platoon, a light machine gun platoon, an 81mm mortar platoon, and the battalion surgeon and his staff.

Following a brief leave, I arrived in Toccoa in mid-August. Disembarking from the Southern Railway train adjacent to the Toccoa Coffin Factory, Lewis Nixon and I were directed to board an army truck for "Camp Toombs." As soon as we arrived at camp, we were ushered into 506th Regimental Headquarters, where we reported to Colonel Sink. He welcomed us to the airborne and informed us that the 506th was an experimental outfit—the first regiment to train civilian recruits into an elite airborne unit. Sink made it clear that he intended that the 506th PIR was going to be the "best damned unit" in the U.S. Army. I had always prided myself in my ability to judge character, and Colonel Sink was truly inspirational. When I first met Sink, I was in awe. He was sitting behind his desk, smoking a cigarette. He came across as having this West Point "better than thou" attitude, which I had always found disconcerting, but I learned pretty quickly that my first impression was wrong. Colonel Sink was an exceptionally competent officer who issued a personal challenge to every incoming officer—he expected officers to set the example and to lead from the front in everything that we did.

I was assigned to Easy Company, 2d Battalion, 506th PIR. When Easy Company formed in July 1942, it listed 8 officers and 132 enlisted men in its table of organization and equipment. The company included three rifle platoons and a headquarters section. Each platoon contained three twelve-man rifle squads and a six-man mortar team squad. Easy also had one machine gun attached to each of its rifle squads, and a 60mm mortar in each mortar team. First Lieutenant Herbert M. Sobel of Chicago, Illinois, was the first member of E Company and its commanding officer. His executive officer was 2d Lieutenant Clarence Hester. Two officers were assigned to each platoon as a safeguard for anticipated casualties and the continued expansion of the U.S. Army. Most were newly commissioned from OCS or from the ROTC contingents from various universities across the country. In addition to me as second platoon leader, Lewis Nixon, Walter Moore, and S. L. Matheson formed the initial contingent of E Company officers. Lieutenants Matheson and Moore commanded 1st and 3d Platoons, respectively.

As had Colonel Sink, Lieutenant Sobel made it crystal clear that he would tolerate no breach of discipline in Easy Company. Sobel informed the officers that Easy Company would be the first and the best in everything it did. He expected Easy to lead the 506th PIR in every measurable category, including calisthenics, road marching, marksmanship, physical fitness, and field training. Sobel intended that Easy Company would be ready when it entered combat. In the interim, he would train the company to a high degree of physical and mental readiness. In contrast to the regimental commander, Lieutenant Sobel did not impress me as a field soldier, but he was the commander and I was determined to do my part to make my platoon the best in the company.

My first day at Toccoa was a shock. I had been in the army for over a year, but all my experience had been at more established military posts like Camp Croft and Fort Benning. All of a sudden, I felt I was back at basic training. Officers' quarters consisted of tar-paper huts, two officers to a hut. Our quarters had no doors, no windows, and no electric lights since the camp was still being constructed. The only electric lights were in the latrine. It was pretty rough, but you expected to have it rough if you were going to be a paratrooper. As I sat there that first night, the mosquitoes ate me alive. I learned a valuable lesson that nothing is ever guaranteed. However, you adjust; you get used to the little things and hope for the best.

Few of the original members of Easy Company survived Toccoa. According to statistics compiled by Lieutenant Salve M. Matheson, an Easy Company platoon leader who eventually moved to battalion and regimental staff, it took over 400 officer volunteers to form the 148 survivors who made it through the following thirteen weeks of training. From over 5,300 enlisted volunteers, 1,800 were selected to continue with the 506th when it deployed to Fort Benning for jump school. You could quit anytime you wanted to. All you had to do was walk down the hill to headquarters and say, "I don't want this." I made up my mind to stick around because I wanted to be with the best. Fortunately I was in prime physical condition and had no problem with the physical aspect of our training. When I joined Easy Company at Toccoa, I stood 6 feet tall and weighed 177 pounds.

Formed into companies, the training began in earnest as officers and men adjusted to military life. The training program was designed to last thirteen weeks. The majority of the initial weeks consisted in getting the men in good physical condition. Since most of the men had just recently entered military service, they were in terrible shape. Daily calisthenics included chin-ups, sit-ups, deep knee bends, jumping jacks, and running. Surprisingly by the end of the first week, the men began responding to the physical demands for airborne troopers. Those who didn't adjust were reassigned from the regiment. Colonel Sink demanded that physical conditioning remain intense—pushing each trooper to the point of exhaustion. Everything was done at double time, including a six-mile run up and down Currahee. Daily obstacle courses, calisthenics, endless hours of physical training, nine-mile marches with and without field packs, bayonets, rifles, and machine guns became the norm. And the training never let up. Private Robert T. Smith noted that the training became more rugged with each passing day. He mentioned the obstacle course that included "all kind of contraptions designed to exercise every muscle in your body."

All enlisted men at Toccoa arrived directly from civilian life for their initial "boot camp" training. Their motivation revolved around additional pay for airborne duty and a desire to be associated with "the best." The 506th was the first unit to have the authority to do this and to keep only those it wished and to send the rest to other army units. That included officers, noncommissioned officers, and soldiers alike. Those who were unable to meet the rigorous standards of airborne troopers were assigned to "W Company" and rapidly assigned to other commands. W Company was a special unit established for incoming troops as well as outgoing troops who failed physicals or who "washed out" during training. Men reached camp in small groups almost daily, and after a much more thorough physical evaluation than they had at their reception centers, they were assigned to one of the units within the 506th PIR. Troopers slept in tents until the army built enough hutments. Officers were initially quartered in unfinished huts with no lights, mud galore when it rained, and so cool every night so that we needed two blankets.

Periodic runs up and down Currahee required the men be in tiptop condition. Rising above the camp's parade ground, Currahee was an imposing sight. Three miles up and three miles down, three or four times a week formed an integral part of our physical conditioning. The run was wicked, a real killer. To move a company up Currahee, you led the company at an airborne shuffle, then, as you felt the ranks falling apart due to stress, you cut the pace back to "quick-time" march. After the ranks closed again, and the troops were breathing normally, you went back to the double-time shuffle. The last mile up Currahee was done more at quick-time than at double-time. In a free-run competition to the summit of Currahee and back to camp, I can't remember anyone who could "run" up Currahee. The record for a round trip up and down Currahee was forty-two minutes; my personal best time was forty-four minutes. I was strictly no runner, just did it by plugging along.

On the days Easy Company did not run up Currahee, Lieutenant

Sobel ordered us to negotiate the obstacle course. As with most of the physical training, the obstacle course was a timed exercise, with each soldier required to complete the course in three minutes. Some of the men never completed the course in three minutes and they were subsequently dropped from the 506th. The obstacles themselves were numerous and varied, but each required a certain degree of dexterity and strength—all designed to build the muscle strength necessary for manipulating parachutes and facing prolonged combat. Arm strength was enhanced by means of crossing a thirty-foot body of water by way of a horizontal ladder that had to be negotiated hand over hand. One particular obstacle that led to many dismissals from the company was a ten-foot-high log wall that had to be climbed without assistance from other members of the company. One officer attempted to catch his breath and to hide behind the wall until the next company came through. He then joined the next company as they passed through. Needless to say, he did not remain at Toccoa for long. Between individual obstacles were hills that had to be run, ditches that had to be crossed, and trenches that had to be jumped. By the time one finished the course, he was physically exhausted. As the weeks wore on, negotiating the obstacle became routine as the individual endurance of each soldier improved dramatically.

To say training at Toccoa was intense is an understatement. Colonel Sink insisted on extremely high standards. Since all personnel were handpicked and could easily be replaced, Sink was determined to create the most elite and best-trained unit in the U.S. Army. Within a week, each company in the regiment became proficient in close order drill, marching back and forth and practicing the manual of arms with our individual weapons. From my experience at Camp Croft and from OCS, close order drill became a pleasant distraction from the more rigorous training. Physical conditioning under realistic conditions proved more demanding. Ten-mile hikes gave way to twenty-five miles through the Georgia countryside. The first night march we made was eleven miles long. Lieutenant Sobel demanded that these endurance tests be accompanied by water discipline: no soldier was allowed to take a sip of water from his canteen until the march was over. In addition to field marches, Regular Army noncommissioned officers delivered lectures on weapons, tactics, and parachute training. One of the things that took some getting used to was bayonet training. The first time you went through the drill, it made you think. The thought of sticking a bayonet into a man was not something you took lightly. I had done a bit of wrestling before, so the thought of unarmed combat did not unsettle me, but the thought of thrusting a steel bayonet into someone—that took some adjustment.

Toccoa also contained mock thirty-four-foot jump towers from which eager troopers developed the necessary skills of jumping, guiding parachutes, and landing. The only thing missing from an actual jump was the absence of the prop blast when exiting the aircraft. After climbing the tower, each trooper was strapped into a parachute harness that was connected to a fifteen-foot strap, or static line. The strap, in turn, was attached to a pulley that rode a cable about sixty feet long to the ground, at which point the soldier landed hard. It was incumbent on the paratrooper to position his body properly when leaving the mock-up door and to develop the proper form and to concentrate on the basic fundamentals of the jump in order to escape injury when he landed. Another training station included the suspended harness, in which troopers were suspended from a device that resulted in various parts of the male anatomy being crunched and pulled in every direction. In the suspended harness, each of us practiced the five points of performance—check body position and count "one one thousand, two one thousand, three one thousand;" check your canopy and your initial oscillation; get your back to the wind; prepare to land; and land.

Training remained demanding throughout our stay at Toccoa. Through thirteen weeks of field training, we experienced the summer heat and red dust so characteristic of western Georgia. Training continued day and night, regardless of weather conditions. Some of the men became demoralized at the pace and the intensity of training. Endless field marches, overnight training exercises in the worst imaginable weather, and exposure to the elements sapped the strength of the faint-hearted. Nor were weekends free, since Saturday mornings were more often than not devoted to inspections of equipment, rifles, barracks, and clothing. Few survived recently promoted Captain Sobel's inspections without incurring some deficiencies. Those who failed the inspections—and in Easy Company most troopers failed—had their weekend passes revoked and were subjected to another run up Currahee.

As the training progressed, leaders honed Easy into a well-disciplined unit within an extraordinarily cohesive regiment. Most of the credit belonged to Colonel Sink, Major Strayer, Captain Sobel, and my fellow platoon leaders. Easy Company met every challenge, exceeded every requirement, as both Sink and Sobel demanded that each company meet the exacting standards that they had established. Those troopers who could no longer bear the strain that our commanders subjected Easy Company were rapidly shipped out. The survivors merely endured.

In early fall, the riflemen in the company traveled to South Carolina and bivouacked and slept in pup tents near Clemson University, where they qualified on the university rifle ranges. Machine gunners remained at Toccoa where they slept in their own barracks and ate in their own mess halls. Lieutenant Salve Matheson ran the machine gun ranges and proved himself an incredible instructor. Both groups spent a full week on the ranges. Every soldier was required to become intimately familiar with each of the company's weapons, ranging from the M-1 Garand rifle to the .45-caliber pistol to the 60mm mortar. Additional training focused on the assembly and disassembly of light machine guns. When inclement weather confined us to the barracks, map and compass reading became the order of the day.

One of the reasons that Easy Company excelled was undoubtedly Captain Sobel. Born in Chicago in 1912, Sobel graduated from Culver Military Academy and became a reserve officer upon his graduation from the University of Illinois. He arrived at the 506th from Fort Riley,

Kansas, where he had been serving as a military police officer. Historian Stephen Ambrose describes Sobel as a "petty tyrant who exuded arrogance." Ambrose wasn't far from the mark. Placed in a position of absolute power analogous to the captain of a ship, Sobel was a strict disciplinarian who ruled Easy Company with an iron fist. To officers and soldiers alike, Sobel became known as the "Black Swan," which soon evolved into "Herr Black Swan" due to his tyrannical methods of command. As company commander, he tolerated no breach of discipline or loyalty, either real or imagined.

I have always felt that for the eyes of the enlisted men, a junior company officer should try to be a reflection of his company commander. Easy Company's junior officers found they simply could not emulate the image of Sobel and live with themselves. Sobel was not just unfair; he was plain mean. As time went by and the pressure shifted from the training of the citizen soldiers to the proving and testing of the leadership in the company, Sobel started to wilt and his disposition grew increasingly impossible. In a bad mood he could go down a line of men during an inspection and find five or six dirty stacking swivels or weapon slings in a row. Then he might switch to finding three or four soldiers with "dirty ears." A man could not pass inspection if Sobel had a grudge against him, and it seemed that our company commander held many grudges.

Every soldier who served in Easy has his share of Sobel stories, many of which are recounted in Ambrose's *Band of Brothers*. Private First Class Burt Christenson recounted his initial meeting with Sobel, which was not unlike my own. Reporting to the commander's office, Christenson recalled that Sobel said: "Each man in this company will learn the importance of discipline and practice it or he won't remain in this unit for long. If you don't complete your assignments or pass inspections, you'll receive company punishment. If you continue to fail to accomplish what I consider is your duty, you'll be disqualified from the parachute infantry." Never an admirer of his company commander, Christenson remembered one incident when Sobel viciously humiliated a soldier whose principal crime was nothing more than it was his turn to be the object of the company commander's scorn. Once during a routine inspection, Sobel was standing in front of Private First Class (PFC) William Dukeman, a model soldier. Dukeman was a strapping six-foot, one inch, well-built trooper. His uniform was always immaculate. Yet Sobel stood there and continued to scrutinize Dukeman. Then suddenly Sobel thrust his face within inches of Dukeman's face and in a normal tone asked, "What size shirt do you wear, soldier?"

Dukeman replied, "Size 15, sir!"

With a scowl on his face, Sobel shouted, "G—damn it, I can put two fingers between your neck and your shirt!"

Dukeman merely responded, "Yes, sir," as Sobel quickly moved to the next man and found similar fault with him.

Yet even Sobel had to chuckle about some of the men's antics on furlough or on weekend passes. Take Private Wayne "Skinny" Sisk, one of the first soldiers to join Easy Company. To win over the girls in the 1940s, Sisk used his smile, wit, and the glamour of being a paratrooper. On one occasion the military police arrested "Skinny" on a Saturday afternoon for making out with his girlfriend along the railroad tracks. When asked by Sobel to explain his conduct, Sisk replied, "The train was coming, she was coming, and so was I."

Suffice it to say Herbert Sobel was a complex and volatile officer, difficult to serve over, impossible to serve under. For those of us who served in the company, he treated us with equal disdain, officers and enlisted men alike. His constant raving that "The Japs are going to get you," and his "Hi-Yo Silver," led to widespread snickering behind his back. Never comfortable in a tactical environment, our commander could not read a map, was constantly lost, and tended to panic when confronted with an unexpected situation. As a result, Captain Sobel rapidly lost the respect of the men. The men did what he ordered because they wanted those wings. Yet they never respected him. If he could not lead men on a hike or on a military maneuver, how could he lead Easy Company in combat? His inability to lead by example or remain calm in a crisis soon became questions that permeated the entire company.

Despite his personal shortcomings, Sobel drove each member of the company to become an elite soldier capable of taking the war to Hitler's Germany. In that sense, Herbert Maxwell Sobel "made" Easy Company by producing a combat company that acted with a single-minded purpose. Carwood Lipton, who would later receive a battle-field commission in Europe, noted that Easy Company was very similar to the groups of men in every company in Sink's 506th save one. Yet there was a difference because Easy coalesced to protect itself against Sobel. In that way, Easy ended up a different way than Sobel intended. Sobel drove us hard and he continued driving us when other companies had already fallen out and gone to the showers. While the other commands within the 506th were getting the hot showers and the early food, we were still out there working, taking an additional lap around the track, and standing at attention to see if anybody was moving. Soon other companies knew of Captain Sobel, including the officers throughout the regiment. No one envied us, but Sobel was producing a magnificent company. Having said that, I would be remiss to disregard the contributions of Easy's first batch of noncommissioned officers who emerged from the ranks: the Carwood Liptons, Joe Toyes, Bill Guarneres, Floyd Talberts, and others.

In Sobel's defense, he was equally demanding on himself. Charged with converting "civilians" into an effective fighting force in a relatively short time, he permitted himself few luxuries. Shortly after he assumed command of the battalion, Major Strayer remembered one instance when he disciplined the company commanders for not showing up on time for staff meetings. To demonstrate his point, he confined the company commanders to the camp area for an entire weekend. Their wives raised holy hell. Sobel was the only company commanding officer who was always on time and did as he was instructed, therefore he was not penalized. To his credit he also stood up for his men to higher headquarters. Prior to Easy Company's movement to the port of embarkation, our battalion commander had the authority to leave any officer behind whom he felt was unsuitable for deployment. When Sobel heard Major Strayer was going to drop one of his officers from the manifest, he went to battalion headquarters and made such a spirited defense that Strayer agreed to keep the officer in the unit and actually pulled him to battalion staff in order to keep him away from troops.

What bothered Easy Company's officers, me included, was not Sobel's emphasis on strict discipline, but his desire to lead by fear rather than example. Each evening he quizzed us on our field manual assignments, which he gave us daily. In his critiques, Sobel was very domineering. There was no give and take. His tone of voice was high-pitched, rasplike. He shouted rather than spoke in a normal way. It just irritated us to no end. Iron discipline the officers could tolerate, but armed with the ultimate authority to dismiss any man in the company, Sobel exceeded the boundaries of acceptable conduct in dealing with citizen-soldiers. If infractions of discipline were not found during inspections, he manufactured deficiencies to prove a point or to emphasize his authority as company commander. To the individual soldiers, Sobel's propensity to find fault was pure chickenshit, so-named by former infantryman and noted author Paul Fussell because "it is small-minded and ignoble and takes the trivial seriously."

At other times, our commander deliberately embarrassed the platoon leaders in front of their men. Not surprisingly, Sobel rapidly emerged as the central target of hate and scorn within Easy Company. One officer summed up our collective appraisal by stating that Sobel was dedicated to doing everything by the book, but he seemed to possess tunnel vision. He could not, or would not, see or anticipate the results of his disciplinary measures on the men. As a result Easy Company gave their loyalty and devotion to their platoon leaders, who in turn took care of their men the best they could and who softened Sobel's dictatorial behavior. Several troopers, including Richard "Red" Wright, Terrence "Salty" Harris, and Lieutenant Walter Moore, however, sought an escape from Sobel's wrath and they volunteered for the pathfinders.

Any relationship between company commander and company officers that existed in Easy Company remained strictly professional. Captain Sobel had no friends within the company and few within the regiment. At the end of the day, he went one way, and we officers went the other, hoping not to run into him at the officers' club. As training progressed through the first half of 1943, Sobel's tactical ineptitude, coupled with his increasing paranoid behavior as our overseas deployment neared, led to the total loss of any confidence that remained in his leadership. So traumatic was my own relationship with Captain Sobel that sixty years after the war, it's still painful remembering my initial meeting with him.

Why then was Captain Sobel retained in command by Colonel Sink and Major Strayer? I suspect the answer lies in Easy Company's performance vis-à-vis the other companies within the regiment. Sobel's hard hand, for better or worse, resulted in a well-disciplined and physically conditioned airborne company. Senior officers tolerated Sobel's erratic behavior because he produced the desired results. One indicator of Easy Company's success within the 506th was reflected in the number of company officers who were pulled up to battalion and regimental headquarters. Senior commanders only assign the most talented officers to headquarters staffs. Colonel Sink and Major Strayer were no exception. Within the first eight months of the company's existence, Lieutenants Matheson, Lavenson, Nixon, and Hester were all reassigned to 2d Battalion staff. Hester, Matheson, and Nixon remained on Strayer's staff until Colonel Sink advanced them to regimental staff. For Matheson, the call to regiment occurred before D-Day. Hester was transferred to 3d Battalion in Holland, while Nixon joined regimental staff during Bastogne. Lavenson was severely wounded outside Carentan. For the remainder of the war, every vacancy in battalion staff was filled by an officer from Easy Company. For that, Sobel deserved a portion of the credit. He was a satisfactory training officer, but he was definitely not a leader of troops. I suspect he did his best, but he was in the wrong job and that was hardly his fault. Having grown up in urban Chicago, he was ill-suited for the outdoor life required for the leader of an elite infantry unit. Nor was he cut out for the field grade officer. Better suited for administrative duties, Sobel stayed in Easy Company until imminent combat conditions dictated his reassignment—but that was all in the future.

Interpersonal relationships and command problems aside, training at Toccoa remained as demanding as ever. After several weeks of intense physical training, Colonel Sink lined up a C-47 Dakota aircraft to qualify his officers before the bulk of the troops arrived for basic infantry training. The airstrip at Camp Toccoa had been constructed by leveling the top of "Dick's Hill," a medium-sized hill that the Le Tourneau Earth-Moving Company had lopped off about halfway up and flattened for an airstrip. The landing strip was very short and built to take care of Piper Cubs, not Army C-47s. The length of the runway required that a C-47, in taking off with a load of jumpers, could just barely get airborne by the end of the strip. To reach flying speed, the pilot had to dive the plane parallel to the downward slope of the mountain. That was a real thrill. To land the plane, the pilot could not stop while going in a straight line, so, as he came near the edge of the mountain, he had to turn left or right, as the wing of the plane extended over the edge of the slope. It was much safer to jump from the plane than to land in it.

To determine who would serve as jumpmaster of the first contingent of officers, Sink conducted a "Junior Olympics." The competition consisted of the best time up and down Currahee, most push-ups, most chin-ups, and the best time through the obstacle course. First Lieutenant Wally Moore was the only man to beat me on that run up Currahee when my legs cramped. I won the overall competition, however, and was rewarded by becoming number one jumper in the first stick to jump at Toccoa. As the aircraft climbed to 1,000 feet, it circled over the drop zone and decelerated to around ninety miles per hour. A Regular

Army sergeant instructed us to "stand up and hook up." Hooking my static line to the anchor cable, I placed my left foot on the edge of the open door. Gazing down to the drop zone, I looked over the cornfields below and placed both hands on the outside edge of the plane. The green light came on and the sergeant yelled, "Go!"

Out I stepped into thin air and the inexorable force of nature took over as gravity carried me downward. It was an exhilarating feeling, but I experienced no sensation of falling. On my initial jump, I almost caught my chute in the high-tension line running through the cornfield that was also our landing field. Having landed safely, I was back up with the other officers until we all made five jumps by evening. We were now airborne qualified and could "blouse our boots," the traditional mark of an airborne soldier. Colonel Sink ran three or four groups of officers through this system of qualification before the plane had an accident while landing on the field. He determined that this method of qualification was too dangerous, so the remainder of the regiment qualified at Fort Benning. That night the officers congregated at the officers' club to celebrate our newly acquired status as airborne officers. The liquor flowed freely and I received my share of good-natured ribbing because I was a teetotaler.

Every soldier who endures basic training emerges with stories that evolve with passing years. Both Sink and Strayer developed innovative training programs to bolster our morale and to foster unit cohesion. Before the regiment left Toccoa, Colonel Sink directed that a final physical test be conducted to eliminate unsuitable men from the regiment. Companies were rotated through the testing center, with noncommissioned officers from other battalions judging the individual stations. One of the men, Burt Christenson, remembered that the day before the test, Easy Company was primed and ready, confident that the men were now in the best physical conditioning of their young lives. On the day of the test, we began with the obstacle course. Each soldier received ten points if he successfully negotiated the course in three minutes. For every three seconds under three minutes, he earned an extra point.

From the obstacle course, Easy Company marched to the push-up area, where each trooper was required to do thirty push-ups for ten points. For each additional push-up, another point was awarded to the contestant. Many members of the company had placed wagers on Captain Sobel's inability to do thirty push-ups, but he successfully passed this station. Next up was the standing broad jump, also worth ten points with additional points for additional distance.

Sink's decathlon continued with the pull-up station, where each trooper had to do six overhand pull-ups to the chin from a hanging position using a horizontal bar. The next event was to run at a ten-foot wall, leap up to catch the top of it, and then pull oneself over for ten points. This was followed by a duck-walk for fifty yards in thirty-five seconds, a feat that was far more difficult than it sounds. The 100-yard dash was next over a field where the green grass was about four inches high. To obtain the required ten points, you had to cover the ground in thirteen seconds, not too hard except by this point each member of the company was near exhaustion. The final event was the one mile run over a half-mile course. When a soldier reached the turnaround point, he shouted his name and received his time. If you completed the mile in six minutes, you received ten points and another ten points if you made the half-mile in three minutes. The men who received the highest scores in Easy Company in the physical competition were Burt Christenson, Gordon Carson, George Rainer, Carwood Lipton, and Robert Van Klinken. Their collective reward included bragging rights in the company and the opportunity to represent the company in the battalion competition the following day.

Much has also been written about the "Hog and Innards Problem" over Thanksgiving. This sounds gross, but it actually wasn't that bad. The setup for the exercise consisted of stringing barbed wire on top of stakes about eighteen inches high. This ended up being like a net, covering an area approximately twenty feet wide and fifty to sixty feet long. The ground was covered with hog entrails—hearts, livers, intestines, the works. And then, to make sure you kept your head and butt down, two .30-caliber light machine guns were set up to fire live ammunition over the top of the barbed wire. The barrels of the machine guns rested on 2" x 4" supports and the legs of the tripods were sandbagged down. For a basic infantry training exercise, this resembled a real combat atmosphere. We had a real incentive to keep our heads and butts down in the hog guts. I thought it was an excellent exercise, and it's one everyone remembered.

The most grueling exercise Easy Company endured during our time at Toccoa was the field march to Atlanta, a distance of 118 miles, during the period December 1 to December 4, 1942. Some reports say the march was 112 miles, others 115 miles. Who cares? It was a killer! Prior to deploying the regiment to Fort Benning, Colonel Sink had discovered a newspaper article that said the Japanese had conducted a forced march of 100 miles in seventy-two hours down the Malayan Peninsula. Determined to demonstrate that his men could better the Japanese mark, Sink selected 2d Battalion to prove his point while 1st Battalion traveled to Columbus, Georgia, by train and 3d Battalion marched directly to Fort Benning from Atlanta to begin airborne training. Lieutenant Sal Matheson, who had joined battalion staff as adjutant, laid out the course for Major Strayer. The march was conducted during unusually severe weather conditions with full field equipment less rolls. Private First Class Smith remembered that the march started out with the assumption that the battalion had landed in hostile territory and had only its regular war rations and equipment. Approximately 100 miles of the march was made over rough and muddy roads, with temperatures dipping below freezing every day. Of the 586 men who initiated the march, only twelve failed to complete the journey. The elapsed time to complete the entire exercise was seventy-five hours and fifteen minutes according to the battalion's letter of commendation, with the actual marching time of thirty-three hours and thirty minutes.

Seven miles outside the gates of Camp Toccoa, a cold winter rain turned to snow as the battalion began its trek toward Atlanta. The first day out, we covered forty-four miles, followed by forty miles on the second day. My worst memory was the morning of the third day. It had been raining the entire preceding day so that when we camped late that night, we were in mud to the tops of our boots. When we lay down to sleep, we were in the mud. I took my boots off and put them by my head in the mud. During the night the temperature dropped dramatically and the mud froze, so when I awoke, the sleeping bag was frozen in the mud and I was stiff and sore all over. But the worst part was that my boots were frozen stiff and I could hardly get them on, even with the laces loosened all the way. The lesson I learned that morning, and I've never forgotten, was to always get your boots or shoes nice and wide and a little on the long side. Your feet always swell under severe stress.

PFC Robert T. Smith described the field march as "the most miserable experience" he ever had. By the end of the hike, Smith's knees and ankles were so swollen that he could hardly walk for three days afterward. Another of Easy Company's men, Gordon Carson, remembered that those four days were the worst four days he had ever spent. Beginning on Tuesday at 7:30 A.M., the company marched in the cold and rain through the mud and rain in the Georgia back hills. We stopped to eat at 12:15 P.M. and resumed the march an hour later, not stopping until we reached the bivouac area at 8:45 P.M. The wind was so high the men couldn't keep their fires going. Tuesday night, said Carson, "was the most uncomfortable night I ever spent in my life." Tuesday, Carson was never colder; Wednesday, he was never more tired. I vividly recall seeing Floyd Talbert, one of our best soldiers, slugging along with his machine gun. I can still see the determination on Talbert's face. Later we developed a personal friendship that transcended rank. Talbert was athletic and dedicated. You knew if your life were on the line, he would come through. Another of my 2d Platoon troopers, DeWitt Lowery, not only carried his light machine gun, but also the company's faithful mascot, "Currahee," in his backpack. Second Battalion had adopted Currahee shortly after the majority of troopers had arrived at Toccoa. He stayed with Easy Company long enough to see all the qualified paratroopers receive their hard-earned wings on graduation day.

Dog and Fox Companies shared equally in Easy's hardships. Private First Class Leonard Hicks of Fox Company remembered the freezing rain that drenched everything and everyone the first day out. As his pain increased, he began hallucinating, claiming that at one point he saw two or three Johnny Rebs watching the battalion as they trudged through the Georgian woods. The miserable weather also affected Fox Company's 1st Sergeant Willie Morris, whose usual enthusiasm was waning as the day progressed. Aided by his buddies, Private Hicks and the remainder of 2d Battalion reached the campus of Oglethorpe University on the evening of the third day.

After "cursing everything the Lord created," the battalion finally reached Atlanta after an overnight halt at the Oglethorpe campus. It was reported that Lieutenant Colonel Robert L. Wolverton, the commanding officer of 3d Battalion and who would later be killed on D-Day, finished his hike in his stocking feet. By now our march was the subject of every newspaper and radio broadcast. Lieutenant Wally Moore's 3d Platoon of Easy Company crossed the finish line with every man crossing the line unaided, so he led the company parade down Peachtree Street to Five Points in the center of Atlanta. The other platoons objected that Moore had violated the "rules of engagement" by having his men remove the barrels of their machine guns for the hike, but 3d Platoon captured photographic honors anyway. The mayor of Atlanta and other dignitaries greeted us and presented the battalion with a key to the city. Following ceremonies at Five Points, we then marched to the train station, only too eager to board the train for the ride to Columbus.

As I look back on the officers and men who served in Easy Company during the war, my thoughts always return to the corps of soldiers who survived Toccoa. To this day I keep a list of the Toccoa men by my desk and I look at it every day. Every trooper who joined Easy Company after Toccoa was a replacement. Many of them made fine soldiers, but they were replacements. Toccoa men are special, and they are always the guys I remember first.

From Benning to Shanks

The period from our arrival at Fort Benning until our deployment to England was characterized by intense training designed to prepare Easy Company for movement to a combat theater of operations. The 1st Battalion of the 506th PIR preceded our battalion to Fort Benning since we spent three days "marching to Atlanta." We were followed by 3d Battalion, which conducted a forced march from Atlanta to Fort Benning. Arriving back at Benning, I recalled the weeks spent in OCS. Not much had changed except the number of soldiers on post and the hectic activity that enveloped the post. Like all companies in the regiment, Easy Company was scheduled to undergo four weeks of airborne training, culminating in jump week, where those soldiers who had not qualified at Toccoa would make the five jumps from a C-47 and earn their coveted jump wings. Supervision of the airborne training was under a highly skilled group of noncommissioned officers, so the men enjoyed a brief respite from Captain Sobel's direct command. Officers were not so lucky since most of us had completed our five jumps at Toccoa.

The first week at Benning was dedicated to physical training, but the entire 506th PIR was in far better shape than the Regular Army cadre who conducted the physical conditioning. Within two days the cadre recommended the regiment move immediately into the next two phases of training, which in today's army is known as "tower week." Hours in the suspended harness apparatus gave way to additional training on the thirty-four-foot towers. Once qualified on these stations, each member of the company made practice jumps from Fort Benning's 250-foot towers. Cadre carefully critiqued landing procedures and the ability of individual troopers to maneuver their parachutes during descent. While the men spent their days in the Frying Pan, the area that housed the billets and training areas, officers participated in classroom instruction and weapons familiarity. In between classes and the Frying Pan, officers learned the rudiments of riding a motorcycle, were taught how to swim, and became "acquainted" with horses.

The final two weeks in December found Easy Company on the drop zone. Weather permitting, the men made all five jumps and earned their wings. The fourth jump occurred on Christmas Eve and, following a rare day off for the holiday, the men made their last jump on December 26. Faced with the ultimate moment of truth, only two men in the entire company froze and refused to exit the aircraft. Each trooper now received a certificate declaring that he was a qualified "parachutist" and had earned the right to wear the silver wings of the parachute soldier. To celebrate the occasion, Colonel Sink granted each trooper a well-deserved furlough and told us to behave ourselves and to return on time following the holiday. I spent my ten-day leave at home in Pennsylvania, where I arrived on New Year's Eve. Home was still a wonderful place, but given my experiences over the past several months, I felt a stranger among friends. At times it seemed that the people at home did not even realize there was a war going on.

As might be expected, a number of the newly minted paratroopers failed to report to duty on time, not unusual considering the rudimentary transportation network in January 1943. To emphasize his displeasure, Colonel Sink called a regimental parade to welcome back the returning troopers. Following his command of "At ease," Lieutenant Matheson read aloud the names of a trooper from each company who had reported late from furlough. As his name was read, the unfortunate trooper was escorted to the front of the formation by two NCOs armed with semi-machine guns. As the regimental drummer beat a mournful tattoo, the officer ripped off the regimental crest from the soldier's sleeve, tore off his wings, and removed the airborne patch from his hat. Then a jeep pulled up and deposited the disgraced soldier's barracks bag at his feet. In front of the entire regiment, the condemned trooper was forced to unblouse his trousers, remove his airborne boots, and replace them with regular shoes. As the drum continued to beat, the noncommissioned officers escorted the dispirited trooper from the airborne area. This ostentatious display was not lost on those who witnessed the ceremony. To be embarrassed by condemnation to the regular infantry was bad enough, but to be relegated to that branch from the airborne regiment in front of friends and comrades with whom you had served for six months was humiliating as hell.

While some may question Colonel Sink's methods, his message was crystal clear. Sink simply would not tolerate any breach of discipline in the 506th PIR. From my perspective the colonel's punishment did not fit the crime, but he had established a standard that I would not soon forget. Several months later while Easy Company was in England, I served as the battalion athletic officer. When the regimental executive officer called a meeting eight miles from the company barracks, I left in what I considered plenty of time to attend. Since my ride failed to show, I was tardy for the meeting. When asked why I was late, I explained, but the executive officer inquired why I hadn't run instead of waiting for the ride. Like Colonel Sink's "drumming-out ceremony," the message was clear—no excuses: "Don't tell me it is someone else's fault. Just get the job done!" Following that incident, I always wore a wristwatch until I was discharged from military service after the war.

Upon our return to Georgia, Easy Company and the rest of the 506th marched ten miles across the Chattahoochee River to take up new quarters in the swamps on the Alabama side of Fort Benning. The troops now enjoyed more spacious accommodations in that they had fifteen men to the barracks instead of the twenty to twenty-four men in the barracks during the Fort Benning phase of training on the other side of the river. Here on the Alabama side, we conducted another parachute jump. The focus of this period was on platoon and squad level field exercises. About the same time, Major Strayer finally received his long-deserved promotion to lieutenant colonel.

Our next move was to Camp Mackall, North Carolina, where we arrived in late February 1943. The camp was formerly Camp Hoffman and encompassed 62,000 acres of wilderness in North and South Carolina. Camp Mackall was named for Private John "Tommy" Mackall, a twenty-two-year-old airborne trooper from Wellsville, Ohio. A member of the 82d Airborne Division, Mackall was the first American paratrooper to be killed in combat in World War II. Following Mackall's death during the invasion of North Africa, the War Department published General Order Number 6, dated February 8, 1943, which officially changed the name of Camp Hoffman to Camp Mackall. Fifty miles from Fort Bragg, North Carolina, Camp Mackall now served as the headquarters and home to the Airborne Command.

At Mackall we conducted four more training jumps, including jumps with full field gear, and spent what seemed an excessive amount of time in the field in preparation for overseas deployment. For much of the time, the weather was considerably worse than it had been during our epic march to Atlanta. With so much time in the field, it was hardly surprising that the men complained about never sleeping in the one-story, heated barracks with mattresses. Now the training was more advanced than previous camps and it centered on platoon and company training, with two- to three-day field problems being the norm. We were drilled mercilessly in specialty arms, with each trooper cross-trained on the other weapons that were organic to a light infantry company. The current standard operating procedures called for the airborne infantry to jump with everything that they would need for three days of sustained combat. Parachute infantry was still in its infancy and developing tactical doctrine on the fly. Consequently, Easy Company experimented with various equipment loads, breaking down crew-served weapons to each member of the crew. Taking a brief respite from the confines of Mackall, we spent the period from May 23 through 28 around Camden, South Carolina, where we conducted a tactical training exercise.

On a personal note, I officially assumed the duties of company executive officer, a position that I had been holding for three months without title. I had been promoted to first lieutenant the preceding October, so my new position was more in line with my rank. As executive officer, my job was to command the company when Captain Sobel was not around and to take care of company administration. I now had six months' seniority as a 1st lieutenant, so I was eligible for promotion, but that was out of the question since there were no vacancies. What I was anxious to see happen was for Easy Company to cross the ocean and to see some action. I was tired of training in North Carolina, South Carolina, Georgia, and Alabama. When this war was over, I wanted to be able to say more than how much I suffered down south.

Now that the men were qualified parachutists and no longer green recruits, Sobel's attempts at intimidation began to recede. There was still an occasional blow-up, such as the time when our company commander was slightly injured during one of the jumps. Returning to the barracks area, Sobel and his first sergeant searched through all the footlockers, clothing, and personal possessions of the men in Easy Company. While the rest of the company remained in the field, Sobel seized all items that he considered contraband. Virtually every soldier had something confiscated. He then published a list identifying the contraband, the offender, and the punishment. When the men returned to the barracks, exhausted, footsore, and dirty after several days in the field, they found their individual possessions in disarray and some valuable personal items missing. For Private First Class Edward Tipper, this "unauthorized seizure" was the proverbial straw that broke the camel's back. He had always disliked Captain Sobel, but now that dislike evolved to outright hatred. Surprisingly, he found himself transferred to company headquarters as Sobel's runner. With Tipper's help, Sobel was able to mislay his maps or compass when he needed them most. It was evident that the men were hoping that their commander would screw up to the point that he would be replaced and would not be in command when Easy Company deployed to a combat theater.

The men's concern about their commander's ability to make rational decisions under pressure was certainly understandable. While at Mackall one night, the company conducted a field exercise in which Easy Company established a defensive perimeter in the woods. Our plan was to remain in position, stay very quiet, and let the enemy walk into our area so that we could ambush them. As we waited for the enemy, suddenly a breeze sprang up and the leaves on the trees started to rustle. Sobel sprang to his feet, shouting at the top of his voice, "Here they come! Here they come!" We all thought, "Ye Gods! I am going into combat with this man. He'll get us all killed."

The men did achieve a degree of retaliation during one exercise, when the medics complained about the absence of realistic training. As a result several men, including Sobel and Lieutenant Jerre Grosse of Dog Company, were designated "casualties" so that the medics could practice bandaging wounds, improvising casts and splints, and evacuating the wounded to the regimental aid station. At night the medics shaved off Gross's mustache and gave Sobel an anesthetic that rendered him unconscious. They then made a small incision simulating an "appendectomy." When Sobel awoke he was livid, but the medics were nowhere to be found and no soldier in Easy Company would testify to what the medics had done. Consequently no investigation was mounted and the incident became yet another in a long list of Sobel stories that persist to this day.

To pass what little free time they had, Easy Company enjoyed a good joke or played poker whenever the opportunity arose. What baked goods that were received from home were routinely shared with the members of one's squad or platoon. Privates "Popeye" Wynn and Darrell "Shifty" Powers, two Easy Company troopers from 3d Platoon, had joined the army together straight from the shipyards at Portsmouth, Virginia. Both were somewhat quiet and withdrawn, but they enjoyed a good laugh as much as their "Yankee" platoon members. Powers recalled one incident when Walter Gordon gave his last cigarette to Floyd Talbert, but then charged him a dime for a match.

By this time, Easy Company had emerged as the strongest company in the regiment and the 506th PIR had become a source of pride to every soldier who wore its regimental patch. One of the popular songs on the radio was called "Geronimo," and it was rapidly adopted as the paratroopers' song. "Geronimo" became the password that paratroopers were supposed to holler when they jumped, but Sink would have none of it in the 506th. At the time the 506th PIR was the only qualified parachute regiment not assigned to an airborne division, so Sink wanted something to set his regiment apart from the rest of the airborne commands. Consequently, when we exited the aircraft, each trooper was to shout "Currahee" to distance himself from the other regiments with whom we had developed a spirited competition, if not a tolerant scorn. As for myself, I had hoped we would ship out as a separate command to avoid six more months of training as a unit of an airborne division, but that decision would be made at far higher pay grades than where I served. In the interim, Colonel Sink also published a regimental magazine to foster unit pride and cohesion.

Other changes in Easy Company occurred during our stay in Mackall. The initial cadre of noncoms who had supervised our training since Toccoa departed to train a new airborne unit that was being formed. To replace them, Sergeants James Diel, Salty Harris, and Mike Ranney were promoted to staff sergeants. Bill Guarnere, Carwood Lipton, John Martin, Bob Rader, Bob Smith, Buck Taylor, and Murray

Roberts were promoted to sergeants. In addition, a number of Easy Company's officers were transferred to battalion staff, including Lewis Nixon, Clarence Hester, and George Lavenson. As I had grown quite fond of Nixon, I was sad to see him leave Easy Company. Only later on did I discover that Lieutenant Colonel Strayer had learned that Nixon was seeking a transfer to get away from Captain Sobel. After discussing the situation with Major Oliver Horton, his executive officer, the battalion commander decided to bring Nixon to staff and made him intelligence officer even though there was no Table of Organization and Equipment (TO&E) slot for a Battalion S-2. It would prove to be one of Strayer's more inspired decisions.

To fill the vacated platoon leader positions, several new officers arrived straight from OCS. One, a tough little Irishman named Harry Welsh, was assigned to the first platoon. Welsh had grown up in the coal regions of eastern Pennsylvania. Always a good athlete, he won state titles in swimming and diving. After Pearl Harbor he volunteered for the paratroopers. He was assigned to the 82d Division where he was broken from sergeant to private six times for fighting. After OCS Welsh joined Easy Company, 506th PIR, we rapidly became close friends and would later bunk together when we reached England.

Prior to leaving Camp Mackall, our battalion conducted another in a long series of physical training tests. Second Battalion scored around 97 percent, which was the highest ever recorded for a battalion. Disbelievers at headquarters thought Lieutenant Colonel Strayer fixed the results, so they ordered us back to the area, where we retested under the supervision of a Colonel Jablonski of the War Department. This time outside observers insisted that all the cooks and service personnel take the test with the infantry companies. Determined to uphold the battalion's honor, the men improved their collective score to a 98 percent passing rate. The Washington observer who verified the test results informed Strayer that his unit had scored higher than any battalion in the entire U.S. Army. Needless to say, Colonel Sink and Captain Sobel were extremely pleased with the results.

At the end of May, our company packed its gear and headed to Sturgis, Kentucky, for a series of field exercises, which took place over three states from June 5 to July 15, 1943. Five days into the exercises, the 506th PIR officially joined the 101st Airborne Division commanded by Major General William C. Lee, one of the airborne pioneers. Brigadier General Don F. Pratt, who would later be killed in Normandy, became Lee's assistant division commander. Brigadier General Anthony C. McAuliffe was assigned as the division artillery commander. In forming the 101st Airborne Division, Army Chief of Staff General George C. Marshall and 82d Airborne Division commander Major General Matthew Ridgway divided the officer complement of the 82d Division to form the initial core of officers for the 101st Airborne Division, now known as the "Screaming Eagles." We were honored to join the U.S. Army's second airborne division, but I would be less than honest if I did not say that we prided ourselves on having been a member of an independent parachute regiment.

The training we received at Camp Sturgis was the most realistic to date as controllers from the War Department supervised the largest combined paratroopers and glider-borne exercises. In spite of Captain Sobel's lack of confidence in the field, Easy Company performed well as part of the Red Forces, which were opposed by the Blue Forces. While senior headquarters digested the lessons of the airborne drop in Sicily and the controversy surrounding the fratricide involving the U.S. Navy's shooting down of twenty-three parachute transports of the 504th Parachute Infantry in the skies over Gela, Sicily, we concentrated on platoon and company tactics. Extended field marches, maneuvering against opposing forces at night, and wading through streams and rivers provided a realism that we had not experienced at Fort Benning or Camp Mackall. Easy Company conducted two training jumps during the exercise, one made with C-47s towing gliders to a release point, before dropping the paratroopers into another drop zone. From this drop zone, we marched several miles, crossed the Cumberland River in boats, and finished the field exercise just outside Camp Breckinridge,

Kentucky. At the conclusion of our field maneuvers, 2d Battalion, of which Easy formed one of the three organic rifle companies, received a special commendation from our new division commander, in which Lee extended his "congratulations on the splendid performance of Colonel Strayer's battalion" in the recent operations. Citing "a high standard of training and competent leadership on the part of the officers and enlisted men" and the "splendid aggressive action, sound tactical doctrine, and obviously well-trained individuals," General Lee stated that he "expected all personnel in the battalion to continue to live up to the fine reputation established by the battalion for soldierly bearing and behavior."

In mid-July, the company moved within the confines of Camp Breckinridge, where barracks and hot showers provided a pleasant break from the dirt and grime in the field. The camp itself was a paradise in comparison to any place where we had been. Camp Breckinridge was in close proximity to a number of large towns and contained its share of large post exchanges (PX), theaters, and service clubs, which provided an outlet for the soldiers who had so recently spent an inordinate amount of time in a field environment. Roughly a third of the men received ten-day furloughs in rotation before moving to Fort Bragg, North Carolina, in late July to prepare for overseas deployment. Upon their return from furlough, the entire 101st Airborne Division boarded trains en route to North Carolina. Fort Bragg was the staging area for deployment to a combat theater. Easy Company was brought up to full strength and each soldier was outfitted with new gear. The company spent a lot of time on the firing ranges, ensuring that their individual weapons were properly zeroed. I busied myself with my normal administrative duties but my anxiety mounted as the departure date neared. As company executive officer, one of my responsibilities was serving as postal officer, a laborious task that consumed much of my time. Still, I was caught up with the impending deployment, though no one knew with any certainty whether we were heading to the Pacific or to Europe.

Reflecting on the previous year's training in Easy Company, I was surprised at just how much I enjoyed the men with whom I served. You would think that after two months of not sleeping on a bed, dirty clothes, and trudging up and down the Tennessee hills, one would relish the peaceful surroundings of Fort Bragg. My only complaint was the emergency rations that they claimed had been especially designed for the paratroopers, K-rations and D-rations, both of which could turn a soldier's stomach in short order. If you read the list of what the rations contained, they sounded great, but to eat the rations over a period of time was more than a normal fellow could take. The meals were just too concentrated.

While at Fort Bragg, Colonel Sink decided that all officers should have a new trench coat–style overcoat. He also wanted the officers' club to stock up on bourbon whiskey. Each officer was assessed for a coat and whiskey. I didn't drink, never did drink, so I'll never know why they picked me for the detail of going to Philadelphia to pick up the coats and whiskey. Buying the coats was no problem. I had a list of the sizes and number of coats that I wanted and the name of the supplier to contact. The bourbon was another matter.

This was wartime, everything was rationed, and I was supposed to buy a truckload of Southern Comfort. I rode around Philadelphia in a taxicab, looked in directories, asked for advice, and got nowhere. I then went back home to Lancaster and called regimental headquarters for advice. The next day Lieutenant Colonel Chase, the regimental executive officer, called and gave me an address in New York City for a distributor for Schenley's whiskey. I took a train to New York, found the distributor, and was introduced to a pudgy man sitting in a chair with his foot on a stool. My initial impression was that this man had gout. He was surrounded by more beautiful, well-groomed secretaries than I'd ever seen in my life. To say that at this point I was ill at ease hardly describes my feelings, but I had a mission—to get that bourbon or face a firing squad. I was in a totally foreign atmosphere: a kid from a Mennonite family background facing a bloated executive with all the beautiful secretaries, and he the only man who could help me. I told him my mission and what I wanted. He smiled and said, "Yes, I could take care of that order." In my view, right then and there, that man did his part in helping to win World War II. I spent the next hour endorsing money orders. I had been so naïve that I had converted my money to small denominations of $20 and $50 money orders.

On August 22, 1943, the entire division boarded trains and headed north to Camp Shanks, thirty miles north of New York City on the Hudson River. The weather was crisp and cool, with the Hudson River Valley arrayed in beautiful autumn colors that reminded me of the hills in southern Pennsylvania. Camp Shanks, built on 2,000 acres in Orangeburg, New York, was the largest World War II army embarkation camp in the United States. Named after Major General David C. Shanks, commanding general of the New York port during World War I, Camp Shanks opened in January 1943. Over the course of the war, 1.3 million soldiers processed for overseas deployment through the camp, nicknamed "Last Stop USA." Fully three-fourths of the soldiers who participated in D-Day and a total of seventeen divisions destined for Europe passed through its walls. En route to Camp Shanks, I sat in a car with Lewis Nixon and Harry Welsh as we discussed our ultimate destination. As we continued north, we knew for certain that we were European-bound. The 506th PIR closed in on Camp Shanks on September 1. As we detrained, the men formed columns of fours and marched to their assigned barracks. Each barracks was twenty by one hundred feet and contained two rows of bunks and three coal-burning pot-bellied stoves that provided minimal heating. The movement to the barracks was a long haul, with each trooper loaded to the gills with equipment. All hoped for a brief furlough to New York City, but the NOCs kept us busy with endless rounds of inoculations. Burt Christenson remarked that he had been given so many shots that his "arms hung from his body like limp rope." When the men were given passes to New York, they were forced to remove their jump boots and their airborne patches from their uniforms for security reasons. Higher headquarters feared that German spies would identify the 101st Airborne Division and ascertain its eventual destination.

Within days Easy Company moved to the port of embarkation. It was a short train ride to the New Jersey docks at Weehawken, where a harbor boat ferried troops to Pier 88. At the pier, troop ships were tied up for boarding. Loading the ship that would take the 506th PIR to England took nearly a full day. In our minds was a letter that Captain Sobel had sent to our parents, in which he extolled the training and dedication of their respective sons and in which he encouraged loved ones to write frequent letters to "arm him with a fighting heart."

One of our officers, Lieutenant Fred "Moose" Heyliger, received notice as we boarded the S.S. *Samaria* that his wife had just given birth to a boy, "Little Moose." The receipt of this news forced the rest of the company to listen to Moose sing songs all night as he celebrated the birth of his son. The rest of us were filled with trepidation, but each trooper took consolation in the fact that he was part of the best damned unit in the entire U.S. Army. As we walked up the gangplank of the *Samaria*, everyone knew that there was no turning back. Easy Company was off to war.

Old Beyond My Years

In early September 1943, Easy Company began its transatlantic passage aboard the British steamer S.S. *Samaria*. As we departed New York Harbor and passed the Statue of Liberty, I wondered if I would ever be coming back. Had I seen my family for the last time? Would we reach England without encountering any German submarines? Knowing that I was in the paratroopers was some consolation even though each of us knew our mission required us to be dropped behind enemy lines and that we would have to fight outnumbered until we could be relieved. None of the men had any combat experience or had any idea what combat would be like. As New York faded on the horizon, I stood and searched my soul, saying a silent prayer that God would allow me to return home.

What I remember most was the filthy condition of the ship. The excessive dirt, the terrible food, and the fact that we washed our mess kits in a garbage pail nearly turned my stomach. Forrest Guth, a trooper from Allentown, Pennsylvania, who had joined the paratroopers with his two friends Roderick Strohl and Carl Fenstermacher, recalled that the prevalent rumor on board was that the British crew consumed American food, while the paratroopers were forced to eat British food. What struck him most was the cooks serving fish chowder for breakfast. After ten days on the S.S. *Samaria*, I felt as though I had lost all my muscle tone, especially in my legs. The thought occurred to me that if we had to come off this ship and go directly into combat, it would have been mighty rough. Arriving in Liverpool on September 15, we were immediately transported to Aldbourne, in Wiltshire, approximately eighty miles west of London on the Salisbury Plain. Aldbourne was a typically quaint English town with houses constructed of brick and stone. Flowers were in bloom and most homes had well-kept yards with colorful gardens. As company executive officer, I commanded the company in Captain Sobel's absence and I handled the administrative and logistical requirements as Easy Company settled into their new billets. Within days of our arrival in England, our troops occupied their new barracks, which were Nissan huts and tarpaper shacks, heated by two large pot-bellied stoves. Officers were crammed into a huge manor house until private housing could be obtained.

Aldbourne would be Easy Company's home for the next nine months, until the unit moved to the departure airfield for the invasion of France. The initial week in the English countryside was dedicated to orientation to our new environment. To ensure American soldiers understood the intricacies of Allied cooperation, the United States War Department distributed a pamphlet to American servicemen who were going to Britain to prepare for the invasion of occupied Europe. This pamphlet's avowed aim was to prepare these young American GIs for life in a very different country and to prevent any friction between them and the local populace. Printed in 1942, the *Instructions for American Servicemen in Britain* attracted a great deal of attention for its candid views of how Britons were viewed on our side of the Atlantic. The booklet cautioned the Americans on how to conduct themselves. In-

cluded were orders not "to fight old wars and to bring up old griev-
ances" from the American Revolutionary period so as Hitler would be
unable "to make his propaganda effective" and separate the Atlantic
partners. If he could do that, his "chance of winning might return." We
were also told not to use phrases and colloquialisms that our allies
might find offensive. Two unpardonable sins would be to comment on
the British Government or politics or to criticize the King. The War Department assured us that the British would welcome us as friends and
allies, but we ought to remember that crossing the ocean did not automatically make us heroes. There were "thousands of housewives in
aprons and youngsters in knee pants in Britain who had lived through
more high explosives in air raids than many soldiers saw in first class
barrages in the last war." In short, our government directed us to behave ourselves and neither be condescending, nor "a showoff" because
Americans were routinely more highly paid than the British Tommy.
Accordingly, Easy Company conducted tours, visited local bars, met
village officials, and generally became acquainted with English customs. We soon found that the English were similar to Americans in
many aspects, but in other ways it was as if we were from different
planets. Plumbing, electric light wiring, furniture, heating, and cooking
seemed light-years behind what I was used to in the United States. Most
Britons had never eaten popcorn, marshmallows, hot dogs, and other
eatables that they characterized as strictly Yank chow. Nor did they
possess the large and varied assortment of expressive adjectives that we
did and often an expression of ours meant something entirely different
to them.

Following our first week in England, officers were billeted in private homes. Looking for an opportunity to escape the crammed conditions of our not-so-spacious manor, I went to a local church where I
was fortunate to meet a family named Barnes. The Barneses had recently lost a son in the Royal Air Force during the Battle of Britain. I
first met this couple following services on my first Sunday in England.
Walking to the adjacent cemetery, I sat on a bench and took time for

personal reflection and simply to enjoy some solitude. As I looked over the cemetery, I noticed an elderly couple tending to one of the graves. They then sat on an adjacent bench and the three of us talked for nearly an hour. They told me their names were Mr. and Mrs. Francis Barnes and that they were paying respects to their son Robert. The Barneses invited me to join them for afternoon tea, and I graciously accepted their invitation. I saw them periodically over the course of the next several weeks, and when our unit requested billeting within the local community, the Barnes family volunteered to host two officers as long as I was one of them.

Along with Lieutenant Harry Welsh, I moved in and the Barneses soon adopted me as a full-fledged member of their family. The Barneses also had a child from London—Elaine Stevens, thirteen years old, a refugee from the London bombing—as a houseguest. Because my sister, Ann, was also thirteen years old, they became penpals. My personal quarters were with the family in a room over their grocery store. The room wasn't big and we slept on army cots, but the comforts of home were a pleasant respite from the crowds and the barracks. While Harry Welsh spent his free time at a pub that was only a stone's throw from our room, I spent my evenings with the Barnes family.

Life with the Barneses suited me perfectly. I greatly appreciated what Francis Barnes and his wife were doing for me. They provided me a home, a family, and a fireplace to come to at the end of a day's training. They adopted me as a son. Francis Barnes was a lay preacher at one of Aldbourne's three churches. On Sundays I always had a special invitation to come to their church. Mr. Barnes would preach the sermon, Mrs. Barnes played the organ, and I wore my best dress uniform and sat front and center. Most Sundays I was the only soldier in church, but I know that without a spoken word, everybody knew my lifestyle.

A typical evening began with Mrs. Barnes knocking on my door before 9:00 P.M. and saying, "Lieutenant Winters, would you like to come down and listen to the news and have a spot of tea?" Sitting around a smoldering chunk of peat in the fireplace, we listened to the

BBC. Afterward, everybody would gather around the table and Mr. Barnes would read a passage from the Bible, then he would say a prayer, after which Mrs. Barnes would serve tea and biscuits or some fresh bread. Around 10:00 P.M., Mr. Barnes would then announce that it was time for bed.

My association with the Barnes family was one of the most enjoyable experiences in my life. They prepared me mentally for the tasks that lay ahead. I had observed their personal suffering at the loss of their son and experienced similar feelings when I lost some of my men in Normandy and the subsequent campaigns. By giving me time to reflect and to study my manuals for the nine months prior to the invasion, the Barneses helped me develop my own personality and hone my leadership skills. This formative period of my life was very important in continuing to build the fundamental characteristics my parents had initiated, and they helped shape my life. Today I realize what the Barnes family did was help me develop the most fundamental element in good leadership—lead by example, live by setting a good example. They lived for nearly ten years after the war, and I still treasure the mementoes that they gave me. Years later I returned to Aldbourne with Stephen Ambrose and excused myself for a few minutes to place flowers on their graves. I then took a minute to reflect on this wonderful couple and sat on the same bench where we had first met so many years earlier.

We were in England to prepare for war, not to tour the countryside, and the days were filled with intense training. Training monopolized six days of the week, with the average week consisting of prolonged marches, marksmanship, and simulated night attacks. Hikes of varying length, some up to twenty-five miles, were conducted, and there was special emphasis on physical conditioning. Map-reading remained an important component of every field exercise and every week Easy Company conducted a two- to three-day field training exercise. Captain

Sobel continued to perform poorly in the field, further exasperating the platoon leaders and the men. He remained as tyrannical, inflexible, and paranoid as he had been at Toccoa. Tension was building within the company, particularly among the officers who bore the primary responsibility for preparing the men for combat.

Nowhere was the pressure more apparent than on Sobel himself. Whereas the punishment he administered in the States was often mean and degrading, in England the punishment passed the point of normalcy to outright cruelty. If a man was late getting back to camp, instead of extra kitchen police (K.P.) duty, he had to dig a six-foot-by-six-foot pit with his entrenching tools at night after the day's training. When the soldier was finished, Sobel would tell him "to fill it up." Our commander's inability to make decisions, coupled with his tactical incompetence, continued to alienate both officers and men alike. While Sobel was partially effective in matters where he controlled everything, he would be utterly helpless in combat where adaptability and initiative were keys to survival. The noncommissioned officers soon began grumbling and dissension spread throughout Easy. While such talk is always detrimental to the discipline in any unit, Sobel was simply not cut out to be a combat leader. While the men could tolerate a tough taskmaster, they were simply afraid to have Sobel lead them into combat. Within two months of arriving in England, things boiled over and I found myself in the middle of it. The ensuing confrontation between Captain Sobel and me brought out the best and worst qualities of leadership within Easy Company.

On October 30, Lieutenant Colonel Strayer was scheduled to inspect Easy Company. Sobel issued me orders to inspect the latrine at 1000 hours, one hour before Strayer was due to arrive. At 0930 hours I also received orders from battalion headquarters to censor the enlisted men's mail. I completed that chore and at 1000, I promptly entered the latrine. To my surprise Sobel was already there, making his own inspection. Without uttering a word, he exited the latrine, walked by me without acknowledging my presence. Behind him walked Private

Joachim Melo, the latrine orderly, wet mop in hand. Melo was soaking wet, dirty, in need of a shave, hair uncombed. He looked (and I am sure felt) like a man who had just finished doing a dirty job. Sobel left without saying a word. I proceeded with my personal inspection and found that Melo had done a superb job. When I walked to company headquarters forty-five minutes later, 1st Sergeant Evans handed me a typed document that demanded my reply by endorsement whether I desired company punishment for failure to inspect the latrine at 0945 hours as instructed by the company commander or whether I requested a court-martial. I immediately proceeded to Sobel's office to clear up the misunderstanding.

"Captain, my orders were to inspect the latrine at 1000 hours."

"I changed that time to 0945," he replied.

"I wasn't informed of the change."

"I telephoned and I sent a runner."

This was too much for me—just another example of the chicken-shit that characterized Sobel's tenure as Easy Company's commanding officer. Captain Sobel was now questioning my integrity and my sense of duty. I could not care less that my punishment was the denial of a forty-eight-hour pass until mid-December. Preferring to stay home with the Barneses where I studied my manuals, I very seldom left Aldbourne anyway. Principle was now at stake. Immediately following Strayer's inspection, which Easy Company incidentally passed with flying colors, I returned to Sobel's office and demanded trial by court-martial. Aldbourne being a small village, within minutes the story spread around the company. Within days Lieutenant Colonel Strayer directed his executive officer to conduct a preliminary investigation and in the interim, he transferred me to headquarters company and appointed me battalion mess officer until the court-martial was resolved. I was heartbroken by the transfer because I was no longer a troop leader, and the general practice was to assign mess duties to those officers who were not up to standard. On reflection, I understood Strayer had little alternative as it would have been detrimental to keep me in Easy Company when the company commander was court-martialing his second-in-command. The transfer in no way eased my pain of leaving the men with whom I had trained for over a year. This was the first time since I had been in the army that I wasn't with field troops or in troop command.

My abrupt transfer to battalion headquarters and headquarters company soon provoked widespread anger among the noncommissioned officers in the company. With Sobel still in command, the NCOs decided to push the issue. I had heard rumblings of a mutiny as soon as my court-martial was officially announced. Sergeants Mike Ranney and "Salty" Harris were the instigators. They called all the NCOs together in the company dayroom to discuss what they were going to do. Only a few of the noncommissioned officers were absent because Ranney and Harris did not want the word to reach Sobel until they had decided on what course of action to take. They invited me to the meeting. I went and told them not to do anything—any mutiny was in itself a court-martial offense. As I was in the middle of my plea asking them not to go through with this mutiny, Sobel walked in the door. Everyone just froze in place; there was not a sound. Ranney was the first to recover his voice and started off with something like, "Now how can we improve our athletic program?" This didn't fool Sobel, I am sure, but without a word, he picked up a book and left. I then excused myself and returned to battalion. After careful deliberation, the NCOs decided to bypass battalion and present a formal protest directly to Colonel Sink, our regimental commander. Each wrote a formal protest against Sobel and turned in his stripes.

Confronted with an insurrection within the ranks of Easy Company and a crisis in command that permeated the entire regiment, Sink summoned the noncoms and really gave them hell. In no uncertain terms, he informed the sergeants that under the articles of war, he could have them shot. Then he transferred Harris from the regiment and busted Ranney to private. Prior to D-Day, Ranney returned to Easy Company, but Harris remained with the pathfinders and played an important role in the upcoming invasion. He would later be killed in action in Holland. The magnitude of the "sergeants' revolt" probably prevented similar disciplinary action to the other noncommissioned officers. Within days Sink assigned Sobel to command the division's new training center at Chilton Foliat and in February 1944, he assigned 1st Lieutenant Thomas Meehan of Baker Company to command Easy. Sobel's stint in Easy Company had come to an inglorious end. 1st Lieutenant Patrick Sweeney of Able Company temporarily took over as company executive officer until I returned to that post on the eve of the invasion.

On November 11, Lieutenant Colonel Strayer set aside my punishment under the articles of war. Shortly thereafter, his executive officer, Major Horton, stopped me and said with a smile, "You gave me one hell of a problem trying to figure out how to squash that court-martial. We had the court-martial manual out and were doing a lot of reading for a couple of days." When I rejoined Easy, it was not as executive officer, but as platoon leader of 1st Platoon. Needless to say I was elated as I regained my troop's leading status. With Sobel's departure, Easy Company once again returned to normalcy. I saw Sobel only once more during the entire war while the battalion was stationed at Mourmelon. I had already been promoted to major when Captain Sobel walked past me on a deserted company street. He completely ignored me and continued on his way. After he had passed me without recognition, I stopped, turned and said, "Captain, we recognize and honor the rank!" Sobel stopped, turned, came to attention, and said, "Yes, sir!" We exchanged salutes and he moved on. My revenge was sweet—Sobel's debt to me had been paid in full!

Colonel Sink's intercession in my court-martial proceedings was the second time that he had personally intervened to salvage my career. I maintained tremendous respect for Sink dating back to Toccoa, when he first observed me leading calisthenics. Then he promoted me to 1st lieutenant, which ensured that I would be assigned as company executive officer. Under ordinary conditions, there was no way that I would have been reassigned to Easy Company based on my recent confrontation with Sobel. I later discovered that the NCOs had personally requested my return. Sink made it happen and for the remainder of the war, he closely monitored my career. I am not sure why he had such a personal interest in me, but he remained the officer instrumental in always advancing me to the next job.

We passed the second anniversary of December 7, 1941, almost without noticing. The Japanese attack had occurred two years earlier, but in some ways it seemed longer. I certainly felt more mature and harder than I was when I entered the service. This airborne outfit left a man with many aches, pains, and bruises. On the plus side, being affiliated with a crack outfit also left each soldier with an equal number of memories: some good, some not so good. In any event, with Lieutenant Meehan in command, a far more conducive command climate permeated Easy Company as we entered the most intense period of training since our days at Toccoa.

Military activity reached a fever pitch as we entered 1944. Everyone anticipated the invasion would take place in the spring. Christmas was a rare day off, and in late February, I took a week's furlough and visited Scotland. After six months in the European theater of operations, I was anxious to see something that reminded me of home. Glasgow and Edinburgh fit the bill nicely. Later I visited Plymouth, Oxford, and London. There were plenty of things to occupy my time: ice-skating, stage shows, nice theaters, and plenty of restaurants. Still it was not much fun traveling or going out over England. The blackout left me stumbling about, getting lost in strange cities, and wishing to God I could get out and do some real fighting. However, I did a bit of shopping for the family, buying my sister a Scottish cap, a lovely silver necklace and locket for my mother, and a pearl-handled knife for my father. In addition, I purchased a "dirk," or stiletto knife, to wear inside my boot. All in all, the leave provided a welcome interlude before the next round of training.

After a long English winter filled with long, dark, and foggy nights, spring finally arrived. Forgotten were the months on end of no sun and the ever-present rain and mud that marked the English countryside. From March through May, Easy Company remained constantly in the field. We conducted night operations, including night airdrops and night attacks. Over the course of the spring, we made five training jumps in England before D-Day. Only one of these exercises, the airborne drop conducted on March 12, was a night jump. To acquaint myself with every weapon, I experimented jumping with a different weapon each time. Normally, when you dropped your weapon in an equipment bundle, you had trouble finding the equipment and assembling the men on the bundle. This was especially true on a night jump. Although we had not received official orders for the invasion, it was fairly easy to determine what was expected. On most of our field exercises, we conducted attacks against gun positions, causeways, bridges, and other potential strong points. Dress rehearsals for the impending invasion included massive airdrops of the entire division, such as Operation Eagle at Newberry on May 12. That jump included 1,050 airplanes and over 15,000 paratroopers. En route to the drop zone, we flew two and a half hours before we exited the aircraft. Fortunately, the company responded well and the men were anxious to get into combat.

Over the course of the spring, most of the brass visited the 101st Airborne Division. First up was General Bernard Law Montgomery, the commander of 21st Army Group, who made it a point to address every division in England—to "binge up" the troops, as he called it. Monty had a knack of addressing the troops in a language that they clearly understood, never speaking down to them or attempting to impress upon them his rank and position. He was a soldier's soldier in every sense of the word. What impressed me most about Montgomery was that he lived a lifestyle that was beyond reproach and easy for his staff to follow. Monty gathered us around his jeep and told us to take off our helmets so he could see our faces. He then said how much he pitied the Germans when they came up against us. Montgomery was quickly followed by the Supreme Commander, General Eisenhower, and U.S. First Army commanding general Lieutenant General Omar Bradley. Prime Minister Churchill joined Ike and Brad to observe the combined Anglo-American jump in late March. Also on the stand was our new commanding general, Maxwell Taylor, who had assumed command of the division when General Bill Lee suffered a mild heart attack and was sent home to the States.

Taylor was an interesting commander but never enjoyed the respect and admiration of his predecessor, the "father of the American airborne." At the company level, I had little contact with the new commanding general until two months prior to the invasion. That encounter was not pleasant and it was reminiscent of how the company fared under Captain Sobel's tenure. On this occasion, it was my job as first platoon leader to secure the division command post and of course I was trying to be on the ball and keep every soldier on the ball, too. General Taylor's standing orders were that every soldier must wear his helmet at all times. One morning I was out checking my outposts when General Taylor exited his tent. Surprised by his sudden appearance, one of my troopers sat up from sleeping and as he did so, his helmet fell off his head. As Taylor drove by, he stopped his jeep, took the man's name, and asked who his platoon leader was. Within hours, I was told to report to division headquarters where I was administered punishment under the articles of war for failure during a recent condition of simulated combat to require a man under my command to wear a helmet. According to the division commander, my actions in failing to strictly enforce the provisions of a training memorandum demonstrated "a lack of full appreciation of the importance this directive bears to safeguarding my command in actual combat." Punishment for my indiscretion was a $25 fine. Twenty-five dollars at that time was a great deal of money and it hurt. I felt that the so-called infraction was unjust, unfair, and unreasonable on Taylor's part. In my opinion the accidental dropping of the helmet hardly required disciplinary action, but I reluctantly accepted the punishment.

The spring of 1944 also had a profound impact on me, both in the personal and professional sense. In April I had sent enough money home to help my parents pay off the mortgage of their home. I was so proud that I could have burst. I had once expressed an interest in finding a farm after I returned from Europe, and Dad said he would keep looking for one. After what I had experienced since I had joined the army, now I was not so sure that I could be satisfied with remaining in a small town for the rest of my life. I knew this idea of thinking that you could go home and adjust yourself to civilian life by just changing your uniform for a business suit was wrong. I no longer thought I wanted to stay around home while I adjusted to civilian life after this cruel war ended. I joked that I might get a job on a tramp steamer as a deckhand or on a liner in some capacity and just sail around until I had seen the world or until I was tired of traveling. Sooner or later I knew that I would have to start looking for a way to earn a living, but the old style of life no longer held any charms for me. Wartime provided few amusements and my stress level increased as the invasion neared.

One of these amusements was an active sports program designed to lessen the apprehension that gripped the company. I served as coach of the basketball team, while Lieutenant Lynn "Buck" Compton, who had joined us in England, served as my assistant coach. Compton had joined the army in February 1943. Standing six feet tall and weighing two hundred fifteen pounds, Compton was every inch an athlete. Prior to entering service, he attended UCLA, where he had played in the Rose Bowl. After graduating OCS at Fort Benning, Compton had been assigned to a demonstration unit on the main post, a common practice since senior officers wanted him to play football and baseball in the athletic leagues that they had established on post. Rather than lead a comfortable life while others were overseas fighting, he volunteered for the paratroopers because assignment to a high-priority unit could not be denied. Compton was an energetic officer, whom I later chastised about gambling with the men. An officer should never put himself in a position where he takes anything from the men. Never abuse them by act or omission. As a commander, a leader must be prepared to give everything, including himself, to the people he leads. You give your time and you strive to be consistently fair, never demonstrating favoritism. In my opinion Compton had jeopardized his position as a leader by establishing an improper relationship with some of his troopers. Compton did not take the counseling seriously, but I felt it my duty to ensure that he understood my feelings on maintaining a professional relationship with the soldiers in his platoon.

In any event, the basketball team was an interesting experience. We had no basketball court, so we could not practice, nor did we have uniforms. When we played a game with one of the Air Corps commands, we traveled to their court. Our fellows played in their long johns if it was cold, or in any shorts that they might have. The Air Corps boys always had beautiful suits and sweat suits to match. Obviously, these had been brought over from the States. Most of the Air Corps teams were usually comprised of ex–college players who enjoyed the soft, cushy jobs of pilot training schools, and who later became pilots. Naturally the men of Easy Company had the edge on making the 506th Regimental team since I was coach. These games were an interesting experience to say the least—the cool-looking, well-coached Air Corps team against those little, raunchy paratroopers running around in their underwear. As I mentioned, we had no practice court, so we had no offensive plays, no defensive plans. We just got out there and ran, and then we would bump and run, and bump again and run some more. By the end of the second half, we had run the Air Corps team into the ground.

One game with our sister regiment, the 501st PIR, in an Air Corps hangar sticks in my memory. It was payday and Colonel Sink stopped by to remind me that it was the 506th's payroll against the 501st's payroll. We had to win. The ensuing game was rough and tough, and with just a few seconds to go, the score was tied. I noticed Sergeant Barlow's [from A Company] legs were shot. He had played a terrific game. He was our playmaker, the leader of the team. I pulled him out and sent in

Corporal "Gordy" Carson. Gordy called for the ball, took a long shot, and made it. He not only won the game for the 506th, but he also saved our payroll. Carson has been a hero to me ever since that night.

Organized athletics were only one means to pass the time as we awaited news of the impending invasion. Together with his friend Paul C. Rogers, Walter Gordon seized upon the idea of composing a simple poem when any member of their platoon became the object of company punishment. Sometimes nonjudicial punishment wasn't required to have a poem dedicated in one's honor. The ridiculous poem was recited as soon as the platoon was assembled. The hapless victim would cringe with embarrassment and more often than not, would explode in anger—much to Gordon's and Rogers's delight. The more embarrassed a trooper would become, the more satisfaction the poem's composers would gain. Sergeant Floyd Talbert proved to be a particularly easy target. Shortly before Christmas 1943, it was decided that the noncommissioned officers would serve Christmas dinner to their men. Mess kits were set aside for the day and plates, tumblers, and flatware were issued. Talbert brought in heaping plates of food. When all were served, he took his seat and was ready to join in the feast. It was only then that he discovered that his knife and fork had been mysteriously removed. The obvious remedy would have been for him to fetch another set of utensils, but that was not Talbert's style. He quickly turned a bright shade of red and shouted a challenge for the culprit to admit to the misdeed. The men continued eating and snickering. Of course the men offered a few choice suggestions as to what Talbert might do with the turkey drumstick that rested on his plate of untouched food. Talbert gave us a great performance and a climax was reached by his storming out of the mess hall without one bite of food. Rogers's eyes met Gordon's because they knew instantly that a poem would be forthcoming. Gordon later met Talbert in the barracks and chided him by suggesting that he had probably forfeited the last Christmas dinner he would ever have on earth. Fortunately Talbert, whom I considered the best soldier in the company, survived the war by many years.

With the invasion now only weeks away, I refocused my efforts for the task at hand. Whether or not I wanted to admit it, the past few months had been a battle of nerves and nobody was any the worse for wear than I. I found refuge in church, having only missed services three times in over eight months. Life with the Barneses also provided a pleasant respite from military duties. I was happy to be an officer, but I wrote one friend back home that it was not all that it was cracked up to be. The social life, for one thing, seemed my principal roadblock to future advancement. I had no desire and I absolutely refused to join in the parties and social gatherings in which most officers participated. Despite the fact that I had been an executive officer for fifteen months, and that I was the only officer left in the company who had started with the unit at Toccoa, I still wore the rank of a 1st lieutenant. But that was okay because I knew my job, my company, the men, and I felt confident that under fire, I had the right answers. Which gets me to the point: I was a "half-breed." An officer yes, but at heart an enlisted man. I worked hard and did my duty as I should, but when it came to play, I was in a bad position and only in athletics with the men did I truly enjoy myself. The happiest days of my army career had been at Camp Croft: good barracks, pretty warm temperatures, and the washroom in the same building. Of course I was only making $21 a month, yet I always had a little money at the end of the month for personal pleasures. Even though I had traveled more and had done more in the past two years, never had I had more fun than during those first few months in the army. Those days seemed as if they had happend in another lifetime.

With the reflection of sixty years, I can say that I was not too concerned about the invasion. I truthfully never wavered as to whether or not I would succeed in combat. I was far more concerned for the safety of the men entrusted to my command. Any success I had as a battlefield commander was based on character, detailed study, and taking care of those troopers. In one letter I painted a beautiful, pathetic, and touching portrait of what leadership consists of. Picture if you will, a small unit exercise in the English countryside on the eve of the invasion. Along a roadside on a cold damp morning sits a private with his machine gun. He has been on the march and fighting for just about twenty-four hours without stopping and sleeping. He is tired, dead tired, so tired his mind is almost a blank. He is wet, hungry, and miserable. As his buddies sleep, he keeps watch, a difficult job when he is so exhausted and knows that when the sun comes up in another half hour, he will once again be on the move. What does he do? He pulls out a snapshot of his girl, who is over 3,000 miles away, and studies her picture. In a state of inner tranquillity, he dreams of days when he can once again enjoy the kind of life she stands for. Down the road comes an officer—it's me. Nobody else would think of being up at a pre-dawn hour. "How's it going, Shep [Howell]? What are you doing?" Then together, we study and discuss his girl's good features and virtues. He asks me to promise that I will ensure he survives the upcoming battle—a promise I cannot make in good faith since I don't know what the final outcome of the battle will be. I can only tell Shep that I will do my best to ensure he comes home safely—a promise that I kept.

When you think about kids like that, and you realize the weight of your responsibility and do something about it, you soon become old beyond your years. In three years, I had aged a great deal. Still only twenty-six years old, I felt that the simpler times of my college experience and the days of civilian life when I did as I pleased, were long past. It must have been a dream, a small and short but beautiful part of my life. Now all I did was work—work to improve myself as an officer, work to improve my soldiers as fighters, and work to develop them as men. The result was that I was old before my time; not old physically, but hardened to the point where I could make the rest of them look like undeveloped high school boys; old to the extent where I could keep going after my men fell over and slept from exhaustion, and I could keep going as a mother who works on after her sick and exhausted child has fallen asleep; old to the extent where if it was a decision or advice needed, my decisions were taken as if the wisdom behind them was infallible. Yes, I felt old and tired from training these men to the point where they were now efficient fighters. I hoped that the effort would mean that more of them would return to those girls in the States than otherwise would have made it back to the comfort of their families and friends.

Now that the invasion was near, higher headquarters suddenly became concerned that our airfields were very vulnerable to German parachute commando-type raids on our lanes and equipment. Steps were taken to organize teams of paratroopers to visit these Air Corps bases and give the pilots basic infantry training. Several Easy Company troopers participated in these visits. Their reports were not always encouraging. On the visit to the 9th Parachute Battalion (British), the evaluator noted that although the individual British Tommy was highly proficient on his assigned weapon, "the general reaction of the British toward us at first was generally expressed in an indifferent attitude." It was not until the American paratroopers took over a major component of the training program, which gave them the opportunity to demonstrate to the British that the American soldiers "knew their stuff," that the British accepted us as their equal. One battalion officer noted that although the British were quite methodical in their training, they were too much on "spit and polish and not quite enough on scouting and patrolling." My job was to teach unarmed combat. My impression of the Air Corps personnel with whom I worked was very poor. If I was going into combat, I was thankful that I was in the 101st Airborne Division. I felt far safer in the company of my paratroopers than with any of the pilots and support personnel.

May 16 was Mother's Day and I made it a special point to order Mom a dozen roses. I also bought a handbag for Mrs. Barnes. She had been like a mother to me for over eight months and she seemed almost like my own mother. I was flat broke for the remainder of the month after these purchases—just like old school days and those days at Camp Croft. While I attended church services the following week, the congregation celebrated what the British called Witsun, or Children's Day.

It sure was enjoyable to watch those kids get up and recite, then recall how I used to be in the same shoes not so many years ago. One little girl about four years old, with a pretty little pink dress and white bonnet-shaped hat, stole the show. She was up and down, yawning, stretching, singing with her music upside down, waving to friends in the audience, and then fussing with her new dress, hat, and shoes. Quite a show! When it was over, I couldn't help but wonder whether or not I would live to share another Mother's Day or Witsun with loved ones. Would I see flowers bloom again the following spring?

On the verge of a major deployment, it was important to hold on to something from home. In my free moments, I often reminisced about life in the States prior to our deployment overseas. That past seemed so distant now. Still, I would not trade anybody back home or anyone in England for tickets for the "big show" [D-Day]. I had worked long and hard for these tickets and now, I was not going to part with them. We were ready.

On May 29, the company marched to the trucks lined up in the village center. Half of Aldbourne turned out to bid us farewell. We were appreciative of our English hosts and had formed a strong attachment to them over the course of the preceding eight months. Due to security, I couldn't say anything to anyone about where we were going, but the residents of Aldbourne knew we were pushing off. The Barneses bade me farewell, knowing without being told that this was the real thing. My own parting with the Barnes family was tearful, but it was time to move toward the departure airfield. As we went down the road in trucks, I can still see my British "sister," Elaine, walking ahead of us and turning to wave goodbye as we drove by. Rumors naturally abounded as to the time and place of the invasion. Lieutenant Meehan and I had actually determined the approximate location of our projected drop zone. While sitting around in our tent one evening, we used our imagination and discussed our previous flight times and course changes. Taking a map and placing a string on Uppottery, we then extended the string and discovered that the pencil crossed the Cotentin

Peninsula in Normandy. If we could figure this out, we wondered if the Germans could do the same thing.

A column in *Stars and Stripes* stated that theaters, ball games, and nonessential business establishments in the United States would close and people would be asked to attend church and pray for us on D-Day. That announcement, coupled with the size and the magnitude of a united feeling like that we experienced when we left Aldbourne, sent chills up and down our collective spines. At home a soldier does not usually think beyond his local acquaintances. Go to another part of the country and it is one's home state, and anyone from your hometown is a buddy. Once overseas, the situation changes dramatically and anybody from the United States is your buddy. So when we felt that way and thought that all those people were sending their best wishes and prayers, you could not help but feel good. As for myself, I wrote my final letter home and told my friend that every night at taps I would meet her at the North Star. The old North Star is a soldier's guiding light when he is lost, alone, and feeling mighty funny in the pit of the stomach. What makes him feel good is when he can look up and know that there is somebody else looking up at the same star.

Easy Company closed on our marshalling area near Exeter, in Devonshire in the mid-afternoon of May 29. Our camp lay in an open field beside the airstrip at Uppottery in southwestern England, approximately ten miles from the coast. Easy Company was billeted in pyramidal-shaped tents. The next day Sink briefed the regimental officers, and the troops spent the day caring for and cleaning their equipment. Ammunition was issued and weapons were checked by ordnance. A band played in each battalion area during the evening.

During our first evening in the marshalling area, the company officers received our initial briefings on our D-Day mission from my friend Nixon, who was now serving as 2d Battalion S-2 (intelligence officer) and Captain Hester, a former Easy Company officer, who was the battalion operations officer. We examined sand tables, routes of advance and egress to the objective areas, and received briefings on the enemy situation and pending weather conditions. I listened closely, but concentrated on the general concept of the operation rather than all the specifics because it was more important to be able to think on my feet than it was to memorize every excruciating detail, most of which would never withstand the initial clash with the enemy. Personally I did very little briefing. I just couldn't seem to get enthusiastic, but I had the situation well in hand.

The 101st Airborne Division's mission on D-Day was to drop in the vicinity of Ste. Marie du Mont and to seize four causeways behind Utah Beach on the Cotentin Peninsula. In all, there were four causeways that connected Utah Beach with the solid ground of Normandy. The concept of operation called for the 502d Regiment to secure the two northernmost exits to facilitate the passage inland of the amphibious forces, principally from the 4th Infantry Division, while Colonel Sink's 506th PIR secured the two southernmost exits. Sink, in turn, planned for 1st and 2d Battalions to land on a drop zone just to the west of Ste. Marie du Mont, which put it about as close to the western approaches of the two lower causeways as was tactically possible. As rapidly as it could complete its assembly, 2d Battalion was to move toward causeway No. 2. Exit No. 2 led from the beach through Houdienville to Ste. Marie du Mont. Securing that causeway was the responsibility of Easy Company with an attached demolition team. This specific causeway was built to a height of an average six feet above the marsh, which was an initial barrier to the westward advance of the forces landing on Utah Beach. The regimental intelligence report noted that over most of the adjoining area, the marsh could be waded, but the entire region was crisscrossed at many points by drainage canals, which though narrow, ran to a depth of eight feet or more. The presence of these streams presented a very real danger. If the force coming by sea was denied the use of the causeways, many hours would pass before the amphibious forces could link up with the airborne forces. The time thus lost might determine the fate of the invading forces at Utah Beach.

On June 1, General Taylor arrived in our area in early afternoon and delivered an inspirational speech to the 506th Parachute Infantry Regiment. Taylor told us to "just give me three days and nights of hard continuous fighting and by then we will have done our part." The following day we assembled the men in the briefing tent and instructed them on the precise details of the impending night jump. On June 3, the officers received Eisenhower's D-Day message and Colonel Sink's order of the day. General Eisenhower reminded us that we were about to embark upon "a Great Crusade to which we have striven these many months." Colonel Sink referred to our impending departure as "the night of nights" and urged us to "strike hard. When the going is tough, let us go harder. Imbued with faith in the rightness of our cause . . . let us annihilate the enemy where found." Both messages were stenciled and packed in bundles of eighteen and were to be delivered to the men at take-off time. We also received $4 worth of "invasion money" and all our British currency was exchanged for French francs. We would not need British pounds where we were heading. Each of the men was also given a dime store cricket—one *click-clack* to be answered by two in the Norman darkness—and the challenge, *Flash*, to be answered by the password, *Thunder*.

I distributed ammunition and grenades to Easy Company on June 3 and the men took hot showers and were given extra cigarettes and candy rations. The tension finally got to Lieutenant Raymond Schmitz, one of Easy Company's platoon leaders. In civilian life Schmitz had been a boxer of some distinction. To break the tension Schmitz asked me to box him. I was no idiot and said, "No, thanks." During the afternoon he kept up the same baiting challenge and I continued giving him the same reply. Finally Schmitz said, "Let's wrestle." Well, I had done a little wrestling in college, so I accepted the challenge. The match was very, very short and ended with Schmitz going to the hospital with two cracked vertebra. He, of course, was scratched from the manifest for the D-Day jump. The rest of that day and right up to the time we strapped on our parachutes, I had a constant line of requests from fellow soldiers asking me with a smile on their face, "Will you break my arm for five dollars?" On June 4 we were in the midst of loading our planes when the word came down that Eisenhower had postponed D-Day for twenty-four hours.

For anyone who participated in D-Day, it was a day like no other in history. Sweating out the $10,000 jump was something that never occurred to us, $10,000 being the standard insurance coverage every solider was required to carry by regulation. We simply relaxed and enjoyed the rest. The mental state of the men was best described in the regimental journal as a mood of "sober expectancy." No one was jubilant, but no one wanted to be left out. Everyone wondered what the jump and the hours following would be like, but every trooper was confident of his own ability to meet the unknown situation. My personal preparation consisted of sewing my escape map into the seam of my jump pants and concealing a short knife inside my boot. A few men in Easy did sweat and they were easy to spot because they kept asking questions about the enemy, situation, and equipment. On the afternoon of June 5, we were told that tonight was definitely the night we would board the aircraft and fly to Normandy. I spent the afternoon getting ready and taking a two-hour nap. After supper, things remained in a great uproar, with everyone getting ready for our initial combat jump. A final check was made of all equipment: the rest was packed away. Next, we enjoyed a last-minute bathroom break, blackened our faces, and checked our weapons. A good number of the men shaved their heads like Mohawk Indians. On the departure airfield, news arrived that Rome had been captured, but we were too intent on the job at hand to be concerned about operations in the Mediterranean.

At 2030 hours, we assembled by planeload and marched off to the hangars. As we passed buddies, friends, and fellow officers, there was usually a stiff smile, nod of the head, or pat on the back, but very few men displayed any emotion at all. It seemed like just another jump, nothing to get excited about. On the way to the hangars we passed some British antiaircraft units stationed at the field, and that was the first time I'd ever seen any real emotion from a limey. They actually had tears in their eyes. You could see that they felt like hell standing there watching us go into battle even though they had been at war much longer than we. At the hangars, each jumpmaster was given two packs of papers containing the messages from General Eisenhower and Colonel Sink, our regimental commander. Each man then synchronized his watch, was assigned a truck, and was whisked off to his respective plane.

At the plane, the first thing I did was unload all the parachutes and equipment and see that each man had his proper equipment. Then, in a huddle, I passed out the poop sheets, gave them the schedule we would have to follow: 2215, in the plane ready to go; 2310, take off; 0120, jump. Good luck, God bless you, and see you in the assembly area. With that done, we went to work harnessing up, and it's here that a good jumpmaster or officer can do the most for his men. For getting all that equipment on, tying it down, trying to make it comfortable and safe, then placing a parachute on top, calls for a lot of ingenuity and sales talk to satisfy the men that all's well. By 2210, all were ready but me: it was no good first getting ready yourself and then helping the men. So, I whipped into my equipment fast and furiously, mounted up, and was ready to go. Thank goodness my main chute opened when I jumped the next morning because I had no place to hang the reserve chute on my harness.

As we climbed aboard the planes, one noteworthy incident ensued. One of the boys, Private Robert "Jeeter" Leonard, had a terrific load. In fact, like others in the stick, I had to push him up the steps into the plane because he carried such a heavy load. Well, "Jeeter" was in the plane ready to go and so was everybody else. I made a final check of all kit bags that held our equipment, and in Jeeter's I found one basic load of M-1 ammunition. Poor Jeeter had everything but his ammunition. The sad part about it was that he just didn't have any place to carry it. So I told him to see me at the assembly area and I would give it to him—which was okay, for there was to be no shooting on the jump field.

At this time I distributed the second round of motion sickness pills, the first having been given at 2200. We had never taken any pills before on any practice jumps, so I directed the men not to question higher headquarters. "Orders are orders. Take them." Headquarters said the pills would eliminate airsickness and the butterflies in each soldier's stomach when he was scared. All was relatively quiet on the departure airfield, just a little bitching about all the equipment we had to carry, but outside of that, there was little conversation. Most of us were just thinking good and hard about the mission at hand and how we would fare in our initial contact with the enemy. My only concern was whether or not I would let my men down once we entered combat. As a fighting company the men were primed and ready to go, and we fully intended that we were either going to win the ensuing battle or be killed.

PART TWO

In the Time of Achilles

The son of Peleus pressed on to win still further glory,
and his hands were bedrabbled with gore.

HOMER, *The Iliad*

Day of Days

Our aircraft took off on schedule at approximately 2313 hours. Second Battalion, 506th PIR, flew in Serial 12, with Easy Company in aircrafts #66–73. Easy Company's headquarters element, led by Lieutenant Meehan, boarded plane #66 piloted by Lieutenant Harold A. Capelluto. Our three platoon leaders, Lieutenants Harry Welsh, Warren Roush, and Robert Matthews, who had assumed command from Lieutenant Schmitz, jumped with their respective platoons. I boarded plane #67 and served as jumpmaster with the stick from 1st Squad of 1st Platoon. A total of seventeen paratroopers were in my aircraft. Lieutenant Bill Sammons piloted our plane. Colonel Charles Young, the commander of 439th Troop Carrier Command, commanded all the aircraft transporting the 101st Airborne Division. Although Young was an experienced pilot and had trained extensively in low-altitude navigation for two years in a tactical squadron as an attack pilot, most of his pilots had only a few hundred hours of flying and this was their first combat mission.

As we departed the airfield at Uppottery, the aircraft climbed to the assembly altitude of 1,500 feet and flew in a holding pattern until the entire formation turned on course at 2342 hours to join the stream of planes converging on the coast of France. Descending to an altitude of 1,000 feet, the pilots maintained course until they neared the Normandy course, at which time they descended to 500 feet. The optimum altitude for a drop was 600 feet at a speed of 100 to 120 knots to preclude excessive prop-wash and needless exposure to enemy fire.

Twenty minutes out, Lieutenant Sammons hollered back and the crew chief removed the door. I immediately stood up and gazed at the long procession of leading planes. With my head out the door, I could see the planes in front and behind us in V of V formations, nine abreast as far as the eye could see. The planes seemed to fill the entire sky. I had seen rows of aircraft on the airfields in England, but now their power filled the night air. Over the coast we encountered a cloud bank that completely obscured the rest of the formation. Since the pilots were not allowed to use their navigation lights, the only visible lights were the dim blue formation lights along the top of the wings. Pilots were now flying on sheer instinct, attempting to maintain the tight formation to avoid collisions with other aircraft. I was somewhat surprised that there was so little antiaircraft fire, but within minutes the entire sky was alive with red, blue, and green tracers. It looked brighter than the Fourth of July. Later Lieutenant Bob Brewer, who commanded the battalion's 81mm mortar platoon, claimed that he had "never seen as much antiaircraft fire as he had seen that night in France."

Off to my right, the plane piloted by Capelluto was struck by antiaircraft fire. Capelluto immediately turned on the green light as tracers went clean through the plane and exited the top of the aircraft, throwing sparks as he fought to stay in formation and to maintain course. Though the clouds obscured my vision, I later learned that the aircraft carrying Lieutenant Thomas Meehan, 1st Sergeant William Evans, and most of the headquarters element, flew steadily onward, and then did a slow wingover to the right. The plane's landing lights came on as it approached the ground. It appeared they were going to make it, but the aircraft hit a hedgerow and exploded, instantly killing everyone on board. If I survived the jump, I would be the company commander.

In my aircraft, Sammons accelerated to evade the enemy fire as I stood in the door with my head down, searching the ground below. This was the first time that I had been under fire and my adrenaline was pumping. As we got closer, I could see the pilots were experiencing difficulty maintaining their formation. Initially the Germans were leading us too far and did not realize that we were flying around 125 miles per hour, but soon they began adjusting their fire. Instead of looking pretty, the fire began to crack as it got closer to our aircraft—and it cracked louder and louder until it hit the tail of our plane. Glancing at the light panel, I waited until Sammons turned on the green light. I yelled, "Go!" just as another burst of 20mm fire hit our aircraft. Within seconds I was out the door, screaming, "Bill Lee," at the top of my lungs. The initial shock of traveling at nearly 150 miles per hour tore my leg bag off, along with virtually every bit of equipment that I was carrying. Jumping immediately behind me was PFC Burt Christenson, carrying one of Easy Company's machine guns. Following Christenson were Private "Jeeter" Leonard, Private Joe Hogan, Christenson's assistant gunner PFC Woodrow Robbins, PFC William Howell, Privates Carl Sawsko, Richard Bray, and Robert Von Klinkin. Luck plays a big role in life. Consider that fact that because plane #66 was overloaded, T/4 Robert B. Smith and Private "Red" Hogan were transferred at the last moment from ill-fated plane #66 to jump with me in plane #67. The last man exiting my aircraft was "Bull" Randleman, my "push man." You always pick a big husky guy as your last man to make sure he is a good "push man." If anyone wanted to change their mind, Bull's job was to give him one push out the door whether he wanted to go or not. No one in stick #67 needed any encouragement.

Our regiment's after-action report described the chaos that resulted from accelerated flight resulting from the heavy enemy antiaircraft fire.

According to the report, out of eighty-one planes scheduled to drop their men into 1st and 2d Battalion's drop zone, only ten had found their mark. Three of the planes had missed their DZ by twenty miles. The planes carrying Lieutenant Colonel Strayer's battalion had simply overshot the mark. "The paratroopers knew it when it happened. Many of them saw three large green 'T's' formed of electric lights pass under us and they recognized the zone markers that had been set up by the regiment's pathfinders. Still, the beacon did not alarm the pilots and they must have flown straight on for several minutes after crossing the drop zone, for when the men at last got their jump signal," the report continued, "the battalion came to earth with its center about five miles from our drop zone." Not one of the 506th Regiment's battalions had a drop pattern that "was as good as the lowest mark that it had established during any training operation. Whether the great spread of the drop pattern contributed materially to the casualty figures was something of a question, but it undoubtedly slowed down assembly and acted as a drag on local operations." Only later did we discover that our planned drop zone had been strongly covered by the enemy with rifle pits and automatic weapons all around its perimeter. Had the drop taken place as planned, it was quite possible "that the greater breadth of the target would have given the waiting Germans a greatly enhanced opportunity for killing." Planned or not, Easy Company was scattered across a wide dispersal area several miles west of our objective.

How the remainder of the regiment was faring was the furthest thing from my mind as I descended to earth. I hit the ground with a *thump*. This was the only jump I ever made that I ended up with black-and-blue bruises on my shoulders and legs for a week afterward. As I lay in a field on the edge of Ste. Mere-Eglise, I could hear the church bell tolling in the night, summoning local citizens to fight a fire that had broken out on the edge of town. Worse yet, I had no weapon because my M-1 and grenades had been ripped off from the shock of the prop-blast as soon as I had exited the plane. In the distance a machine gun was firing into the night sky as other paratroopers descended into the

Norman countryside. Fortunately, there was more sound than fury in the reception that greeted me as I landed. My initial thought was to get as far away from that machine gun as possible. Armed only with the knife that I had stuck in my boot, I struck out in the general direction where I thought my leg bag had landed.

Despite this deplorable situation of landing in enemy territory without a rifle, I still wasn't scared. Don't ask me why. Fear paralyzes the mind but I needed to be able to think clearly, especially when men's lives were at stake. Though I had been apprehensive whether or not I would measure up, the long months of training now kicked in. Before jumping, I'd thought of cutting the top of my chute off and using the silk as a raincoat, both protection against the cold and for camouflage. But now, the only thing on my mind was to get the hell away from those machine guns and that town. Just as I started off, trench knife in hand, another paratrooper landed close by. I helped cut him free from his chute, then grabbed one of his grenades, and said, "Let's go search for my equipment." He was hesitant of taking the lead even with his tommy gun, so I said, "Follow me!"

It wasn't long before we were far enough away from that machine gun that we started to feel a little more secure. To retrieve my equipment would have taken us near the road where another machine gun was shooting down, so I said, "The hell with it, let's go." We started to move north away from the town of Ste. Mere-Eglise, which we identified a few minutes later when I cricketed and received an answer from one of my platoon sergeants, Staff Sergeant Carwood Lipton. Lipton had run across a sign post that read STE. MERE-EGLISE. I studied my map and as soon as I realized where Ste. Mere-Eglise was with respect to our drop zone, I ascertained our approximate location. With that in mind, I looked at the direction of the flight of the rest of the planes and determined the fastest route to Utah Beach. We then hooked up with Lipton's crew, so our group now numbered about twelve men as we started down the road in the direction where our objective lay astride causeway No. 2. Before too long we merged with a larger group of about fifty men from the 502d Regiment with a colonel in charge, so I attached my group to his. The rest of the night was spent walking down the road while the senior officers tried to find the way to their objective. My intention was to remain with the 502d until we reached the beach, then cut loose and head south to our own objective. To separate now and travel with twelve to fifteen men would be foolish if I could stay with fifty more. The only real excitement during the night was when we ran into four horse-drawn wagons of Germans carrying additional harnesses and saddles. Most likely the saddles belonged to the reported Russian cavalry in the area. We destroyed two wagons and killed several Germans before the others escaped into the darkness. We traveled on until we came across some more dead Germans astride a destroyed wagon. I was still looking for a weapon and soon discovered an M-1 under the wagon seat. Finally armed, I was happy once again. I picked up a few more combat essentials as we moved a little farther along. By the time our body eventually joined the battalion, I had a revolver, a belt, a canteen, and lots of ammunition, so I was ready to fight, especially after I bummed some food from one of the men.

About 0600 in the morning, we bumped into Captain Jerre Gross of Dog Company from our battalion. He had approximately forty men, so we joined forces and headed south toward our objective behind Utah Beach. In a few minutes we encountered our battalion staff, so 2d Battalion, 506th Parachute Infantry Regiment, was once again a fighting unit, though it was considerably under regular strength. The fact that Colonel Strayer had been successful in assembling over 200 men was largely the result of the work of his operations officer, Captain Clarence Hester, Easy Company's first executive officer. Hester had landed with the leading elements of the battalion. He rapidly ascertained that his stick of paratroopers had spread over about 1,000 yards during the descent, so he walked back 500 yards in the direction the planes had come, thinking this would put him at about the center of his small group. There, he put up a string of amber bundle lights in a tree. The signal did its work: officers and men began to find their way into the position. Still unsure of his precise location, Hester dispatched Lewis Nixon to prowl the nearest village. A considerable group had gathered around Hester while Nixon conducted his reconnaissance. In a little over one hour, Hester's force included a communications platoon, a machine gun platoon, approximately eighty men from 2d Battalion Headquarters Company, ninety men from D Company, six men from F Company and eight men from E Company. By 0330, Strayer arrived and he took command from Hester.

After we linked up with Strayer's force, Easy Company now consisted of nine riflemen and two officers (myself and Compton) armed with two light machine guns, one bazooka (no ammunition), and one 60mm mortar but no base plate. Since we still had received no word from our company commander, I immediately assumed command of Easy Company. We ran across a lot of dead Germans as we moved toward our objective, but very little fire. Suddenly some heavy artillery rounds landed near the head of the battalion after they moved into a small town called Le Grand Chemin, several kilometers behind Utah Beach. The column stopped and we sat down, content to rest after traveling cross-country for the past several hours. In about ten minutes, Lieutenant George Lavenson, the battalion adjutant, came walking down the line and said, "Winters, they want you and your company up front."

So off I went, still not sure of the whereabouts of our commander, Lieutenant Meehan. Up front I discovered most of the battalion staff including Captain Hester, Lieutenant Nixon, and Lieutenant John Kelly from D Company in a small group talking things over. Kelly had deployed his platoon forward to a position where he could observe the suspected German artillery position, but he could do nothing about stopping their fire. As battalion operations officer, Hester pointed to where an enemy machine gun was located and approximately where a four-gun battery of 105s was situated. That was all he knew. Captain Hester turned to me and said, "There's fire along that hedgerow there. Take care of it." That was the sum of my orders—no detailed battle plan, no intelligence summary, nothing but a specific task to be accomplished without delay. Easy Company's mission was to silence the battery.

Conducting a mental estimate of the situation, I viewed any infantry assault on the battery as a high-risk opportunity since our air forces had failed to destroy the artillery battery in the preliminary bombardment prior to the seaborne invasion. Our key would be initiative, an immediate appraisal of the situation, skillful use of the terrain, and our ability to destroy one gun at a time. The first thing I did was to have everybody drop all equipment except ammunition and grenades, for that was all we would need if things went from good to bad. While the noncommissioned officers prepared the men for the assault, I conducted a hasty reconnaissance of the enemy position. A leader gains an advantage in combat if he is able to appraise the terrain and the situation quickly and correctly. Crawling along a hedgerow, I moved to a position where I could get a better view of the enemy position. The guns appeared to be set in a trench in a hedgerow covered by machine gun fire from across an open pasture. The battery was firing directly down causeway No. 2 in the direction of Utah Beach, where the initial waves of the 4th Infantry Division were already landing. Anticipating that it would be too costly to conduct a frontal attack across an open field, I determined our chances of success would be greatly enhanced if we could hit the enemy on the flank and silence one gun at a time.

Returning to the company, I assigned specific missions to each man. First I placed one of Easy Company's two machine guns in a position where they could provide us covering fire as we moved carefully into position. Next I divided our detachment into two units, one led by Lieutenant Buck Compton, the other remaining with me. Compton moved down one hedgerow with Sergeants Guarnere and Malarkey to get as close to the first gun in the battery as possible, while I led my unit down a parallel hedgerow. Compton also sent Sergeants Lipton and Ranney to a concealed position to put flanking fire on the enemy while my detachment crawled across the open field to approach the first gun.

When my group, consisting of Corporal Joe Toye, PFC Robert "Pop-eye" Wynn, and Private Gerald Lorraine from regimental headquarters, reached the hedge that led to the enemy position, we stopped. Here I placed a second machine gun to engage the first gun that was firing point-blank at us. I gave the gunner instructions not to fire unless he saw a definite target so he would not give his position away. Then we worked our way up to Compton's hedgerow. Here, I spotted a German helmet and I squeezed off two rounds. I later found a pool of blood at this position, but no Jerry (German). Next I sent Compton with two men along the hedge to throw hand grenades at the enemy position while the rest of us supported him with covering fire. I fired occasionally to fill in spots when there was a lull in the covering fire due to putting in new clips. Compton took too long getting his detachment into position and we spent more ammunition than we should have, but in return, we received no enemy fire.

Just as Compton was ready to hurl his grenades, I started across the field with the rest of the assault team so that we jumped into the position together as the grenades exploded. Simultaneously, we hurled additional grenades at the next position. In return we received substantial small arms fire and grenades from the enemy. As we approached the first gun, "Popeye" Wynn was hit in the butt and fell down in the trench. Rather than complaining that he was hit, he apologized, "I'm sorry, Lieutenant, I goofed. I goofed. I'm sorry." My God, it's beautiful when you think of a guy who was so dedicated to his company that he apologizes for getting hit. Now, here was a soldier—hit by enemy fire in Normandy on D-Day, behind the German lines, and he is more upset that he had let his buddies down than he was concerned with his own injury. Popeye's actions spoke for all of us.

At the same time, a Jerry potato masher (hand grenade) sailed into the middle of our group. We spread out as rapidly as possible, but Corporal Joe Toye of Reading, Pennsylvania, just flopped down and was unlucky enough to have the grenade fall between his legs as he lay face-down. It went off as I was yelling at him to "Move, for Christ's sake, move!" He just bounced up and down from the concussion, but he was unhurt and ready to go. By now, a couple of the men had tossed grenades at the Germans, so we followed up our volley with a mad rush, not even stopping to look at Wynn. Private Gerald Lorraine and Sergeant Bill Guarnere accompanied me as we pounded into them. Both troopers had tommy guns and I had my M-1 rifle as we moved into position. Just then three Jerries left one of the guns and started running in the direction of Brecourt Manor. It took only a yell to alert Guarnere and Lorraine, and each immediately fired on his respective man. Lorraine hit his man with the first burst. I squeezed a shot off, which struck my man in the head. Guarnere missed his target, who now turned and started back toward one of the guns. He had only taken two steps when I put a round in his back that knocked him down. Then Guarnere settled down and pumped him full of lead with his tommy gun. We had just finished off these three men when a fourth German emerged from the wood line about one hundred yards away. I spotted him first and had the presence of mind to lie down and attempt a good shot. I killed him instantly. This entire engagement must have taken about fifteen or twenty seconds since we had rushed the initial gun position.

Expecting a counterattack, I flopped down and gazed down the connecting trench to the second gun position, and sure enough, there were two Germans setting up a machine gun. I got in the first shot and hit the gunner in the hip; my second shot caught the other soldier in the shoulder. By that time, the rest of the men were in position, so I directed Toye and Compton to provide supporting fire in the direction of the second gun. Then I retraced my steps, looked over Wynn, who was still sorry he had "goofed off," and told him to work his way back toward battalion headquarters since I couldn't spare anyone to help him.

When I returned to the assault team, Compton, who had been fooling around with a grenade, yelled, "Look out!" We all hit the ground for cover, but there was no protection from the grenade. None of us could get out of the trench, and right in the middle of our position was a grenade set to explode. It burst, but for some reason nobody was hurt. Then, a Jerry, scared to death, came running toward us with his hands over his head. We had captured our first prisoner. We were too busy to escort him to the rear so one of the men hit him with some brass knuckles, and he lay there moaning for about a half an hour. No sooner had this occurred than I spotted three Germans, who for some reason were walking to the rear of our hedge, in a very informal manner, swinging their mess kits. These soldiers were obviously machine gunners protecting the rear of the 105mm cannon crews. I got two of our men into position and we set our rifle sights for about 200 yards. Somebody must have yelled at the Germans because they stopped and tried to listen. That's when I gave the order to commence fire.

It was now time to assault the second gun, so we reorganized for the assault team. In our initial attack, I noticed that as we approached the gun position, German machine gun fire from across the open field behind the battery slackened as we got closer to the actual gun position. Call it a sixth sense, but I decided that if we moved quickly and laid a strong base of fire support, the assault team would only be exposed for a minimal amount of time. Leaving three men at the first gun to maintain supporting fire, we then charged the next position with grenades and lots of yelling and firing. Within seconds we had captured the second gun. I don't think anyone got hurt that time, but we did pick up those two Germans I had injured when they tried to put the machine gun in operation. By now we were running low on ammunition and I needed more men since we were stretched far too much for our own good. Those machine gunners whom I had requested from battalion had never arrived, so I sent a runner to headquarters for some additional firepower.

The sixth sense that had kicked in while taking the second howitzer helped me develop the plan to charge the next gun. After about half an hour, the machine guns from battalion finally arrived, and I put them in place and prepared to assault the third gun. Two soldiers from another company joined us for the assault. On this attack, one of those men, Private First Class John D. Hall of A Company, was killed. We took the gun position, capturing six prisoners in the process. As the German soldiers advanced toward us down the connecting trench with their hands over their heads, they called, "No make me dead!" I sent all six prisoners back to headquarters and at the same time asked for additional ammunition and men. Finally, I spotted Captain Hester coming forward and went to meet him. He gave me three blocks of TNT and an incendiary grenade. I had these placed in the three guns we had already captured. Hester then informed me that Lieutenant Ronald C. Speirs of D Company was bringing five men forward to reinforce Easy Company.

While waiting for Speirs to arrive, I went about gathering documents and stuffing them in a bag. I discovered a map in the second gun position, showing all 105mm artillery positions and machine gun emplacements on the Cotentin Peninsula. I immediately sent the map to battalion and supervised the destruction of the radio equipment, range finders, and other pieces of German equipment. We also discovered belts and belts of machine gun ammunition that contained "wooden bullets." This was the only time I remembered seeing wooden bullets. Perhaps the Germans were short of ammunition, but that was the least of my concerns.

Finally Speirs came forward with a contingent from Dog Company and led the assault on the final gun in the battery. Joining Lieutenant Speirs was Sergeant Bill Guarnere, one of the most consistently brave men in Easy Company. Having just been informed that his brother had been killed in action in Italy, "Wild Bill" Guarnere fought like a man possessed. In a savage attack, Speirs captured the gun and promptly disabled it. In the process he lost "Rusty" Houch, who was killed when he raised his head to throw a grenade into the gun position, and Leonard G. Hicks, who was wounded. With the entire battery now destroyed, we now withdrew because the machine gun fire that we were receiving from the manor house and other positions remained intense. I pulled our own machine guns out first, then the riflemen. I was last to leave, and as I was leaving, I took a final look down the trench, and there was this one wounded Jerry trying to put a machine gun into operation. I drilled him through the head. On our way back, I came across Warrant Officer J. G. Andrew Hill, who had been killed working his way up to help us. In all, we had suffered four dead, six wounded, and we had inflicted fifteen dead and twelve captured on the enemy. German forces in the vicinity of the battery had numbered about fifty. About three hours had passed since I had first received the order to dispose of the battery.

Even though Easy Company was still widely scattered, the small portion that fought at Brecourt had demonstrated the remarkable ability of the airborne trooper to fight, albeit outnumbered, and to win. This sort of combat typified the independent action that characterized the American airborne divisions that jumped in Normandy. Once the battle began, discipline and training overcame our individual and collective fears. As the bullets cracked overhead, our natural adrenaline, coupled with the elements of surprise and audacity, compensated for some foolish mistakes we had committed during the conduct of the assault. At times we had needlessly exposed ourselves to fire and we had charged through a hedgerow without having a clear picture as to what was on the other side. Carwood Lipton later characterized the battle as "a unique example of a small, well-led assault force overcoming and routing a much larger defending force in prepared positions." Don Malarkey, who manned the 60mm mortar, concurred, stating that the success of the day's battle undoubtedly saved numerous lives on the beach. Lipton later gave me far too much credit for our success. Long after the war, he stated that the action at Brecourt was the most outstanding example of a combat leader reading a situation, forming a plan to overcome almost impossible odds, organizing and inspiring his men so that each would confidently handle his part of the plan, and leading his men in the most dangerous parts of the operation. Our success, however, was due more to our training and the unflinching courage of Easy Company than to my personal leadership.

For the action at Brecourt Manor, Compton, Guarnere, and Lorraine received Silver Stars for their role in destroying the German battery that we later discovered was the 6th Battery, 90th German Regimental Artillery. Thirty dead horses in the area confirmed the fact that the battery had been horse-drawn, which was not unusual in the German Army at the time of the war. Bronze Stars were awarded to Toye, Lipton, Malarkey, Ranney, Liebgott, Hendrix, Plesha, Petty and Wynn, all members of our little band. What pleased me most was that every soldier who participated in the assault was duly recognized by senior headquarters. I received the Distinguished Service Cross from Lieutenant General Omar Bradley at a ceremony the following month.

Years later, I heard from a junior officer who had come off Utah Beach on the very causeway that had been under fire from the German battery. The officer was the commanding officer of a medical detachment that landed with the fourth wave. Upon landing, this officer found a wounded Captain John Ahearn, the commanding officer of Company C of the 70th Tank Battalion. Ahearn's tank had been disabled by a land mine. As Ahearn left his tank, he inadvertently stepped on another mine. The medical officer found Ahearn behind a barbed-wire fence, his legs mangled, lying in a mine field, and calling for help. Walking through the mine field, the medic picked up Ahearn, threw him across his shoulders, and carried him to safety. Years later this same medic took time to write me a nice letter in which he admitted that he had always wondered why the artillery fire on the causeway had suddenly stopped so early in the morning. He graciously thanked me and said he would have never made it from the beach had Easy Company not knocked out those guns. That medical officer was Eliot L. Richardson, who later became attorney general in the Nixon administration and who was one of fifteen Americans to receive the Presidential Medal of Freedom in 1998.

Another soldier who noticed that the enemy artillery fire slackened considerably was Sergeant H. G. Nerhood, a platoon sergeant in the 4th Infantry Division, who landed in the second assault wave. Each time he moved his men forward, the artillery fire fell right on top of his platoon. Nerhood's platoon leader figured there was an enemy forward observer calling down the artillery barrage on his position. He looked in vain to see if he could determine where the observer was hiding. Nerhood recollected, "I just wanted to get the hell out of there. Another barrage came down and my platoon leader was hit. I called for the medic to tend to the lieutenant and ordered the platoon forward. We ran thirty or so yards and the barrage came down again, killing five more men in my platoon." After another shell exploded so close that it shook the ground on which Nerhood was laying, "Slowly the shelling stopped and we were able to move inland. Later in the day our operations officer told us that some fellows from the parachute infantry had taken out the guns firing on us."

Nerhood seldom discussed the war in his later years, but his grandson persisted until the Normandy veteran finally acquiesced. His grandson recorded the conversation and wrote me in 2005, "My grandfather was on the beach getting his butt kicked. Your men were at the guns, kicking butt and saving his, along with hundreds more. Had you not succeeded, I might not be alive this day to tell you how deeply grateful I am that Easy Company accomplished its mission and saved the lives of a lot of men that day." H. R. Nerhood and Eliot Richardson were but two soldiers who survived Utah Beach because of the destruction of the Brecourt battery.

When we left the field in front of Brecourt Manor, I took my first shot of hard cider. I was thirsty as hell and I needed a lift, and when one of the men made me the offer, I shocked them by accepting. I thought at the time it might slow down my train of thoughts and reactions, but it didn't. Soon Lieutenant Harry Welsh and Lieutenant Warren Roush came down the road with about thirty more men. I organized them into two platoons and had them stand by until I could direct the armored forces coming from the beach. When the tanks arrived, accompanied by Lewis Nixon, I directed them to the field that had witnessed our baptism of fire. Climbing aboard the lead tank, I

pointed out the location of the enemy machine guns to the tank commander. The tankers then swept the hedgerows and the manor house
with their .50-caliber and .30-caliber machine guns. Armed with superior firepower, they made quick work of the enemy positions.

By mid-afternoon Brecourt was secured and the Germans began
withdrawing in the direction of Carentan. For the first time since the
action had begun, I took time to reflect upon what Easy Company had
accomplished. No longer confined to the trench, I could now walk
across the open pasture in front of the manor. I remember very clearly
promising myself that someday I would come back and go over this
ground when the war was over. As I was making myself that promise,
I became conscious that there was somebody behind me. Turning my
head to see who was following me, I saw Lipton, with a smile on his
face. Probably the same thought was going through his head.

Now that the enemy had left the premises, the de Vallavieille family, led by Colonel de Vallavieille, a sixty-nine-year-old World War I veteran who had fought at the Marne and Verdun, emerged from Brecourt
Manor. Wounded three times during the Great War, Colonel de
Vallavieille had already lost two sons to the Germans during the 1940
campaign. Accompanied by his wife and two sons, Michel and Louis,
the family was ecstatic at their liberation after four years of living
under Nazi occupation. Stepping into the entry of the courtyard,
Michel raised his hands over his head, alongside some German soldiers
who had remained behind to surrender. Regrettably, an American paratrooper shot Colonel de Vallavieille's son in the back, either mistaking
him for a German soldier or thinking he was a collaborator. Carted off
to the nearest aid station, Michel received a blood transfusion and became the first Frenchman evacuated from Utah Beach to England.
Michel de Vallavieille not only survived the war, but he later became
mayor of Ste. Marie du Mont, as well as the founder of the museum at
Utah Beach. He repaid his liberators a hundredfold by honoring their
memory.

In one of my subsequent visits back to the farm of Louis and

Michel de Vallavieille, they asked me if I had seen any civilians in the field on D-Day. I responded, "No," and they took me to the center of the battlefield and showed me a huge sinkhole, probably forty to fifty feet deep and full of trees and bushes. It seems that a farm worker, his wife, and three children, went into the hole when the battle began and remained there for two days, huddled out of sight. That haven was one hot spot—fire going overhead from all directions—but the family was safe and snug as long as they kept their heads down. What a nightmare it must have been for that poor family on D-Day morning.

With the fighting over, Easy Company soon departed for its next objective just a few miles south of Ste. Marie du Mont, where General Maxwell Taylor, our division commander, had established his command post. Easy Company settled in for the night outside the small village of Culoville, which now served as our battalion headquarters. After seeing to the men and placing outposts on our perimeter, I went on a night patrol by myself, if for no other reason to collect my personal thoughts. Approaching a tree line, I heard enemy troops marching down a path directly toward me. The sound of hobnailed boots told me they were German soldiers. I hit the ditch and as they passed, I smelled the strong odor of German tobacco for the first time in my life. Even though I didn't smoke, I clearly recognized the difference between American and German tobacco. The entire episode was too close for my comfort, but I gave the U.S. Army a vote of thanks for giving us good boots with rubber soles and heels, and not the hobnailed footwear of the enemy.

At long last, D-Day was over. Our success had been due to superb leadership at all levels and the training we had experienced prior to the invasion. Add luck to the equation, and Easy Company comprised a formidable team. On reflection, we were highly charged; we knew what to do; and we conducted ourselves as part of a well-oiled machine. Because we were so intimate with each other, I knew the strengths of each of my troopers. It was not accidental that I had selected my best men, Compton, Guarnere, and Malarkey in one group, Lipton and Ranney in the other. These men comprised Easy Company's "killers," soldiers who instinctively understood the intricacies of battle. In both training and combat, a leader senses who his killers are. I merely put them in a position where I could utilize their talents most effectively. Many other soldiers thought they were killers and wanted to prove it. In reality, however, your killers are few and far between. Nor is it always possible to determine who your killers are by the results of a single engagement. In combat, a commander hopes that nonkillers will learn by their association with those soldiers who instinctively wage war without restraint and without regard to their personal safety. The problem, of course, lies in the fact that casualties are highest among your killers, hence the need to return them to the front as soon as possible in the hope that other "killers" emerge. This core of warriors survived, at least until the fates finally abandoned them, because they developed animal-like instincts of self-preservation. Around this group of battle-hardened veterans the remainder of Easy Company coalesced. Other leaders emerged as the war progressed, but the best leaders were those who had endured combat on D-Day and matured as leaders as they gained additional experience.

As for myself, I never considered myself a killer although I had killed several of the enemy. Killing did not make me happy, but in this particular circumstance, it left me momentarily satisfied—satisfied because it led to confidence in getting a difficult job done with minimal casualties. Nor did I ever develop a hatred for the individual German soldier. I merely wanted to eliminate them. There is nothing personal about combat. As the war progressed, I actually developed a healthy respect for the better units we faced on the battlefield. But that was all in the future. For the time being, I was just happy to have survived my baptism by fire. I had always been confident in my own abilities, but the success at Brecourt increased my confidence in my leadership, as well as my ability to pass it on to my soldiers.

Evening allowed a few minutes of quiet reflection. With our outposts in place, I stretched out to catch a few hours sleep, even though the rattle of German small-arms fire continued throughout the night. The Germans were evidently not as tired as we were because they fired their machine guns all night and hollered like a bunch of drunken kids having a party. Before I dozed off, I did not forget to get on my knees and thank God for helping me to live through this day and to ask His help on D+1. I would live this war one day at a time, and I promised myself that if I survived, I would find a small farm somewhere in the Pennsylvania countryside and spend the remainder of my life in quiet and peace.

6 Carentan

There was no pause after D-Day. Easy Company was put on alert to continue the advance around 0500, but we remained in defense while waiting for the regimental order to move out. The projected route was south from Culoville through Vierville to Ste. Come du Mont, then across the Douve River into Carentan. As we were getting ourselves pulled together for another day, Captain Hester, battalion operations officer, came to see me at dawn with a message. "Winters, I hate to do this to you after what you went through yesterday, but I want Easy Company to lead the column toward Vierville." Since Hester was speaking for my battalion commander, I immediately complied with the order.

The sequence of march was E Company, battalion headquarters, followed by D and F Companies. Since we were first in the battalion order of march, we followed 1st Battalion, but before too long they were fired on from the rear between Beaumont and Angoville au Plain.

A lively engagement ensued during which our battalion destroyed two companies of enemy paratroopers. Approximately 140 prisoners were taken and 150 Germans were killed. The majority of prisoners belonged to the 6th Parachute Regiment. Their regimental headquarters had deployed them to their present area about two weeks prior to D-Day. Many were extremely young; some were overage. They did not physically appear to be first-class troops, though their ammunition supply was plentiful and their equipment was good. The majority of the prisoners seemed willing to talk. This lack of discipline changed as we began our drive toward Carentan.

On June 7, General Taylor visited battalion headquarters and complimented the troops on the excellent job they had just finished. Meanwhile, Easy Company attacked and secured Angoville with the help of two light tanks. We were now placed in reserve with our principal responsibility being defense of the 506th Regimental headquarters. Later, I was told of the hard fight around Ste. Come du Mont that Dog Company had that day, and I heard that Captain Jerre Gross, the company commander, had been killed. Gross had been conferring with his battalion commander when an artillery shell struck a nearby tree, killing him instantly. Lieutenant Joe McMillan assumed command of D Company and remained the commanding officer for the rest of the war. In my estimation, he was the best company commander in 2d Battalion. Also killed was Lieutenant Colonel William Turner, 1st Battalion's commanding officer. When Turner raised his head out of a tank turret, he was suddenly shot dead by a sniper, in plain sight of many of the men on the forward line. Combat in Normandy was proving an extremely dangerous business.

During this time one of our major problems was the disposition of dead bodies. The countryside was now littered with dead Germans, abandoned vehicles, and smashed equipment. Dead cattle and horses lay everywhere, often with their legs grotesquely pointing toward the sky. Within days, their carcasses began to bloat and smell in the sweltering June heat. Regiment hired French civilians to burn and bury these animals, but the stench was overpowering. Work details also buried German soldiers where they found them, sometimes in mass graves. Grave registration officers collected and identified American dead, who were temporarily interred at unit cemeteries. Later many of these bodies were interred in the American cemetery that sits atop the bluffs overlooking Omaha Beach.

In addition to the destruction of livestock, the Norman agriculture suffered dramatically during the campaign in Normandy. The Calvados and La Manche departments of Normandy form a richly agricultural region best known for its lush pastureland as well as its apple cider. Ample rainfall ensures that the landscape remains green for most of the year. Dairy products include milk, cream, and various cheeses like Camembert, Livarot, and Pont l'Eveque. The agricultural production declined not only because of direct destruction from shelling and bombing, but also because crops and livestock went days and weeks without proper care and attention. The dairy industry, which once characterized Norman agriculture, virtually ceased to exist in early June 1944. Once the fighting moved toward the interior of France, however, the Norman countryside returned to its pre-invasion state and today it remains one of the country's most prosperous agricultural regions.

Another problem that we encountered in Normandy was the French cognac and Calvados, a distilled apple brandy that is usually drunk between courses to clear the palate and then as a finale to a good meal. If not aged ten to fifteen years, Calvados will take the skin off your throat, as many Allied soldiers discovered within days of the invasion. Both cognac and Calvados lay in abundance in every Norman village and farm. Lieutenant Harry Welsh had found a barrel of cognac, and I was convinced that he attempted to drink it all by himself. On one occasion he passed out in the middle of a road and there he was, lying on his reserve parachute, propped up in full view of the enemy. The Germans began zeroing in on Welsh and I had to get out there and grab him and pull him off the road. My God, he was lucky. There were times when I talked to Harry and I realized later that he hadn't heard a word that I had said—and it was not because his hearing was bad. We got that problem straightened out in a few days.

Sleep was still tough to get at night for a variety of reasons. Actual fighting or even the anticipation of combat created constant tension among our soldiers. Equally bothersome were the huge mosquitoes that inhabited the swamps in front of Carentan. Prior to the invasion the Germans had flooded the countryside in a futile effort to discourage Allied planners to conduct airborne operations. The flooding caused large, stagnant pools of water, which proved a fertile breeding ground for swarms of mosquitoes that dive-bombed us every evening. In our advance toward Carentan, you could see pillars of mosquitoes extending several hundred feet into the air. There was no escape since our troops were not equipped with mosquito nets.

Nor was the climate overly hospitable. Days are long in June and July, with the darkness limited to six or seven hours before dawn breaks the eastern horizon. A light drizzle falls over Normandy during most of the spring and summer months, and 1944 was no exception. At night the temperatures fell so much that each trooper wore additional layers of clothing. Climactic conditions changed as rapidly as the tides that swept the Norman beaches. It was not unusual to have one dry day in five. Censorship forbade the mention of any specific town in the vicinity of the operation, but many an American paratrooper began his letters home with the origin listed simply as "Cold and Wet in Normandy."

Higher headquarters also hindered our ability to catch a few minutes' rest. In one case, battalion headquarters alerted the company to prepare for a gas attack that never materialized. Additionally, the German *Luftwaffe* (Air Force) finally appeared in the skies over Carentan and strafed our forces preparing to attack that city. Actually, we had a few precious days to catch our breath, and we needed that rest. We had been under a lot of pressure since word had come down on June 5— "We go tonight." None of us had had much sleep on the flight to Normandy, then we were engaged all day on D-Day, caught a doze or two that night, then fought all day June 7 and half that night. In Normandy it was not unusual to have less than six hours of sleep during the first four days of combat.

The respite, albeit welcome, did not last for long. By June 10, soldiers from the 29th Division, who had landed at Omaha Beach, linked up with the 101st Airborne Division northeast of Carentan, a town of approximately 4,000 that lay astride the main road artery running to Cherbourg at the tip of the Cotentin Peninsula. To take the town, our division commander, General Taylor, devised a three-pronged assault: the 327th Glider Infantry Regiment would attack from the north; the 501st PIR would assault from the northeast, while Sink's 506th PIR conducted a night march, swinging around Carentan to the southwest. H-Hour for the divisional attack was scheduled for dawn on June 12. To reach the line of departure, our battalion conducted a night march over unfamiliar terrain—a task that presents its own share of challenges under the best of circumstances.

Easy Company had spent months and months training at night. For all his faults, Captain Sobel had seen that the men were highly proficient in conducting nocturnal patrols and movement. The problems associated with forced marches across country, through woods, night compass problems, errors in celestial navigation, had all been overcome in the months preceding D-Day. Prior to the invasion, Easy Company had experienced every conceivable problem of troop movement under conditions of limited visibility. We had so much experience in night attacks that we had actually learned to see better at night. Not so surprisingly then, the troops were completely at ease as we prepared for the attack on Carentan. It was my observation that the leaders who experienced the greatest difficulty in handling night movement were regimental and divisional staff officers and personnel. They had "crapped out" on the training problems and did not get to the field day after day and night after night as frequently as had the troops and junior line officers. These shortcomings were evident on D-Day. These staff officers encountered major problems getting oriented and finding their objectives. The numerous hedgerows we found in Normandy only compounded their problems. The junior officers and enlisted soldiers, on the other hand, found their way around and attacked their objectives with ease. As we moved into our assault positions on the evening of June 11, this same lack of training on the part of staff officers once again led to widespread confusion.

At dusk on June 11, 2d Battalion set out across the marsh for Carentan. Our route took us over a bridge, where we turned west across the fields to railroad tracks. The going was very rough as we crossed swampy areas and hedgerows. I knew the battalion would have a difficult time finding its way to our objective. Part of the problem was that regimental headquarters assigned routes to individual battalions and companies as they traversed the countryside. During this movement, 2d Battalion continually broke contact with its organic companies. Once physical contact is lost, ill-disciplined units sacrifice noise discipline in an effort to reestablish contact with the unit immediately to their front. The primary reason for the disruptions occurred when the head of the column would negotiate a tough section of territory, and then take off at an accelerated pace, with no consideration for the rear elements traversing the same tough bottleneck. Additionally, regimental headquarters repeatedly altered the boundaries between the 1st and 2d Battalions. All told, it was a rough night. We stopped, dug in, set up machine guns and bazookas, moved out, over and over. We finally crossed the Douve River in front of Carentan around 0200 on the morning of June 12.

About 0530 on June 12, 2d Battalion was straightened out and deployed for the attack, and Easy Company was finally on its assigned road. Colonel Strayer's scheme of maneuver called for an assault with two companies abreast. He placed Fox Company on our left flank and set up his battalion headquarters to the rear of Easy Company. Dog Company constituted the battalion reserve. The attack was scheduled for 0600. Our battalion was attacking down a road on the southwest side of Carentan. We realized later this meant we were in a position to cut off or trap the German troops that were being forced from Carentan by the remainder of the division. All in all, General Taylor had devised a well-planned attack by his 101st Airborne Division. If the 2d Battalion could take that road intersection leading south from Carentan, the Germans would be forced to use the swamps and flooded areas in their retreat or face annihilation.

With respect to Easy Company, I deployed my first platoon on the left, second on the right, and placed my third platoon in the rear. The road down which we were scheduled to attack toward that T-intersection was straight, with a gentle downward slope, and had shallow ditches on both sides. All was quiet as Lieutenant George Lavenson, the battalion S-1 (personnel officer), decided to relieve himself. He left the road and went into the field between E Company and F Company. I remember seeing a profile of his white fanny as I moved up the road toward Carentan. A shot reverberated in the distance and Lavenson was hit in the rear end. He was later evacuated to a hospital in England before being transferred to a medical facility in the United States for further recuperation. En route to the States, his plane went down. George was a smart officer, a good ex-E Company man; we hated losing him.

I positioned men on both sides of the road and prepared to move out in order to secure the intersection. Lieutenant Welsh led 1st Platoon at the head of the company column. Precisely on schedule, I hollered to Welsh, "Move out!" Just as the attack started, a German machine gun, located in a building at the foot of the hill, started to fire up the road. The German gun crew was in a perfect position, at the perfect time, to wipe out our entire attack. From the left-hand-side of the road, Welsh pushed six men toward the intersection. They went straight at that intersection and the enemy machine gun. The enemy fire, however, was very effective. Our men on both sides of the road kept low profiles in the ditches, heads down, and then they froze in place, leaving Welsh and his six men assaulting the intersection alone. To my rear, Colonel

Strayer and his staff, including Captain Hester and Nixon, could see what was happening. They, in turn, were hollering at me: "Get them moving, Winters, get them moving."

I struggled out of my harness to rid myself of excess equipment so that I could run, since it was obvious what needed to be done. Standing in the middle of the column on the right-hand-side of the road, I hollered, "Move out, move out!" This did no good; everyone had his head down. This was the one and only time in the war that I really blew my top and physically "kicked ass." I came out of that ditch with only my M-1 in hand, and hollering, I ran to the head of the column, kicked ass on the left side of the road, then ran to the right side of the road, back and forth, screaming at the top of my voice, "Get going!" I will never forget the surprise and fear on those faces looking up at me. With me running around on the road like a wild man, the German machine gun seemed to zero in on me. I was a wide-open target. The bullets snapped by and glanced off the road all around me. For a short time, I had the feeling of being "blessed." That feeling didn't last too long, for I was to find out in a few minutes that I wasn't so blessed.

As the men finally renewed the advance, Sergeant Talbert passed me and called out, "Which way when we hit the intersection?"

"Turn right," I ordered.

Finally the rest of the column advanced, and we started to clear the houses on both sides of the intersection. Before long, we had the intersection under control when Welsh and his team tossed some grenades and killed the machine gun crew that had been firing steadily since our attack had begun. The Germans now withdrew from the intersection and headed south. They still had a surprise in store for us. Knowing exactly where we were, they fired prearranged mortar and machine gun fire at the intersection. Our casualties started to mount up fast. I received a slight wound when I picked up a fragment from a machine gun ricochet, which went through the tongue of my boot and into my leg. After the fire died down, I immediately established a company defense. Expecting a counterattack, I checked our ammunition supply and redistributed ammo. Next I walked to the aid station, which had been set up in a courtyard about twenty meters to the rear, to check on our casualties. There the medic picked around my leg with tweezers, extracted the fragment, cleaned the wound, and put some sulfa powder and a bandage on it. I left the top of my boot unlaced and went back to work.

In taking the intersection, Easy Company sustained ten casualties. Among our wounded were Sergeant Lipton, Ed Tipper, and "Burr" Smith. Another casualty was Private Albert Blithe, who was in the aid station sitting with his back against the wall when I entered to have my wound cleaned. I did not notice any wounds, so I asked, "How are you doing, Blithe?"

"I can't see! I can't see!" he replied.

I remember trying to comfort him by saying, "It's okay, Blithe, relax. They'll soon have you out of here, and they'll send you back to England."

As I started to move away, Blithe stood up, saying suddenly, "I'm okay. I'm okay. I can see now."

As soon as Blithe regained his vision, he immediately returned to duty. If you think about that for a minute, that boy had been paralyzed by fear, yet he had the guts and dedication to stick to his buddies in Easy Company. As soon as he relaxed and pulled himself together, he returned to the front rather than taking the easy way out with an evacuation. Sometimes all a soldier needed was a calm voice reassuring him that everything was fine. In Blithe's case, he rejoined the company and was wounded in action during the upcoming fight. After World War II, he served in the 187th Airborne Regiment in the Korean War, where he was awarded a Silver Star and the Bronze Star. By the time he retired from military service, Blithe was a company first sergeant.

Though the Germans were sure to counterattack, I had every reason to be proud of the work that Easy had accomplished in capturing Carentan. Later in the war, in recalling this action with Major Hester, he made a comment that has always left me feeling proud of Easy Company's action that day. As battalion operations officer and later as 506th Regimental S-3, Hester had been in a position to see another company in a similar position caught in machine gun fire, freeze, and then get severely cut up. Easy Company, on the other hand, had moved out, gotten the job done, and had not been deterred by that machine gun. Far more humbling to me was a letter I received years later from Sergeant Talbert. Referring to the attack at the intersection, he wrote, "Seeing you in the middle of that road, wanting to move, was too much. You were my total inspiration. All my boys felt the same way." "Tab" was far too generous with his compliments. His own action at Carentan personified his excellence as both a soldier and a leader. He helped clear that intersection and carried a wounded Lipton to safety. Later when the Germans finally counterattacked, Talbert was everywhere, directing his men to the right place, supervising their fire, before he himself was wounded and evacuated.

As soon as the regiment and the division assembled, we began to pursue the retreating Germans. For the first two miles, there was little or no resistance. Then we ran smack into heavy enemy fire. The Germans had established a defense on the high ground to the west of Carentan. They had excellent fields of fire and heavy hedgerows for protection. Under fire, the 506th was committed to the right-hand side of the road, with 2d Battalion on the right flank, and with Easy Company on the right side of the flank. Our mission was to anchor the railroad tracks that ran along the edge of the flooded area, southwest of the town. Other than at Bastogne, the confusion in getting our men into position was as bad as we were ever to see. At one time I found Easy Company troops firing into troops of another battalion. Later we had some tanks show up for support, and they began firing into our own line. By dark, however, order had been established. We were immediately resupplied with food, water, and ammunition.

As had occurred on D-Day, our lines witnessed wild confusion that evening. The retreating enemy hollered and shot bursts from their burp guns throughout the night. Shortly after midnight, a German patrol crossed in the middle of the field between the two lines and fired their weapons. The sound scared the hell out of me. For a few minutes I half expected a full-blown night attack. On one of our outposts, Sergeant Floyd Talbert took his pistol and gently tapped Private G. H. Smith on the head to wake him. Smith was so confused and scared to be awakened so suddenly that he turned and bayoneted Talbert. Needless to say, Talbert's wound became the subject of another of Walter Gordon's poems when we returned to Aldbourne. In later years Gordon recalled that when Talbert referred to "The Night of the Bayonet," he would always say, "I could have shot the bastard six times as he lunged toward me, but I didn't think we could spare a man at the time."

At approximately 0530, all hell broke loose as we prepared our final attack to drive the enemy from the outskirts of Carentan. Both sides opened up with artillery, mortars, machine guns, and rifle fire—everything we had, and I am sure everything they had. There was a hail of firepower going in both directions. Under that intense fire, our sister company broke and ran. They did so without permission from battalion headquarters. Their withdrawal exposed Easy Company's left flank, as well as Dog Company's right flank. With their flank in the air, D Company also retreated. Easy Company was now alone on the front line, with the flooded area on our right flank, nobody on our left flank. We held fast. A German tank attempted to break through the hedgerow on our left, where Fox Company had initially been positioned. Lieutenant Welsh and his bazooka man, Private John McGrath, ran out in that open field, right in the path of the oncoming tank. As the tank exposed its belly as it penetrated the hedgerow, Welsh and McGrath sent a bazooka round through its unarmored underbelly. In the meantime, battalion had pulled F and D Companies together and pushed them forward about 150 yards, closing the gap somewhat on the left flank, but still leaving us isolated. By mid-afternoon we were finally relieved by the 2d Armored Division, consisting of approximately sixty tanks and fresh infantry. What a wonderful sight it was to see those tanks pouring it on the Germans with their heavy .50-calber machine guns and

then plowing straight into the enemy hedgerows with all those fresh infantry soldiers marching alongside the tanks as though they were on a
maneuver back in the States.

Over the course of the war, 2d Battalion, 506th PIR, participated
in many battles, but without a doubt the toughest fight of the war was
the German counterattack on Carentan on June 13, 1944. On this day
the regiment was pushed back and almost overrun by the enemy. A
friend in the States had once written, "If you're ever in a tight spot, remember you must come back." June 13 was about the "tightest spot"
of the war for Easy Company. That we held our position when the
other companies ran served as a tribute to the fighting spirit of the
American paratrooper.

Now that we were relieved, Easy Company returned to Carentan.
As our column reached the main road back to town, we marched up a
gradual slope, still within long-range distance of the enemy machine
guns. Corporal "Bull" Randleman was immediately in front of me
when an enemy machine gun crew found their range. After another
burst from the machine gun, I could hear bullets hitting the road. Randleman let out a yell, "Damn, I'm hit!" With that, he fell out of line and
started to tear off his harness and musette bag. Bull soon felt moisture
running down his back. Naturally, he assumed it was blood and he prepared for the worst. It turned out that a spent bullet had penetrated his
musette bag and the extra canteen of water inside it. That was a break
for Easy Company because we could ill-afford to lose any more good
men, and "Bull" was a good man.

That night, I slept in a hotel between sheets. The men were billeted
in houses. For the next five days I took it easy as my leg had grown stiff
and sore. The medics cleaned the wound again and kept me on sulfa
tablets. While I recovered, Harry Welsh temporarily assumed command
of the company.

On June 20, Easy Company returned to the main line of resistance
south of Carentan. We remained on the line for the next eight days, but
our only action was to send out patrols every evening. The Germans

did the same. On one of our daylight patrols led by Sergeant Guarnere, Blithe was point man when he spotted a German sniper in a tree. Just as he did in training, he automatically said, "Bang, bang," instead of dropping to the side of the road and putting his rifle on the sniper. The German reacted first and shot Blithe through the collarbone. The rest of the patrol recovered Blithe and then withdrew to Easy's lines.

After a week of patrolling aggressively, Easy Company was pulled off the line and placed into a reserve position on June 28. On June 29, we moved to a position near Cherbourg, where General Taylor visited the company. He mentioned how pleased he was that Easy Company had held the line outside Carentan. We appreciated his comments, but the company was far more appreciative to no longer be under direct fire from the enemy. The respite from combat also allowed us time to reflect on our initial engagements with the enemy and to take stock of our losses. Three weeks of continuous combat had exacted a heavy toll on Easy Company. We had ten casualties on June 12 in the attack on Carentan, and another nine on June 13 in the defense of Carentan. All told, our ranks had been reduced 47 percent, having incurred sixty-five casualties, either killed, wounded, or sick since D-Day. On June 30, Easy Company numbered only seventy-four officers and men present for duty. Normandy had been an extremely costly campaign.

Being pulled from the front line also gave us a chance to collect our personal thoughts. The French people, for instance, had become friendlier as the Germans were pushed farther back. To those who had lost everything, it must have been hard to feel anything but hatred. Everyone had lost at least a little by our invasion, yet all seemed to take great pride in flying their national flags after four years of occupation. They waved to us as we went by and called, "Viva la France!" or they gave us the thumbs-up or "V" for victory sign. It seemed like the feeling was the same the world over. On the whole, however, we did not sense that rural Normandy suffered much under the German occupation. The occupation was far worse in the cities like Caen and Cherbourg, where the Nazis routinely executed members, real or imagined, of the French

Resistance. In the country, dairy products were still plentiful, and few soldiers experienced problems in procuring fresh eggs and milk. Overall, the French natives we encountered as we moved toward Carentan had all the meat and butter they could use. Bread was one of the few commodities that were rationed.

Easy Company also had its share of visitors during our final weeks in Normandy. Colonel Sink arrived to congratulate Easy Company on its achievements. In tow with Sink was Colonel Joseph H. Harper, the commander of the 327th Glider Infantry Regiment from the 101st Airborne Division. Sink was proud as hell and wanted me to explain how his regiment had silenced the battery at Brecourt. I simply replied that we had laid down a base of fire and then maneuvered against the artillery battery, knocking one gun out at a time.

Another visit to senior headquarters was not so pleasant. Supreme Allied Headquarters' combat historian S.L.A. Marshall immediately began conducting after-action reports on the combat in Normandy as soon as there was a lull in combat. In publishing his subsequent *Night Drop*, he alleged that less than 20 percent of the soldiers actually fired their weapons in combat. Marshall obviously had not visited Easy Company, because all its troopers had been decisively engaged. Moreover, Marshall concentrated on the experiences of West Point officers and paid scant attention to those front-line officers who had not graduated from the U.S. Military Academy. Had he spoken to a more comprehensive group of junior officers, he might have drawn different conclusions. My personal encounter with Marshall was relatively brief. He pulled me into a tent with all the senior officers to discuss Easy Company's role on D-Day. There was a hell of a lot of brass in that tent, all anxious for Marshall to make them famous. I couldn't have cared less. I simply related how we established a base of fire and attacked one gun at a time. Because the interview meant absolutely nothing to me at the time, I told my story as quickly as I could and departed. As a result, Marshall didn't say anything special about Easy Company—and what he did say was totally fabricated. Marshall downplayed the contribution of the men and claimed that Strayer's 2d Battalion had kept the German battery "entertained at long range while Captain R. D. Winters hiked to Utah Beach, borrowed four Shermans (tanks) from the 4th Infantry Division, and sicced them on the enemy guns." I don't know what action Marshall was describing, but it sure wasn't the destruction of the battery at Brecourt Manor.

That did not alter my personal admiration of Easy Company during the Carentan campaign. At Brecourt Manor only a small portion of the company had fought the Germans. In destroying that battery, we undoubtedly saved hundreds of American lives on Utah Beach. Carentan was the first battle in which Easy Company had participated as an intact unit. There, Easy had spearheaded the attack into the city and maintained their line when other units withdrew. The enemy counterattack had struck as we were still moving into our defensive positions. We were ill-prepared to meet their attack, but our training and discipline allowed us to repel the German attack. The other members of Easy Company and I were now seasoned combat veterans, though I was careful not to make any false assumptions concerning our battle worthiness based on a single campaign. Our collective experience, however, led to confidence—a degree of self-confidence, despite the fact that operations around Carentan had frequently resulted in mass confusion.

From a strictly personal perspective, my self-confidence increased immeasurably as the men gained confidence in my ability to lead and to think under pressure. On several occasions, they mentioned to me, "God, I am glad to see you!" During most of our time on the front line, our line was stretched very thin. Individual soldiers were under tremendous pressure and intense fire. Just showing up and asking, "How's it going?" meant a lot to them—just reminding them every once in a while you needed to lift your head and to return fire. Success breeds confidence, and Easy Company's success in Normandy instilled the confidence that they would succeed and live to fight another day. At the same time, I could not help but think that had I trained the men harder, if I had done a better job, maybe more of my men would have come home.

On July 1, I received notification that I had been promoted to captain. Gratified as I was, the promotion seemed secondary to the opportunity to take a warm shower and to visit Cherbourg. Later I found a laundry and had everyone's clothes washed. I footed the bill. The next day General Omar N. Bradley, the First (U.S.) Army commanding general, presented me the Distinguished Service Cross. On July 10, the company moved to the vicinity of Utah Beach to be evacuated back to England. Seeing the beach for the first time with that vast armada of ships as far as the eye could see in every direction, and seeing the American flag on the beach, left me feeling weak in the knees for a few moments and brought tears to my eyes. I have never looked at our flag since without that memory in my mind. Today, I think of that moment when I hear people debate and demonstrate over the right to burn the flag. That night we camped in a field near the beach, before climbing on board the LST (Landing Ship Tank) on July 11. We arrived at Southampton the evening of July 12. The next morning we boarded a train, and by noon we were back in Aldbourne.

What a wonderful feeling it was to see friendly English faces! It was like returning home. Awaiting us was all our back mail that had been held while we were in Normandy. That afternoon we distributed new uniforms and weapons to each member of the company. Our old weapons had been left in Normandy. On July 14, I delivered a short lecture to the company about keeping their feet on the ground and avoiding trouble while they were on furlough. Within fifteen minutes, there was not a single soldier in camp, as each departed for a week's furlough. My leg was still sore and stiff, so I remained in Aldbourne a few days, visiting my adopted parents and simply resting in the laziest manner I knew. The Barneses, of course, greeted me as if their own son had returned. Having heard about Easy Company's exploits on the BBC and about my receipt of the Distinguished Service Cross, Mrs. Barnes hugged me and said, "I'm so proud of you. I just knew you would do good."

Still, England required time to adjust from no longer being in a combat zone. At times I was awakened at night by church bells that made me stop a moment. The sound brought back memories of the last time I heard church bells ringing: that had been in France, on D-Day, around 0100 in the morning. What had followed of course was history, but the bells sure gave me a funny feeling. Machine gun fire and rifle fire didn't scare me, but those bells, and the memory of being all alone with only a knife for protection, gave me an eerie feeling of being hunted down by a pack of wolves.

Like most of my soldiers, I visited London where I discovered what it was like to hear and to be on the receiving end of those V-1 buzz bombs. We had seen Hitler's latest "wonder weapons" in Normandy outside of Carentan. At the time they had looked like falling stars, only the falling stars were traveling the wrong way. In Normandy we had been told that when you see one, note the time and take an azimuth reading to determine its origin. In London we were now told that was okay if you could hear the motor running, but to run for an air-raid shelter if the motor had turned off. After what we had experienced in Normandy and when you are dead tired, lying in a bunk on the third floor of a Red Cross building, that part about running for shelter in the middle of the night was for the birds. London was relaxing, but before long I was back in Aldbourne to catch up on some correspondence before the troops returned from furlough. I had asked Staff Sergeant James L. Diel, who had been serving as acting 1st sergeant when the company command group was killed on D-Day, to compile a list of men who had either been killed in action and wounded, along with their home addresses and next of kin. I wrote a note to each, but it was a very difficult job.

As for myself, I relaxed the best I could. Combat had made me tense, particularly since my decisions now meant life or death to the members of my command. Commanding soldiers in combat requires a personal detachment from the men themselves. In a sense, command is the loneliest job in the world. Looking at myself in the mirror, I could see how much I had changed. I could sense it. Another thing that affected me was the importance of discipline—the necessity of instilling discipline in my troops and getting the job done in combat. One thing about combat was that a lot of men you thought were men were just petrified mummies and when they were not petrified, they shook like bowls of jelly. With that in mind, I directed Easy Company to smuggle back from Normandy all the .30-caliber ammunition they could find because I knew that when we returned to England, I would have to train the replacements. I wanted live ammunition, which I could not obtain for training purposes. And I wanted to use that ammunition to put those replacements under live fire. The only way to gain experience for overhead fire was to maneuver under realistic combat conditions. To instill fire discipline and to prepare the replacements for combat, I conducted company live fire field problems. It was dangerous business that scared the replacements and veterans alike. Had anyone been hurt, it would have been my neck. But the training paid huge dividends and fortunately we did not suffer any casualties as we prepared for the next operation. Later on, during the Holland and Bastogne campaigns, time after time Easy Company maneuvered under fire very effectively.

In an attempt to escape the tension that combat had caused, I developed a heavier than usual exercise regimen and I attended church on a regular basis. There were only a few days that I didn't run two to three miles, do eighty push-ups, sixty sit-ups on a foot locker, a couple of splits, and some leg and trunk exercises after the day's work was over. As a result I kept in pretty good shape—not what I'd call wrestling shape, but good enough for army work. Physical activity kept me mentally alert, built up my endurance, and kept me supple.

Another thing I noted about being overseas and away from home was that I found myself not giving a damn about trivial things. Maybe I was spoiled. If I received mail, good, but it didn't bother me one way or another if I didn't. The only value about receiving mail is that it temporarily took my mind off my work and back to the land I dreamed of all the time. Writing was no longer a high priority. Then, what was there to do when I would get home? What I needed instead was to get out and run, or walk, or sing, or do something to alter my frame of mind. It usually resulted in a run. On Sundays, I prepared for church, buttons shined, boots polished, and ribbons in neat rows on my tunic. I considered it a very special privilege to be able to go to church and I didn't want to miss the chance. If combat had taught me anything, it taught me what was essential in life and what wasn't. In my prayers before D-Day, I had always thanked God for what He had done for the world in general and asked that others would be given a break in the future. I had also thanked Him for a lot of things that I now found to be insignificant. The only thing I asked for now was to be alive tomorrow morning and to survive another day. That was all that mattered—that was the only thing as far as wanting anything for myself. All other things had become extra, nonessential, and I could not be bothered or burdened with nonessentials. Not when battle was the payoff.

7

Holland

The next two months passed quickly as Easy Company refitted and absorbed a number of replacements. While many of the wounded veterans convalesced from their wounds suffered in Normandy, I concentrated my efforts on reorganizing our company and platoon headquarters. Lieutenants Harry Welsh and Buck Compton were promoted to first lieutenant, with Welsh now serving as my executive officer and Compton as second platoon leader. New officers assigned to the company included T. A. Peacock, Robert B. Brewer, and John Pisanchin. Lieutenant Charles Hudson, an officer from A Company, received a battlefield commission and joined Easy as an assistant platoon leader. So did Lieutenant Edward Shames, a former operations sergeant, who had built the sand tables we used in planning our airdrop into Normandy. Shames was the first noncommissioned officer to receive a battlefield commission from 3d Battalion.

Because the regiment was in desperate need of officers, I had the opportunity to recommend one man from E Company for a battlefield commission. I immediately recommended 1st Sergeant James Diel, who had served as my company 1st sergeant during the campaign in Normandy. As his platoon leader, I had worked closely with Diel in the States and during our stint in England prior to the invasion. Diel was by no means the biggest, strongest, toughest guy in the outfit. He was not an athlete, but he possessed a command voice, a command attitude, and he took no backtalk or guff from any soldier. He was what I called a "can-do" man. Give him an order and you could forget about it; he got the job done. He was the kind of soldier who made any outfit look good, and he made a platoon leader's job easy. Diel was also a self-starter, highly motivated, entirely dependable, and he had a no-nonsense, low-key leadership style that commanded the respect of the men. Diel performed commendably in Normandy and I was confident that he was ready for the next step. While I knew that Easy Company would be losing a first-class leader and that I would be losing a good friend, recommending 1st Sergeant Diel for a battlefield commission was the highest honor I could bestow on him for a job well done. As it was customary that noncommissioned officers who received battlefield commissions were reassigned within the regiment, Diel transferred from Easy Company to Able Company, where he served with distinction until he was killed in action in Holland at the bridge in Zon on September 19.

Selecting noncommissioned officers for promotion was an easy task. The chief strength of Easy Company had always been its core of NCOs. These enlisted men had been thoroughly tested at Toccoa, had been tested again during jump school at Fort Benning, had been hardened during further training in the States and in England, and then had proven their mettle in actual combat. Consequently we were able to restaff E Company with no discernible loss of leadership or morale, despite the fact that we had lost our entire company headquarters plus many other men in Normandy. To fill the hole left by Diel's promotion, I selected Staff Sergeant Carwood Lipton as the company's new first sergeant. Lipton looked like a first sergeant should look. He acted like a senior noncom—he was smart, mature, self-disciplined, and dedicated to Easy Company. Moreover, he led by example—exactly what I expected from my first sergeant. In addition, he commanded the respect of the men. After I announced my decision, I received a letter from Ed Tipper, who was still in a hospital back in the States. He told me that in his opinion, "Lipton was the best noncommissioned officer in the whole army." To fill the hole made by Lipton's transfer to company headquarters, I assigned Sergeant Talbert as platoon sergeant of 1st Platoon. Again it was an easy choice, particularly after his performance in Normandy.

Promotions were also in line for several of the other Toccoa men. Leo D. Boyle was advanced from sergeant to staff sergeant and served as my right-hand man in company headquarters, where his principal responsibility was to help train the new replacements we would be receiving. Boyle was a couple years older than the average company noncommissioned officer. He was many years older as far as maturity was concerned. Perhaps his marriage to a local Aldbourne girl a month before D-Day had something to do with his maturity and fatherly instincts. As his platoon leader at the time, I had given Sergeant Boyle permission to marry his girlfriend. First Sergeant Evans served as his best man. Also promoted to staff sergeant were Bill Guarnere, the second platoon sergeant, and Robert T. Smith. I had been Guarnere's platoon leader in Toccoa. I had recommended him for promotion to corporal and later I had recommended him for promotion to sergeant as a squad leader. Guarnere was a natural leader and one of the most respected noncommissioned officers in Easy Company. At Brecourt, he had done a magnificent job and I had recommended him for the Distinguished Service Cross. (The recommendation was subsequently downgraded to a Silver Star by higher headquarters as division seemed reluctant to approve too many recommendations for high awards for enlisted soldiers.) As it worked out, Guarnere and Lieutenant Compton were the only two men from Easy Company to receive Silver Stars during the entire war. Smith had also performed well as squad leader in Normandy. Due to his demonstrated leadership and self-discipline, I assigned him to be company supply sergeant to fill the shoes of Staff Sergeant Murray Roberts, who had been killed in action. Also promoted to sergeant were Kenneth Mercier, Bull Randleman, Arthur Youman, Don Malarkey, Warren Muck, Paul Rogers, and Myron Ranney. Ranney had been a sergeant and had been busted to private first class for his role in the Sobel mutiny. Joining the NCO ranks were Pat Christenson, Walter Gordon, John Plesha, Darrell Powers, and Lavon Reese.

The next task was to train the replacements who had recently arrived to bring the company back up to its authorized strength. The first thing we did was fire our new weapons to ensure that all rifles were properly zeroed before the next operation. With Staff Sergeant Boyle's help, we developed a rigorous training schedule that included some field exercises for the benefit of the replacements. The older survivors of Normandy were generally given the easier jobs on these exercises. Many who were still recovering from wounds were given lighter duty. Before our next mission Private First Class "Popeye" Wynn and Private Rod Strohl rejoined the company although both still suffered from wounds incurred in Normandy. After Wynn had been evacuated from Utah Beach following our fight at Brecourt, he recovered in a field hospital in England. When informed that if he stayed away from Easy Company for ninety days, they would send him to another company in the 101st Airborne Division, he became edgy to return. He persuaded a sergeant who released the patients to send him back to Aldbourne with papers authorizing light duty. He returned to Easy Company around September 1 and tossed the papers when the company was alerted for another air drop on the Continent.

Popeye and the other veterans of D-Day were particularly tough on the replacements, cutting them no slack during the two weeks we trained for our next mission. Noncommissioned officers like Johnny Martin, Bull Randleman, and Bill Guarnere refused to get too close to the replacements, some of whom were no more than mere boys. As for the newly arrived troopers joining the regiment, they were justifiably in awe of the Normandy veterans, who formed a nuclear family of their own. Somehow they stood apart from the newer members of the company. To this day, those who made Easy Company's initial combat jump into Normandy sit at separate tables during the company reunions.

On August 10, the 101st Airborne Division conducted a general review for General Eisenhower at Hungerford. Ike expressed his tremendous satisfaction for the 101st Airborne Division and told us that he expected we would soon return to the fight. Meanwhile we took care of more mundane matters. In Normandy we ate K-rations, which contained a little packet of lemonade for the lunch ration. The stuff was terrible; everybody threw the packet away. What we did not know was that the packet of lemonade contained all the vitamin C requirements. After going for a month in Normandy without any vitamin C in our diet, just about every trooper suddenly developed cavities. I went to see the regimental dentist, "Shifty" Feiler. He drilled out the cavities and slapped in the fillings. His drill was a foot-pedal-driven apparatus. My teeth were killing me. The next night I was rolling in pain. I couldn't think straight, nor could I go on sick call with a combat jump coming up anyday and run the risk of not leading the company. I had no intention of being marked L.O.B. (Left Out of Battle) because of dental work. On the other hand, I was wondering how I could function in combat with that pain. Fortunately the scheduled jump near Paris was called off, so it was back to Aldbourne and a real dentist. It so happened that the dentist hailed from Harrisburg, Pennsylvania, not far from my home in Lancaster. He drilled out the fillings and announced, "This is bad. Feiler has cut the nerves in both of these molars. They are perfectly good teeth, and if we were back in Harrisburg, I could save them. But under the circumstances, when you might be going into combat any day, the only thing I can do is pull them." I never went back to "Shifty" Feiler and have sworn never to visit any doctor nicknamed "Shifty" again.

Over the course of the next thirty days, we were continually on alert for redeployment to the Continent. On August 17, Easy was notified and briefed for a drop near Chartres to cut off the retreat of the Germans who had escaped the Falaise-Argentan pocket, but D-Day (August 19) came and went. On August 31, we returned to the marshalling area, this time to jump into Belgium behind the Maginot Line. That operation was scrubbed on September 4. In the interim between the two missions, I quietly celebrated my third anniversary in the army. As I looked back, it seemed like a lifetime in some respects and as if I had aged way beyond three years. In other respects it hadn't felt that long and I had been pretty lucky up to that point. There were not many men in Easy Company who had done as much in the same period of time. I figured that if I stuck in the paratroopers for another two or three years, put my money away at about the same rate as I had been, I would have a pretty darn good haul when the war was over. What I most wanted to do was to get back in action. Letting some other guy do the fighting for me just did not feel right.

On September 10, we were back in the marshalling area, this time for Operation Market-Garden, General Bernard L. Montgomery's strategy to bridge the lower Rhine River and to establish a lodgment area within Germany itself. The airborne component of the operation was code-named "Market" and was the largest airborne drop of the war, far exceeding D-Day in the number of troops and aircraft. If the operation succeeded, my friend Captain Lewis Nixon, now serving on battalion staff, expected that the war would be over by Christmas. At our briefing we were told that the 101st and the 82d Airborne Divisions would be attached to the British 2d Army, a prospect that did not sit well with the men. The 101st Airborne Division was assigned four bridges to secure in Eindhoven and one over the Wilhelmina Canal at Zon. The mission of 2d Battalion was to assemble on the eastern edge of the drop zone and to proceed directly to Eindhoven to seize three vital bridges with the support of the balance of the regiment. If we could seize our bridges and the 82d could capture their bridges over the

Maas River at Grave and the Waal River at Nijmegen, a British armored column from XXX Corps would advance up "Hell's Highway" to join the British 1st Airborne Division at Arnhem. Hell's Highway was a two-lane, hard-surfaced road than ran approximately fifty-five miles between Eindhoven and Arnhem.

Compared to Normandy, the jump on September 17 was relatively easy. Regimental headquarters company, 1st and 2d Battalions closed at Membury Airfield by September 15. Unlike D-Day, Easy Company and the entire 506th jumped in broad daylight several miles north of Eindhoven. Approximately five minutes from the drop zone, the regiment encountered heavy flak from German antiaircraft batteries on the ground. Regimental headquarters' planes were the heaviest hit. Colonel Sink and his executive officer, Lieutenant Colonel Charles Chase, nearly suffered the same fate as Easy Company's commander on D-Day when both of their aircraft were struck by enemy antiaircraft fire as they approached the drop zone. As Sink saw a part of the wing dangle, he turned to his men and said, "Well, there goes the wing," but nobody seemed to think much about it. Both Sink and Chase landed safely and promptly organized the regiment to advance on their objectives. The only danger I personally felt was the need to get off the drop zone as quickly as possible in order to prevent getting hit with falling equipment. Since the drop zone was so concentrated—the entire 506th used a single DZ—it was literally raining equipment: helmets, guns, and other bundles. The march off the drop zone was long, hot, and dusty. We took far too long to get to the objective. I couldn't help but think, *Next time, drop us on the objective.*

As our battalion moved down the main road toward Zon, we encountered little resistance. The order of march was D Company leading, followed by E Company, battalion headquarters, and F Company. Battalion had a column of men on each side of the road, when suddenly a German 88 artillery piece fired down the road and we heard German machine guns open up. We sustained no casualties as D Company covered the right side of the road, while E Company took the left side. We pushed forward and were about twenty-five to thirty yards from our first bridge over the Wilhelmina Canal when it blew. For the second time that afternoon, we were caught in a hail of debris, this time of wood and stone. I remember hitting the ground with Nixon on my left. As the stone and timber came down, I thought, *What a hell of a way to die in combat!* Had we been dropped closer to the objective, we could have secured the bridge before German engineers had prepared it for demolition.

In any event, we were up in an instant and Easy Company provided covering fire as 1st Battalion crossed the canal. In the front of that battalion was the commanding officer, Major James La Prade, tiptoeing from rock to rock, trying to make his way across the canal without getting wet. He had his .45-caliber pistol in one hand as he tried to maintain his balance. It struck me as funny. I thought to myself, *For God's sake, man, carry an M-1 rifle if you're expecting trouble. Give yourself a little firepower. Furthermore, carrying an M-1 makes you look like another soldier, not an officer. Snipers like to look for officers.* Three months later La Prade, now a lieutenant colonel, was killed at Bastogne. As for E Company, we crossed the canal by dark, and I slept in a wood shed that night to keep out of the rain. Later, the Royal Engineers of the 14th Field Company laid a 110-foot long Bailey bridge over the Wilhelmina Canal for the tanks to cross once Hell's Highway was secured.

The following day, the 506th renewed its advance toward Eindhoven, a city of 100,000 residents. As we approached Eindhoven, Colonel Sink ordered 2d Battalion, with F Company leading, to the left flank of the regiment. F Company was stopped cold, and E Company was sent to the left flank of its sister company. During the subsequent attack Lieutenant Bob Brewer, Easy Company's 3d Platoon leader, was hit. I had sent Brewer to lead E Company in the attack. The field in front of Eindhoven was flat, with absolutely no cover. There was a slight rise in elevation as we approached the town. Brewer had dispersed his platoon in perfect formation: scouts forward, no bunching up. The formation was perfect except for one thing. Brewer was way out front with the scouts. Being a tall man, about six-foot-three, waving his arms and hollering, he looked like an officer. Brewer was a perfect target. I could see it coming; everyone could see it coming. I hollered over the radio, "Get back. Drop back. Drop back!" No radio contact. He just kept going ahead. Suddenly, a single shot rang out and down he went down like a tree that had been felled by an expert lumberjack. The bullet passed through his throat just below the jawline. I was sure he was dead. At that moment, I didn't have time for pity. Without a pause, I kept driving the company across that field as fast as we could go. I never looked back. We reached Eindhoven without further resistance. As for Brewer, he miraculously recovered and later joined Easy Company at the end of the war.

After Normandy, I wondered if I would ever find any elation in war. When we entered Eindhoven, however, our biggest problem was pushing the troops through the crowds of people that greeted our men. Having suffered over four years of occupation by the Nazis, the reception by the Dutch population of the first Allied soldiers they had seen since April 1940 was unrestrained. It must have been similar to the outpouring of emotion that greeted our troops when they liberated Paris in late August. The streets of Eindhoven were literally engulfed with civilians, smiling, waving, and offering the men drinks and food. Many residents brought chairs from their homes and encouraged our soldiers to sit down and rest for a while. This reception contrasted sharply with what we had encountered in Normandy, where we had been suspicious of snipers posing as French civilians. I was still afraid of snipers after just having seen Brewer get hit, so I put my map case under my pants belt. I next pulled my fatigue jacket over the map case and the binoculars, to conceal both. I then turned the collar of my jacket up to conceal my rank. I tried as much as possible to look like just another GI, which was why I always carried an M-1 rifle. It just felt good knowing that I could take care of myself in all situations.

Easy Company soon pushed through the crowd and secured the

bridges over the Dommel River. I figured the party could wait until later. Not getting to that first bridge before it was destroyed on September 17 had left us feeling that we had failed to do our part in accomplishing the assigned mission. However, the guilt didn't last long, since the forward elements of the British armored column did not arrive until the afternoon of September 18. Then they promptly halted in the center of town, set up housekeeping, and proceeded to make tea. This lack of urgency for the need to push on to the 82d at Nijmegen and their comrades at Arnhem left us feeling a bit bewildered. By 1830, the main body of the British Guards Armored Division started passing through Eindhoven from the south. This completed the mission assigned to the 506th at the start of the operation. That night, I set up outposts as Colonel Strayer established his battalion headquarters in the center of Tongelre, a suburb on the east side of Eindhoven.

While we consolidated our forces, the enemy remained active. The First Allied Airborne Army had dropped into a hornet's nest. German troops prepared for an immediate counterattack to sever the lone road that ran from Eindhoven to Arnhem. On September 19, two days into the operation, Easy Company, with a platoon of tanks attached for support, was given the mission of advancing toward Helmond, eight miles east of Eindhoven to make contact with the enemy. As we departed Eindhoven, the Dutch were out again, cheering, waving flags, offering food and drink. We crossed the line of departure and passed through Nuenen, a small village whose chief claim to fame was being the birthplace of Vincent van Gogh. No sooner had we departed Nuenen than we encountered heavy fire from enemy tanks. The Germans destroyed several of our tanks and pinned down the company so quickly and tightly that we found it impossible to advance. Most of the men took cover in ditches adjacent to the road since we only had a few buildings that we could use as cover to set up and return fire. All we could do was to maintain fire until night. Then we broke off the fight and crawled back through the ditches until we could consolidate the company and return to Eindhoven. Nixon arrived late in the afternoon with enough trucks to haul the company back to town. The Germans had administered a tremendous beating to American paratroopers who had started the day fully confident.

As soon as we returned to Eindhoven, the German air force gave the center of the city a terrific pounding. The image of that aerial and artillery bombardment remains seared in my mind to this day. The Dutch, who just that morning had been so happy to be liberated, and who had cheered us as we marched out toward Helmond, were now inside, closing their shutters, taking down their flags, looking dejected. It was a sad sight. They obviously felt that we were deserting them in the face of a determined enemy advance. Large fires continued burning in the town, and it wasn't until the morning before Eindhoven's residents brought the fires under control. To the population of this city, their world seemed to be coming to an end. We, too, felt badly, limping back to town. For the first time, Easy Company had been forced to retreat. Without sufficient armor support, our position was tactically impossible. Besides, we had ascertained the enemy location and determined their intention. I immediately settled the men down for the night and made my way to battalion headquarters to report. As I walked in, everybody seemed to be in a jovial mood and enjoying a scrumptious dinner. Lieutenant Colonel Strayer saw me, turned, and with a big smile asked, "How did it go today, Winters?"

"Sir, I had fifteen casualties today and took a hell of a licking."

I wasn't smiling either. Needless to say the mood of the party changed abruptly. The only good news concerning our recent engagement was the return of "Bull" Randleman the next morning. Randleman had been reported as missing in action. Wounded and cut off from the rest of Easy Company, he took refuge in a vacant barn and waited until nightfall. Before long, a German soldier entered the barn to scout it out. "Bull" bayoneted him and concealed the body with hay. Then he covered himself and hid until the following morning when he was rescued by soldiers from A and D Companies.

Randleman was typical of the NCOs in Easy Company, and the

fact that he had stood on his own two feet, behind enemy lines, and had not lost his composure said a lot about the company's ability to function in combat. Private Tony Garcia, one of his squad members, described Randleman as "big and tough: tough not only against the Germans, but also in a milder way with his squad." "Bull" talked slowly, but he had a commanding presence. If you needed to get the company up in the morning, you did not need a bugle. You just put Randleman in the middle of a field and told him to have everybody fall out. That was all you needed. No matter what kind of job you gave him, he got it done. He was extremely dependable. And the men loved him.

After two days in defense, Easy Company received orders to mount its men on trucks and move toward Uden on "Hell's Highway" in anticipation of a German attack. We were part of a two battalion–size force under command of Lieutenant Colonel Chase, the regimental executive officer. Easy Company only had sufficient trucks to carry half of the company, so I commanded the first serial. Captain Nixon and Lieutenant Welsh accompanied me as we approached Vechel. No sooner had we passed through Vechel en route to Uden, a scant four miles away, than the Germans severed the road in two places. Lieutenant General Brian Horrocks, commanding the British XXX Corps whose mission it was to secure Hell's Highway, later referred to the German attack as his "Black Friday." The German assault also left us isolated. I turned to the men and said, "Men, there's nothing to get excited about. The situation is normal. We are surrounded!" Together with three British tanks that were caught in town with us, we remained surrounded for the remainder of September 22 and for the next two days. I reported our dispositions to Colonel Chase, who immediately directed me to establish a defense in Uden. Roadblocks were set up on all roads entering Uden. To coordinate the defense, Nixon and I climbed the church tower. We climbed as high as we could go, to where the church bell was suspended. From here we could observe the battle taking place in the vicinity of Vechel.

It was not long before we noticed a German patrol of platoon strength moving through an orchard on the southeast side of Uden. We ran down the tower and I grabbed a couple of rifle squads and sped off to intercept the patrol. We hit them hard and they withdrew. I returned to the tower to enjoy my catbird seat, watching enemy tanks approach Vechel under tactical air support from the *Luftwaffe*. I couldn't believe that with all this action going on, no one was coming toward us at Uden, just a few miles away. The bliss of this front row seat did not last. A German patrol must have spotted Nixon and me, or, at least suspected that somebody was in that tower. They sent a long shot our way and it literally "rang our bell," which was right over our heads. We came down the stairs of that tower so fast that our feet did not touch the steps more than two or three times. After we hit the ground, we enjoyed a good laugh just thinking about how we must have looked coming down.

At the road junction on the south end of Uden, I established a company strongpoint in a store adjacent to the road. The plan was simple: In case of attack, we would make a stand. If they brought tanks against us, we would drop composition C charges and Molotov cocktails on the tanks from the second-floor window as they passed the strongpoint. There was no talk of retreat or withdrawal and certainly nobody thought of surrender. That evening, around 2200, I decided to check all my roadblocks one last time before settling down for the night. Lieutenant Welsh was in charge of the roadblock on the northwest side of the town. On the left-hand side of the road junction, there was a large home that sat well back from the road. This would make a good command post (CP) for the roadblock, and that was where I had wanted the CP to be located. On the right-hand side of the road junction, there was a tavern. When I reached the road junction, I found a British Sherman tank in place, as we had agreed. However, I could not find a single Easy Company trooper in position. Damn mad, I went to the house where I had wanted the CP, figuring that everyone was inside. I knocked on the door, and a maid answered. I couldn't speak Dutch; she couldn't speak English. Somehow, she got the message that I wanted to see "a soldier." She escorted me down a hallway and opened the door to a large, lavishly furnished living room. The sight that greeted my eyes left me speechless. Sitting on the floor, in front of a large, blazing fire in a fireplace, was a beautiful Dutch girl, sharing a dinner of eggs with a British lieutenant. She smiled, he turned, and over his shoulder asked me, "Are my tanks still outside?" My reply to that question did not improve Anglo-American relations.

I returned to the road junction, went across the street, and found Welsh and his men sacked out on top of the bar at the tavern. Lieutenant Welsh and I sometimes had different priorities when it came to combat. Harry and I talked this whole situation over and I left, satisfied that we would have a roadblock set up to my specifications and that I could get a good night's sleep without worrying about a breakthrough. We remained in defensive positions until the afternoon of September 24, when the rest of the 506th arrived in Uden. That afternoon, however, the Germans cut the road again, this time south of Vechel, just north of the village of Koevering.

At 0300 the regiment was ordered to return from Uden back to Vechel in order to open the road again. In a heavy rain, the regiment launched an attack five hours later south of Vechel. Our battalion was initially in reserve, but by early afternoon Strayer committed 2d Battalion on a flanking action to the left. We had half a squadron of British tanks in support. Even with Easy Company in the lead, our advance was slow. Captain Nixon accompanied me as we scouted the terrain, planned, and executed each move of the flanking action. The pathway we selected was solid and firm, good traction for the tanks. On our right was a stand of woodland. The woodland cover ran out about 350 yards from the highway. To reach that highway, we had to cross 350 yards of open ground with absolutely no cover or concealment.

I dispersed the company in the same formation I had used on entering Eindhoven: scouts out, two columns of men spread out, no bunching up. About halfway across the field, we suddenly encountered machine gun fire from German Royal Tiger tanks and troops from the 6th German Parachute Regiment. Everybody immediately hit the ground. I turned to my left rear where Staff Sergeant Guarnere was located and ordered mortar fire on those machine guns. Guarnere was already giving the range and direction to Sergeant Malarkey, who was in the process of setting up his 60mm mortar. Malarkey was the only man on that field at that point who was not flat on his stomach. Next, I ordered the machine guns to establish a base of fire on that roadway and also on the enemy tank that by now, we could all see, was dug in hull-defilade on the side of the road.

While this action was occurring, I turned to check out Nixon, who was on my left side. He had a big smile on his face as he examined his helmet. A machine gun bullet from that initial burst had gone through the front of his helmet and grazed his forehead, leaving only a brown mark on his forehead before exiting through the side of his helmet. The bullet never broke the skin. This stroke of luck meant that Nixon was one of the very few men of 2d Battalion who jumped in Normandy and went through the entire war without receiving at least one Purple Heart.

From a personal standpoint, I would have been devastated had Nixon been killed. As a leader you do not stop and calculate your losses during combat. You cannot stop a fight and ask yourself how many casualties you have sustained. You calculate losses only when the fight is over. Ever since the second week of the invasion, casualties had been my greatest concern. Victory would eventually be ours, but the casualties that had to be paid were the price that hurt. In that regard Nixon seemed a special case.

As different in temperament as Nixon and I were, he was the one man to whom I could talk. He provided an outlet that allowed me to unburden myself as a combat leader. "Nix" and I completely understood each other. We possessed a common understanding about leadership, of how troops should be employed, and how battles should be fought. On reflection, Nixon always seemed to be around. We had

known each other from our days in Officer Candidate School at Fort
Benning and at Toccoa, but our friendship was not cemented until Normandy. After the fight at Brecourt, I had requested additional ammunition for my men. When none arrived, I went to battalion
headquarters myself, where I saw Colonel Strayer and his staff studying the map that I had found on one of the guns. I blew my top, which
was totally inappropriate considering my rank. Nixon, however, was
instrumental in obtaining that ammunition. Later, when we were
aboard the LST returning from France, he approached me and asked
that I deliver a lecture on leadership to the rest of the officers at battalion. That caught my attention. We remained good friends for the remainder of the war.

My job now was to maintain that base of fire while we pulled the
company back off that field. We did it by extracting the riflemen first.
They then set up a base of fire while the machine gunners pulled back.
I next went to the edge of the woods and climbed one of our tanks to
talk nose to nose with the commander. I told him there was a Tiger
tank, dug in hull-defilade, across the highway. I then suggested, "If you
pull up behind the bank on the edge of the woods, you can be hull-
defilade and you can get a shot at the Tiger." I got off the tank, and the
next thing that happened amazed everybody. The first tank, along with
another tank to its left, plowed straight through the stand of trees,
making a terrific roar on their way to the edge of the field. As the commander hit the edge of the field, he wheeled his tank to the left to line
up for a shot on the Tiger. *Wham!* The Tiger laid a shot that left a
crease in the Sherman's cannon barrel and glanced off the hull. The
British commander threw his tank in full reverse, just as the Tiger sent
a second round dead center through the turret. The Sherman tank exploded, throwing out the commander. The Tiger made one more shot,
dead center, and knocked out the second British tank. Several paratroopers rushed to the aid of the tankers, pulling wounded British soldiers from their vehicles. One of the tankers was missing his arm;
another's body was on fire. Such was the intensity of the fight.

I now withdrew the company back into the edge of the woods. We continued to exchange machine-gun fire with the Germans along the road. Nixon brought up the 81mm mortars from battalion headquarters company and we raked the roadway until dark. The two British tanks continued to burn and ammunition continued to explode most of the night. During the night, I could hear the German tanks start their motors and move about. I was hoping they were pulling out. Nixon, somehow, found a bottle of schnapps and drank it all by himself.

The next morning, September 26, Easy Company moved out. Without any resistance, we covered that same 350 yards to the highway. Either Malarkey's 60mm or the battalion's 81mm mortar fire had made a direct hit on one of the machine gun nests. One of the dead German troopers lying in the gun position had on a beautiful, brand-new pair of paratrooper-style boots. I needed a new pair of boots by now, so I sat down and put the sole of my boot against the sole of his to compare sizes. Too bad—they were not big enough. We then marched back to Uden in the rain, not reaching the city until after dark. By now we were exhausted. The last ten days had been mighty tough. In the span of a week and a half, Easy Company had been in continuous combat and had sustained twenty-two casualties.

The Island

Now that Uden was secured, Easy Company and the remainder of the 101st Airborne Division received orders to move to the "Island," a long narrow area north of Nijmegen between the Lower Rhine and the Waal Rivers. The ground between the dikes of the two rivers was flat farmland, dotted with small villages and towns. The dikes along the rivers were twenty feet high and the fields were crisscrossed with drainage ditches that were covered with heavy vegetation. There were roads on the top of the dikes and narrow roadways through the adjoining farmland. The farming was concentrated and lush with fields of carrots, beets, and cabbages, interspersed with fruit orchards. For the upcoming operation the 101st Airborne Division was attached to the British XII Corps. On October 2, the 506th PIR moved by trucks over the bridge at Nijmegen and was the first unit of the 101st to move to the Island. Intelligence reported that the German 363d Volksgrenadier Division was in the vicinity, and received orders to clear the Island. The

363d Volksgrenadier Division had been cut up in Normandy, but now had been reinforced and was anxious to return to battle.

The following day our regiment relieved the frontline positions held by the British 43d Wessex Infantry Division, which was covering a line of approximately six miles in length. The 43d Division had suffered heavy casualties in their attempt to seize the crossings of the Lower Rhine and to evacuate the British 1st Airborne Division that had jumped at Arnhem. As we approached the forward positions, the British Tommies were withdrawing in trucks. Taking a good look at them, I had never seen more thoroughly dispirited soldiers. Two weeks of combat had totally drained their morale and had thoroughly demoralized the troops. Colonel Strayer's 2d Battalion now dispersed its line on the south bank of the Rhine, covering an area of over three miles in length, starting at a point one-half mile east of Heteren and extending two and a half miles west of Randwijk toward Opheusden. The 3d Battalion lay on our right flank with 1st Battalion in reserve. Easy Company held the right of the battalion line, with Dog Company on the left flank, and Fox Company in reserve. Colonel Strayer established battalion headquarters at Hemmen, a village just to the rear of our front lines. Each company had responsibility to cover one and one half miles of front, far in excess of the normal distance for company defensive positions. The line could only be covered by strategically placing outposts at the most likely avenues of enemy approach and where I calculated enemy infiltration would occur. Company headquarters would keep contact with these outposts by means of radio, wire, and contact patrols. I placed the second and third platoons on line and kept my first platoon in reserve. Easy Company's entire complement of personnel consisted of five officers and 130 enlisted men present for duty.

There was little action the first two days but around 0400 on October 5, the enemy attacked in strength with machine gun and mortar support on our flank, striking 3d Battalion headquarters and killing the battalion commander. Simultaneously on our front, a patrol of four men led by Sergeant Art Youman, left Randwijk to observe enemy activity and to adjust artillery fire from an outpost on the south bank of the Rhine River. The patrol included Youman, and Privates First Class Roderick Strohl, Jim Alley, and Joe Lesniewski. The patrol returned at 0420 with all four wounded by small-arms fire and hand grenades. Alley had caught the worst of it. He had thirty-two holes in his left side, face, neck, and arm, and would spend the next two months in the hospital. Everyone in the patrol was out of breath. One look at them and you knew that they had been in combat and had faced death in the night. There was absolutely no question about it. Strohl reported that they had encountered a large body of Germans at the crossroads three-quarters of a mile east of Easy Company's command post. In his estimation, the Germans had achieved a major breakthrough of our lines. Strohl also reported that the enemy had a machine gun that was firing randomly to the south. As they had approached the machine gun, his patrol had come under fire.

Due to the potential seriousness of the situation, I decided to investigate myself. Taking Sergeant Leo Boyle from the company headquarters (he carried the SCR 300 radio), and one squad from 1st Platoon, which at this time was still the reserve platoon, I organized the patrol and started off as fast as possible to analyze the situation. As we approached the crossroads, I could see and hear intermittent machine gun fire, with tracers flying off toward the south. This firing made no sense to me because I knew there was absolutely nothing down that road for nearly three and half miles—and that would be the 2d Battalion headquarters at Hemmen.

At this point I halted the patrol and tried to make contact with the Canadian soldier who was our forward observer for artillery support. I wanted the observer to place a concentration of artillery fire on that crossroads, but I could not raise him on the radio. Leaving the patrol in charge of Sergeant Boyle, I conducted a short reconnaissance myself to determine which was the best way to get closer to that crossroad. I saw that the river side of the dike had a ditch about two to two-and-a-half feet deep that ran parallel to the dike road. This would provide us better cover. Leaving two men as guards for our rear and right flank protection, I took the remainder of the squad up and over the dike to the north side. We then followed the ditch toward the crossroads and the machine gun. Approximately 250 yards from the crossroads, I again halted the patrol and crawled up the ditch by myself to scout out the situation. As I got closer to the crossroads, I heard voices and observed seven enemy soldiers silhouetted against the night sky, standing on top of the dike by the machine gun. They were wearing long winter overcoats and distinctive helmets. I crawled until I was about twenty-five yards behind them in the drainage ditch at the bottom of the dike. I thought to myself, This is just like the movie *All Quiet on the Western Front.*

I returned to the patrol and informed them of the enemy dispositions. The instructions were clear: "We must crawl up there with absolutely no noise, keep low, and we must hurry." I could see that we would not have the cover of night with us much longer. We reached a position about forty yards from the machine gun as dawn approached. I halted the patrol and instructed Sergeant Dukeman and Corporal Christenson to set up our machine gun. I then went to each man and in a whisper assigned each a target on the German machine gun crew with instructions to fire on my command. Next I stepped back and raising my voice a bit louder, said "Ready, Aim, Fire!" The rifle fire was good, but our machine gun fired a bit high. Three Germans started running for the other side of the dike. I joined in with my M-1, as did everybody else. In short order we accounted for all seven enemy soldiers.

No sooner had we eliminated the German gun crew than we started receiving some light rifle fire from the east side of the roadway that ran from the dike to the river. I immediately withdrew the patrol down the same ditch by which we had approached the crossroads for about 200 yards to another drainage ditch that ran parallel to the roadway from which we were receiving the rifle fire. I had one major problem because the Germans on the other side of that roadway were at least combat patrol–size and I only had one rifle squad at my disposal.

I radioed Lieutenant Harry Welsh at the company CP to send up the balance of 1st Platoon and also 1st Lieutenant Frank Reis from the battalion headquarters company with his section of light machine guns. At this time we received some rifle grenade fire from the direction of a culvert that ran under the road to the river. Without any direction, the men immediately returned that fire and destroyed the German position. In the ensuing exchange, we lost Corporal William H. Dukeman, a man we all respected. "Duke" was a Toccoa man who was beloved by everyone in the company.

While waiting for the rest of the platoon to join us, I went out fifty yards into the field between the two lines to contemplate the situation we were facing. After careful reflection, three things were immediately apparent: first, the Germans were behind a good solid roadway embankment. We were in a shallow ditch, with no safe route for withdrawal. Second, the Germans were in a good position to outflank us to our right and catch us in the open flat field with no cover. Lastly, if the Germans had a force of any size, they could advance right down that roadway south and there would be nothing to stop them until they hit the battalion command post. Determining that we could not stay where we were but refusing to retreat, I decided to attack. To surrender the initiative to the enemy was indefensible. I figured that when you are in a faceoff, the guy who gets off the first shot usually wins. There was really no other decision to make other than to take the battle directly to the enemy. I asked God to give me strength.

By the time the balance of the first platoon arrived, full daylight reached our position. I called Lieutenants Reis and Peacock, the latter being the leader of 1st Platoon, and Staff Sergeant Floyd Talbert together and gave them the following orders: "Talbert, take 3d Squad to the right. Peacock, take the left with 1st Squad, and I'll take 2d Squad right up the middle. Reis, I want your machine guns placed between the columns and I want good covering fire until we reach that roadway. Then, lift your fire and move up and join us. Fix bayonets and get in line as quickly as possible. Peacock, when everybody is in position, I'll give you a hand signal and you drop a smoke grenade to signal our jump-off."

I then assembled the second squad and explained the plan. Don Hoobler was standing right in front of me. When I said, "Fix bayonets," he took a big swallow. I can still remember seeing his Adam's apple make a difficult trip up and down his throat. Hoobler's adrenaline was flowing.

My adrenaline was pumping, too. I had never been so pumped up in my life. On the smoke signal, the base of fire commenced and all three columns started their dash across the 175 to 200 yards of level field. I was a good athlete in school, but I am sure that I ran that 200 yards faster than I had ever run 200 yards in my life. Hidden in the grass were strings of barbed wire, about the height of the tops of our shoes. I tripped once or twice but continued running. Oddly enough, I seemed to be floating more than running as I rapidly outpaced everyone else in the platoon. When I reached the road leading to the dike, I was completely alone, oblivious to where the rest of the men were located.

The roadway tapered from being twenty feet high at the dike to a level of about three feet in front of me. I simply took a running jump onto the roadway. Good God! Right in front of me was a sentry on outpost, who still had his head down, ducking the covering fire from Lieutenant Reis. To my right was a solid mass of infantry, all packed together, lying down at the juncture of the dike and the road, on which I was standing and which led to the river. They, too, still had their heads down to duck under that base of fire. Since it was already cold in October, the enemy were all wearing their long winter overcoats and had their backpacks on, all of which hindered their movement. Every single man was facing the dike and I was in their rear. I realized what the size of a company formation of paratroopers looked like and I knew this was much larger than one of our companies. Other than a lone sentry, who was directly in front of me, the rear of this mass of men was about fifteen yards away and the front of the company was no more than an additional fifty yards from my position.

I wheeled and dropped back to my side of the road, pulled the pin of a hand grenade, and tossed it over. At the same time, the German sentry lobbed a potato masher back at me. As soon as I threw the grenade, I realized that I had goofed. I had kept a band of tape around the handle of my grenades to avoid an accident in case the pin was pulled accidentally. Fortunately, the enemy's grenade also failed to explode. I immediately jumped back up on top of the road. The sentry was still hunched down covering his head with his arms waiting for my grenade to explode. He was only three or four yards away. After all these years, I can still see him smiling at me as I stood on top of the dike. It wasn't necessary to take an aimed shot. I simply shot from the hip. That shot startled the entire company and they started to rise and turn toward me en masse. After killing the sentry, I simply pivoted to my right and kept firing right into that solid mass of troops.

The movements of the enemy seemed surreal to me. When they rose up, their reaction seemed to be so slow. When they turned to look over their shoulders at the sound of my firing, it was in slow motion, and when they started to raise their rifles to fire, they seemed so lethargic. I cannot give you a reason for this mental trance that I was in other than to say that everybody around me seemed out of synchronization. I was the only one who seemed normal. I never experienced anything like this in combat before or since. I immediately emptied the first clip of eight rounds, and still standing in the middle of the road, I put in a second clip. Still shooting from the hip, I emptied that clip into the enemy. By now I could see some of the Germans throwing their rifles to their shoulders to start shooting at me, but they were caught up in the pushing and shoving so they were unable to get a good shot at me. Most of the mob was just running away. After finishing the second clip, I dropped back to my side of the road for cover. Looking to my right, I could see Talbert sprinting to reach the dike. Crouched over, he was still a good ten yards from the road. Right behind him was Sergeant Rader, running straight up the road with that long stride of his. My column was still struggling to reach the road. Tripping over the wire, they were at least twenty yards away. Lieutenant Peacock was leading his column, but he was also about twenty yards from the road.

Not waiting for the remainder of the platoon, I inserted a third clip and started popping up, taking a shot or two, and then dropping back down. In the meantime, the Germans began running as best they could, but those long winter overcoats and packs shortened their strides as they ran away from me along the foot of the dike, toward the east. By now, Talbert, Rader and his crew were in position and they immediately commenced a deadly accurate fire. "Fire at will," I commanded. You could not have written a better script than this. Talbert's and Rader's squads had a duck shoot straight into the rear of that mass of retreating men. It was virtually impossible to miss. Without effective leadership to calm them down and to make this battle organized chaos, the enemy's retreat disintegrated into a rout.

At this time, another German company arrived from about 100 yards away, east of the road crossing. They had been in the vicinity of the windmill adjacent to the river. When they joined the company that we had routed, the increased mass of troops produced a target-rich environment. My column by now had reached the road and PFC Roy W. Cobb placed his machine gun and delivered long-distance fire on the retreating Germans. Cobb was a hard-nosed individual if you ever saw one, a regular army man who clearly understood combat. Cobb's fire was extremely effective, as was the fire of Talbert's squad, since Talbert had a straight shot at a distance of 250 yards. Peacock's group, on my left, now engaged the enemy, inflicting six dead and nine prisoners on the retreating Germans. As the enemy fled along the dike to the roadway leading back to the river, we could observe their withdrawal at all times. I now called artillery support and we maintained effective fire on the Germans as they ran as fast as they could toward the river.

My immediate intention was to pursue them toward the river and cut off their retreat. I requested an additional platoon from battalion, and they ordered a platoon from Fox Company to come to my support. While waiting for the platoon to arrive, we reorganized. My casualties were one man dead and four wounded. Tech/5 Joseph D. Liebgott had been slightly wounded in the arm, but he was ambulatory so I assigned him the mission of escorting seven German prisoners to the rear. Liebgott had earned the reputation of being one of Easy's best combat soldiers, but we had all heard stories that he was very rough on prisoners. Liebgott was one of Easy Company's "killers," so I deemed it appropriate to take a bit of caution. When he heard me say, "Take the prisoners back to the battalion command post," he replied, "Oh boy! I'll take care of them." In his exuberance, Liebgott stood up and paced back and forth and he was obviously very nervous and concerned.

I stopped him in his tracks. "There are seven prisoners and I want seven prisoners turned over to battalion."

Liebgott was highly incensed and started to throw a tantrum. Somewhat unsure of how he would react, I then dropped my M-1 to my hip, threw off the safety, and said, "Liebgott, drop all your ammunition and empty your rifle." There was much grumbling and swearing, but he did as I had ordered. "Now," I said, "you can put one round in your rifle. If you drop a prisoner, the rest will jump you." One of the German prisoners, an officer, evidently understood this exchange. After the officer comprehended my orders, he relaxed and sat down. Liebgott returned seven prisoners to battalion headquarters that day—I personally checked with Nixon.

When the platoon from Fox Company finally arrived, I distributed ammunition and then made plans to advance toward the river. I intended to set up a base of fire, and then move half the unit forward 100 yards, stop and set up another base of fire, and then have the second half of the platoon leapfrog 100 yards. We would again establish a base of fire and repeat the maneuver in this manner to the river, a distance of 600 yards. At the river end of this road was a ferry that connected the village of Renkun on the north side of the Rhine with a factory on the Rhine River's south bank. Obviously, the Germans had used this crossing to get these two companies to the "Island" from Arnhem. Now they wanted to return to the ferry to withdraw across the river.

We conducted four leapfrog movements with little trouble other than receiving a light concentration of artillery fire, which fell harmlessly on our left flank. As we reached the factory buildings, we were hit by an attack on our right rear flank by a force that I estimated at seventy-five men. Looking at my tactical position from the factory, I realized that I was getting myself into a bottleneck. By now, Easy Company was really close to the river and we were looking up at the German artillery and mortar positions. And now, on my right rear flank, I had what was left of those two German companies pinching in on my flank and attempting to cut off the withdrawal of my two platoons. I decided it was better to call it a day, withdraw, and live to fight tomorrow. Consequently, we withdrew to the dike, leapfrogging in reverse, but always laying down a base of fire.

All went as planned, but just as we were pulling the last groups over the dike, the enemy cut loose with a terrific concentration of mortar and artillery fire right on that crossroads. They had that point zeroed in just perfectly. Before we could move the troops either right or left away from the crossroads, we suffered eighteen casualties, all wounded. I grabbed the SCR 300 radio and went to the top of the dike to try and return some artillery on the Germans. I put the radio down by my left shoulder and was coordinating artillery fire as rapidly as I could. I also called battalion and asked for medics and ambulances to extract the wounded. Lieutenant Jackson "Doc" Neavles, the assistant battalion surgeon, replied and wanted to know how many casualties. I told him we needed help for "two baseball teams." Neavles wasn't very sharp where sports were concerned, and asked me to put that message in clear language. I replied, "Get the hell off the radio so I can get some more artillery support, or we'll need enough for three baseball teams."

About that time a concentration of mortar rounds hit right behind me and I heard a *ting*. I took off my helmet to examine it, thinking I'd been hit on the helmet. There was no sign of damage, so I put it back on and then I noticed that the antenna to the radio sitting by my left shoulder had been clipped off right at the top of the radio. Eventually, the artillery and mortar fire ceased, but we had suffered far too many casualties to continue the engagement. Fortunately none was killed in weathering that mortar and artillery concentration. Sergeant Leo Boyle was one of those hit. He had been my right-hand man all day, and he was in a foxhole right behind me when he was hit. That was the end of the war for Boyle, a very good, loyal friend. The ambulances came and picked up the wounded. I set up a couple of strong points to cover the crossroad, but did not put one on the crossroad since the Germans had already used the intersection as a target reference point. About this time Captain Nixon showed up and asked me, "How's everything going?"

"Give me a drink of water," I replied as I sat down on the edge of the dike. Until that point, I had not realized how exhausted I was. He handed me his canteen and as I went to lift the canteen, my hand was visibly shaking. I'd often seen Nixon's hand shake when he had one too many drinks, but this was the first time that I had ever seen my own hand shake. Nixon's shaking hands were the result of guzzling a shot of Vat 69 and was due to the shock of his nervous system gearing up. I felt my shaking hands were the result of my nervous system settling down, recovering from exertion and excitement.

How we had survived, I had no idea. We were certainly *very* lucky, as we had probably faced 300 plus troops. Fortunately the German leadership was abysmal. This was a far cry from what we had experienced in Normandy, where the enemy marksmanship and grazing fire inflicted a far greater number of casualties on Easy Company. At no time during our current battle had there been any evidence of German commanders directing well-aimed and concentrated fire until their artillery had opened up as we reached the river. This lack of fire discipline was seen originally by the indiscriminate firing of the machine guns early in the morning. Once we had eliminated the enemy machine gun crew, the Germans magnified their mistakes by letting our initial squad get away with sitting in that open field, waiting for the balance of the platoon and the machine gun section to come forward from the company CP. While we waited, we were located in a shallow trench—they had a road bank for a firing line. We sat there for at least one hour without the enemy exercising the slightest bit of initiative. Additionally, the German officers allowed their company to bunch up in one gigantic mass once the battle started. Finally the Germans compounded their errors by permitting us to pin them down with two machine guns while the remainder of 1st Platoon made a dash across 200 yards of a perfectly flat field. To allow roughly thirty-five men rout two companies of elite troops hardly spoke well of the leadership of the enemy.

In my estimation, this action by E Company was the highlight of all Easy Company's engagements during the entire war and it also served as my apogee as company commander. Easy's destruction of the German artillery battery at Brecourt Manor on D-Day was extremely important in its contribution to the successful landing at Utah Beach, but this action demonstrated Easy Company's overall superiority, of every man, of every phase of infantry tactics: patrol, defense, attack under a base of fire, withdrawal, and, above all, superior marksmanship with rifles, machine guns, and mortar fire. All this was done against numerically superior forces that had an advantage of ten to one in manpower and excellent observation for artillery and mortar support. Since early morning, we had sustained twenty-two casualties from the fifty-five or so soldiers who were engaged. Nixon and I estimated the enemy casualties as fifty killed, eleven captured, and countless wounded. I guess I had contributed my share, but killing never made me happy. Satisfied, yes, because I knew I had done my job; but never happy.

There was no superior officer or staff officer present to witness any part of the engagement. Therefore, it was up to me to write up the account. Describing this action, I intentionally wrote the entire narrative without once using the word *I*. My reason was simple—I wanted to ensure that all credit went to the men who deserved it. I was not bucking for a personal decoration or any personal acknowledgement of my abilities as a combat commander. On October 16, I recommended that 1st Platoon and the first section of the light machine gun platoon of Head-

quarters Company be cited for gallantry in action. In compiling my recommendation, I noted that 1st Platoon had spearheaded the company
attack at Carentan. In Holland they had led the attack on Nuenen during which fifteen men of the platoon were killed or injured. Now they
had been instrumental in the destruction of two companies of SS
troops. God, I was proud of these men! Eleven days later, Colonel Sink
issued a regimental general order that cited 1st Platoon, Easy Company
for "their daring and aggressive spirit and sound tactical ability"
against a vastly superior enemy force. That citation was reward enough
for me.

My real satisfaction lay in the eyes of the men. In a sense, Staff
Sergeant Talbert was representative of the entire company. From that
day onward, there was a look in his eye of respect, and a look in my
eye of respect for him and the others who had participated in the attack. The key to a successful combat leader is to earn respect, not because of rank, but because you are a man. In a letter dated after the
war, Tab attempted to summarize our relationship: "The things we had
are damn near sacred to me." The feeling was mutual as October 5
sealed feelings of camaraderie and friendship that were beyond words.
You can't describe it. You have to live through it, but you never question it.

October 5 marked my last combat action as commander of Easy
Company and the last day that I fired my weapon in combat. On October 9, Colonel Sink assigned me to 2d Battalion headquarters to serve
as battalion executive officer. First Lieutenant Fred Heyliger temporarily assumed command of Easy Company until First Lieutenant Norman
S. Dike Jr. arrived from regimental headquarters to assume command
of the company with which I had served for two years. Heyliger had
been an 81mm mortar platoon leader in Headquarters Company of 2d
Battalion. He had two combat jumps to his credit and was well respected in Easy Company.

Leaving Easy Company was the hardest thing I had done in my life.
Life in an infantry company is extremely intimate and the result is that

men share their collective experiences each and every day. As I reflected on my two years in the company, from a platoon leader at Toccoa to Easy's commanding officer since D-Day, I knew that I was leaving the greatest group of men with whom I had ever served. From the tyrannical tenure of Captain Sobel through my relief, Easy Company had trained and fought as a cohesive unit. At Toccoa, Sobel had constantly screamed at the men and he forced each soldier to stand on his own. You were not supposed to help one another. If you did, Sobel withheld your pass and placed you on extra duty. He was trying to wash the men out. This brought the men closer together as they helped each other with their sprains, in carrying heavy equipment, such as crew-served weapons, mortars, and base plates. Easy Company had to work together to get through each day, and this cohesion intensified as the weeks passed. In time, I noticed that when the men started receiving packages from home, they shared within their squad and within their platoon. When we deployed to England in 1943 the cooperation manifested itself even more when the noncommissioned officers mutinied because of their fear of going into battle with Captain Sobel. The rebellion was based on true fear of what lay ahead. Fortunately Colonel Sink had intervened to defuse a highly dangerous situation. And later, of course, when we entered combat, the men continued to share the good and the bad, the tough times and the easy times. From D-Day onward, combat further cemented the closeness that united Easy Company. Stress and combat created a special bond that only exists in an infantry company at war. Hardship and death brought the men together as close as any family or any husband and wife. It was this bond that made Easy Company "a band of brothers" that exists to this day. I was fortunate enough to have been a part of it, but the cohesion that existed in the company was hardly the result of my leadership. The company belonged to the men—the officers were merely the caretakers.

PART THREE

In War's Dark Crucible

Soldiers are citizens of death's grey land,
Drawing no dividends from time's tomorrows.

SIEGFRIED SASSOON, *"Dreamers"*

Interlude

I moved to battalion on October 9 to assume my new duties as battalion executive officer to Lieutenant Colonel Strayer. My transfer was part of a large-scale reorganization of the 506th PIR by Colonel Sink. Following the engagements on October 5, Sink transferred a number of officers within the regiment to a variety of command and staff positions. Of the nine rifle companies within the 506th, four received new commanders. In addition to Easy Company, new commanders arrived to take command of each of 1st Battalion's line companies. Many of the transfers resulted from battlefield casualties. Others occurred because officers failed to measure up to the strain of combat. Still other officers seemed incapable of making decisions. I found myself highly critical of any leader who failed to lead by example. You could see similar feelings in the eyes of the men. The first thing they did when a new platoon leader arrived was to "size him up," to determine if he had the mettle. The biggest problem lay with replacement officers. We desperately needed good officers who were technically and tactically proficient. Unfortunately, battlefield casualties required us to accept a number of replacements who simply were not up to par, but there was no alternative. We needed bodies to fill the ranks.

As excited as I was about the new responsibility, my transfer was bittersweet since it entailed leaving Easy Company. Orders were orders; there was no room for looking at it any other way, but I would be less than truthful if I said that the day I left Easy Company was not a tough day. I was now simply the battalion executive officer, a staff officer with no command authority. I was no longer creative; I felt that I had "lost my men." I knew all the men in Easy Company personally. I had been their leader and had been with them since they had joined the army. At battalion, you don't really know or work with the individual paratrooper. You deal with the officers and the leaders. In Easy Company, we had shared our lives as soon as we joined the airborne infantry. It was this shared experience that created the cohesion and the loyalty within the company, a loyalty that was not always transferred to battalion or more senior headquarters.

On battalion staff I had ample opportunity to reflect upon my two plus years as a member of Easy Company, especially the past four months when I had been privileged to serve as its commander. Naturally, I had made my share of mistakes, but they were sins of omission rather than commission. My principal error had been a tendency to fall into a particular habit. Although I did not realize it at the time, I tended to develop a routine when attacking the enemy. I usually deployed 1st Platoon on the left, 2d Platoon on the right, and 3d Platoon in reserve. I continued this method of deployment throughout the war. As you might expect, the first two platoons incurred the greatest number of casualties, which is why sixty years after the war, the survivors of 3d Platoon far outnumber their sister platoons. This bothers me a lot. I should have aligned the platoons differently and altered the tactical formations.

Only later did Strayer inform me of the reasons behind my transfer. In early October, Colonel Sink had called Strayer to his command post and informed him that he was going to make Major Carl Buechner, his logistics officer and a West Point graduate, a battalion commander in order for Buechner to receive the prerequisite experience for more senior command. He was doing this even though Major Oliver Horton, the 2d Battalion executive officer, was senior to Buechner with respect to date of rank and service within the regiment. In Strayer's opinion, this was nothing more than the West Point Protective Association at work. Strayer informed Sink that he did not agree that Buechner was the man for the job. In the past Buechner had demonstrated a lack of common sense in dealing with the men. Strayer argued forcibly that Horton had earned the promotion and ought to be given a chance, but Sink was adamant and directed that Major Horton report to regimental headquarters to be advised of the situation. Colonel Strayer then returned to his own headquarters and advised Horton that if the regimental commander insisted on putting Buechner in command over him, that he, Horton, should demand a court-martial. Sink relented and assigned Horton to command, leaving a vacancy in 2d Battalion. Strayer then returned to regimental headquarters and requested that I be assigned as his executive officer. Regrettably, Major Horton was killed in an attack above Opheusden on October 5. Strayer considered Horton one of the most outstanding officers in the 506th PIR and later named his son after him.

I found life on battalion staff extremely boring in contrast to commanding Easy Company. My principal responsibility now lay in providing logistical and administrative support to the battalion. My tactical job was to line up other people to make the attack or to maintain a position. As executive officer, I could no longer let myself become involved in a firefight. That was a company commander's or a platoon leader's primary responsibility. My new position was one of a counselor, a guide, and a leader. Battalion staff required new responsibilities and I made the necessary adjustments as rapidly as possible.

During the third week in October, battalion headquarters received

a visitor from the First British Airborne Division. Lieutenant Colonel
O. Dobey, also known as the "Mad Colonel of Arnhem," had been captured during Market-Garden, but he escaped and was rescued by the
Dutch Underground. Now Dobey was attempting to coordinate the rescue of approximately 140 men on the north side of the Rhine. The
group included eight to ten Dutch civilians, five American aviators, and
over one hundred British paratroopers who had evaded their German
adversaries when the enemy destroyed the British airhead in Arnhem.
The mission to extract the British soldiers fell to Easy Company. First
Lieutenant Fred Heyliger, temporarily in command of the company,
served as the patrol leader. As battalion executive officer, I had no
hands-on part in the planning or the execution of the patrol other than
to provide the necessary support. Heyliger did an absolutely superb job
and all Allied soldiers were safely returned to friendly lines on the night
of October 22 and the morning of October 23. All twenty-four men of
Easy Company who participated in the extraction were later com-
mended for their "aggression, spirit, prompt obedience of orders, and
devotion to duty." The British remembered Heyliger's contribution and
leadership of the patrol by awarding him the British Military Cross.

Within a week of "the rescue," the 101st Airborne Division's area
of responsibility was enlarged, causing the 506th to shift east along the
river, taking over the area formerly held by the 501st PIR. Second Battalion headquarters moved to Schoonderlogt, west of Elst. Military action during this period was confined to reconnaissance and combat
patrols. The Germans still held the area along the railroad tracks on
our side of the Rhine, south of Arnhem. The sword hanging over our
heads at all times lay in the fact that the enemy controlled the high
ground north of the river. Thus, they could observe every move we
made during daylight hours, and they could, at their will, deliver a
mortar or artillery concentration whenever the target we presented was
worthy of the expenditure of ammunition.

On October 31, I called 1st Lieutenant Heyliger on the telephone
and suggested that at night the two of us make an inspection of Easy

Company's outposts because for the past week the Germans had been aggressively patrolling through E Company's sector. "Moose" readily agreed and about 2100 hours that evening, I arrived at his command post. First Lieutenant Harry Welsh, leader of 2d Platoon, held the sector of the line facing east. His CP was located in a barn about fifty yards west of the railroad tracks, along which the Germans maintained their outposts. This was an extremely active sector, so we telephoned Welsh to advise him that we were en route to see him. Welsh was an excellent platoon leader, but on this occasion, he failed to notify his outposts that we were approaching their position. As Moose and I proceeded down the path leading to the command post we were walking shoulder to shoulder, for the pathway was only about six to seven feet wide. The path was slightly raised, so there was a drop of approximately three feet into a drainage ditch on each side of the pathway. Heyliger felt we were getting close to the platoon CP when suddenly we received an order to "Halt!" Moose was a calm, easygoing officer, but when he took an extra deep breath, I immediately tensed. I knew Moose had forgotten the password. He started to identify himself, but before he had a word half out, *Wham, wham, wham!* We were looking straight down the barrel of a rifle spitting fire at us from a distance of ten yards.

Instinctively, self-preservation reflexes had me diving into the ditch on the left-hand side of the road as I saw that rifle spewing lead. Lieutenant Heyliger dropped to the road with a moan. I thought for a moment that we had run into a German patrol; that rifle had fired so fast that it could have been a German machine pistol. Then I heard footsteps running away. I crawled out of the ditch, grabbed Moose, and pulled him over to the shoulder of the path. He had been hit in the right shoulder and left leg. His calf looked like it had just been blown away. I immediately started to bandage the leg. In a few minutes I heard footsteps running toward us and I recognized Harry Welsh calling us in a low voice, "Moose? Dick?"

Welsh and a few Easy Company men were a welcome sight. Moose was in desperate need of help. We bandaged him as best we could and gave him several shots of morphine to ease the pain. By the time we evacuated him off the line and into an ambulance, Heyliger had lost so much blood that he was nearly comatose. A whitelike pallor covered his face. As he left for the hospital, I said, "I hope he makes it." Heyliger survived, but for him the war was over. In command for less than a month, he had fallen victim to a senseless case of fratricide so characteristic of undisciplined soldiers rushing to the front before they were properly trained. Now safely back in England, he wrote me a letter, thanking me for taking care of him that night. He went on, "Jesus, they put casts right over my wounds and it smells as if a cat shit in my bed. I can't get away from that stink." Moose remained in the hospital until his discharge in 1947. He suffered terribly from that wound for the remainder of his life. And to the day he died over a half century later, he still could not recall the password.

With respect to the soldier who shot Heyliger, I arranged for his immediate transfer from the company. He was only doing his job, but it was apparent that he was very nervous as we approached the outpost. Normally a soldier on the outpost would duck down and hope to recognize a silhouette before commencing fire. The trooper who shot Heyliger, whose name I don't care to remember, was obviously scared to death. He failed to take any precaution before he opened fire. Where I transferred him, I neither know nor care. He had to live with what he did for the rest of his life. At the time, however, I wasn't thinking about his future. I was thinking about the morale of Easy Company. Under no circumstances could the trooper remain with the company.

Easy Company and 2d Battalion remained on the front line for long periods of increasing boredom punctuated by short bouts of intense activity. The Germans seemed to have abundant ammunition and they held the high ground for observation. Not a day or a night passed that they did not let us know that they knew exactly where we were located. At times British Typhoons (tactical aircraft) fired rockets on German artillery positions. Tactical air support was a magnificent sight to behold. It was wonderful seeing the enemy get pounded after what they had been doing to us for the past month. Active patrolling filled most of our days. Replacements came and went.

Nor did the climate make our stay in Holland very enjoyable. It rained nearly every day, resulting in mud everywhere. Water filled the foxholes, leaving everything and everybody soaking wet. Staff Sergeant Robert Smith laconically said that "it must be some job for the Dutch Chamber of Commerce to paint a good picture of this country." In Smith's estimation the weather wasn't just bad, it was unusually bad. Reflecting upon Easy Company's history, he said that rain and bad weather seemed to follow him wherever he went. When Smith arrived at Toccoa from California, it was raining, and it seemed that every time Easy Company started on a march or field exercise, the floodgates opened. On the march to Atlanta, it "rained, sleeted, and snowed all the way. Camp Mackall treated us pretty well and so did Breckenridge and Bragg—at least when it rained there, there was always sunshine to dry us out. England gave Easy Company a wet welcome and kept us in it." France was more pleasant, but the Dutch weather plagued Easy Company with daily rain. Not being able to escape from the mud and rain grew increasingly depressing as the days went on. Still, the tension of patrolling and the probability of close combat kept us on our toes. In an atmosphere where danger was pervasive, we lived life to the fullest.

After several months, I finally had the opportunity to attend church. It wasn't fancy, but it was church. The chaplain conducted services in a barn with cows and horses crunching hay and adding a delightful aroma to the setting. Another ray of sunshine was the radio, which played on occasion. About all we received was a German station that had a female announcer, whom we called "Arnhem Annie" or "Dirty Gertie." Her daily repertoire reminded us what to bring if we were captured, what a dog Eisenhower was, and how President Roosevelt's family was ruining the country. "You are as far as you are going, Yanks. . . . Just bring your toothbrush, overcoat, and blanket and the war will be over for you," was her usual theme. Next Annie announced the names of those Americans who had been recently captured, telling us how nice it was, since for them the war was over. Between broadcasts, we listened to some pretty good American recordings of dance bands.

Administrative and punitive duties also provided pleasant distractions from combat. When you accept a military commission, 2d lieutenant is the bottom of the officer ladder. Accordingly, junior officers perform myriad inconsequential and mundane tasks. A battalion executive officer occupies a similar position. As the battalion's senior staff officer, my responsibilities frequently demanded that I preside over courts-martial. Ever since the onset of Market-Garden, looting had become a major problem on both sides of the line, ours and the Germans'. In mid-October the British had evacuated Dutch civilians from their homes on the Island. For the next month and a half, British and American troops, as well as Dutch civilians, routinely entered the Dutch villages in our sector. Moreover, we had switched units in and out of these homes on numerous occasions so it was impossible to identify a unit single-handedly responsible for the widespread looting. The men had been sitting there looking at these personal items for several weeks and naturally they seized many of the private possessions that had been left behind when the residents fled to safer surroundings. The rampant problem caused by looting made court-martial duty a very demanding job. Day after day, I presided over men charged with looting. I knew these men; they had earned my highest respect as men, as combat soldiers. They were my friends and yet, I had orders from my superiors: "This looting must stop." The usual punishment resulted in six months confinement and forfeiture of two-thirds pay.

What little enjoyment I had resulted from my daily contact with Nixon and the members of the battalion staff. Now operating as battalion operations officer (S-3), Captain Nixon had always been a hard man to wake up. On one morning, I needed to get an early start to visit one of the companies, so I sent a runner to wake up Nixon. Nixon, as usual, could not be talked into getting out of his sleeping bag, so I personally went to his darkened room. The shutters were closed and without ceremony, I grabbed his feet while he was still in his sleeping bag and threw them over my shoulder. I asked him, "Are you going to get up?"

"Go away, let me alone," he mumbled.

I looked over at the bureau and saw the water pitcher was half full. Still holding his feet over my shoulder, I grabbed the pitcher and threatened again. "Are you going to get up?"

Again he yelled, "Go away."

So I said, "I am going to let you have it!" and with that I started the pouring motion.

At that instant, Nixon opened his eyes and started to holler, "No! No!"

It was too late. The contents were on the way, and with his, "No! No!" I realized the content of the pitcher was piss and not water.

Nixon came sputtering and laughing from his sleeping bag in a hurry. We both agreed that we better alter our plans and visit those showers we had been hearing about in Nijmegen.

By the end of the month our turn finally came to be pulled from the line. On November 25, Canadian troops relieved the 101st Airborne Division. After seventy days on the front line, the division had suffered 3,301 casualties. The casualties in the 506th PIR alone totaled 176 killed in action, left 565 wounded, and 63 missing for a total of 31 percent of the regiment's strength. Easy Company had jumped into Holland with 162 officers and men and had come out of Holland with 113 effectives. E Company had suffered six dead: Corporal William H. Dukeman Jr., Corporal James D. Campbell, PFC Vernon J. Menze, PFC William T. Miller, PFC Robert van Klinken, and Private James W. Miller. Operation Market-Garden and the defense of the Island had proven a costly campaign that had failed on the strategic level. Field Marshal Montgomery's scheme to end the war in the fall of 1944 had utterly failed. At the tactical level, however, we had won the battles, but our success was tempered by our inability to dislodge the Germans from their positions north of the Rhine River. For the present 2d Battalion, 506th PIR was just happy to board trucks that would take them to the village of Mourmelon-le-Grand in France, where both airborne divisions would rest and recuperate for the final campaign to crush Nazi Germany.

Camp Mourmelon on the outskirts of Mourmelon-le-Grand was located approximately nineteen miles from Reims. Second Battalion remained at Mourmelon for three weeks—three weeks of relaxation, three weeks of recuperation following two and a half months on the front line. For the men in our battalion, the respite from combat arrived none too soon. What the paratroopers needed most was sleep. A good night's sleep did wonders for every soldier. Collectively, the men didn't need a week or a month to get back in shape. All they required was a couple of good nights of rest, a few hot meals, a periodic shower, and they were as good as new. The three weeks at Mourmelon-le-Grand served as a godsend after the previous two months of combat. Men received passes to visit Reims and Paris and got in their daily fights with the 82d Airborne Division. The two airborne divisions were wonderful in combat, but somewhat difficult to handle when the fighting halted. On furlough they misbehaved, particularly when a trooper from another command spoke ill of the Screaming Eagles or paratroopers in general, but that could be expected after what the men had experienced since D-Day.

As with the troops, what I needed most was sleep and time to collect my thoughts. I found consolation and relief in reading the Bible. I was no authority on the Book, never intended to be, so when I read it, it was not necessarily to improve my mind or to learn the proverbs so I could impress somebody by quoting chapter and verse, but just for relaxation and atmosphere. To escape the daily monotony at Mourmelon, I traveled to Paris on a short leave in early December. What a town it was! The City of Light was really all that the brochures said about it. Even after taking into consideration the fact that I had not been around civilization for some time, Paris was still some city. I joined a tour and took in the sights. That was about it. I also learned more than I wanted to know about the number of nuts and bolts in the Eiffel Tower and how many French citizens had been beheaded by the guillotine, as well as all the rest of the information a combat soldier doesn't need to know for battle. I watched a couple of good shows, bought some clothes, and best of all had the opportunity to sleep between two sheets on a bed with springs and even had the luxury of taking a hot bath.

I certainly didn't raise hell, never did, and had no intention of doing so in the future. Why not? First and most important, I had my own conscience to answer to. Next, I refused to dishonor my parents, and thirdly, because I was an officer in the U.S. Army. I was damn proud of it and with the rank and position I held. I would not think of doing anything to bring discredit to my outfit, my paratroopers, my boots, my wings, my airborne patch, or to the army. I enjoyed Paris but it was nice returning to the battalion. In a sense it was ironic that I should have to return to 2d Battalion to get some peace. Most soldiers felt the same. It was wonderful letting loose, but it was enjoyable only as far as they could see the sites with their buddies. Soldiers draw comfort being in close proximity to their fellow soldiers.

What was less obvious at the time was how much Holland had changed me as an individual. I attempted to express my feelings to my penpal DeEtta Almon, with whom I had frequently corresponded since I had entered the army. Somewhat embarrassed that I had not written a lengthy letter since I left Aldbourne, I began the letter asking her if she remembered "that two-headed paratrooper who used to write on occasion." My lack of correspondence was something I could not honestly explain. Since the day that we jumped into Holland, I had not written more than three or four short letters. I couldn't say I hadn't had the time, although I had been darn busy. The thing was, I couldn't get into the mood. As near as I could explain, it went something like this: I received a number of letters that I truly enjoyed reading, looking at the photographs, smelling the perfumed envelopes. Next, I promised myself, "Yes, I'll write her the first chance I have, but right now I must study this manual," or do this or that. Or if I couldn't find something to do or an excuse, I just relaxed. Don't ask me why I had suddenly reached a point where I could no longer write. It was not my friend, my parents, or anyone else—it was just me. After watching men fight and die with increasing regularity, I no longer found anything to say that was worth saying. In truth, I noticed myself becoming increasingly distant. And if I had nothing worthwhile to say, why write? When I did take time to correspond, my letters no longer focused on abstract thoughts and mundane adventures. In truth I found myself lecturing on leadership and more serious topics.

In a subsequent letter, I addressed DeEtta's question concerning the composition of my dreams. These, too, had changed. Having commanded soldiers in combat, I now dreamt of leading patrols, fighting Germans, outmaneuvering, outthinking, outshooting, and outfighting the enemy. The dreams were tense, cruel, hard, and bitter. Combat comprised about 80 percent of my nightly dreams. But in a sense, the dreams paid huge dividends. Sometimes when I repeatedly dreamt how to solve a particular problem, I arrived at a viable solution. And crazy as it might seem in the cold morning light, it usually worked. In fact, to date those dreams had always paid off. I knew that this was not what my friend wanted to hear, but this was the reality. As for the other 20 percent, well 10 percent revolved around the happiness and pleasure of a nice warm, comfortable home, good chow, and all the pleasures of a kid. The other 10 percent focused on future operations and plans for happiness. Believe me, I intended and hoped to see the day when I could enjoy life a little more and relax. On reflection, I wonder why she maintained a correspondence that was becoming increasingly one-sided.

Easy Company was now under direct command of 1st Lieutenant Norman Dike, an inexperienced officer from division staff whom his superiors felt needed frontline duty. The senior officer in Easy Company, in terms of length of service, was Harry Welsh, who had joined the regiment at Camp Mackall, North Carolina in April 1943. After six months of combat in Normandy and Holland, there were no original Toccoa officers remaining in the company. All had been killed, wounded, or transferred to battalion or regimental staff. The heart of the company, as always, was the corps of seasoned noncoms, and their ranks were rapidly thinning. Most of the Toccoa men were now platoon sergeants and squad leaders. So much depended on this ever-decreasing group of noncommissioned officers. In that sense Easy Company was not unlike any other company in the battalion. Casualties had drained the leadership of the airborne division that had first entered combat on D-Day.

Over the course of early December, several wounded officers returned to 2d Battalion, including Lieutenant Buck Compton, who had been hit in the attack near Neunen. Other vacancies in the officer ranks were filled by replacements too young and inexperienced to lead effectively. Having said that, the job of a replacement officer with an outfit that had served in combat had to be one of the toughest jobs in the world. You can't earn respect until you have measured up in combat. The majority of the replacement officers simply failed to meet that test.

Also returning to the battalion were some of the original Toccoa men and the veterans of two combat jumps. James Alley, who had been seriously wounded on the dike during our defense of the Island in October, went AWOL from the Replacement Depot to rejoin Easy Company. He arrived just two to three days before we departed for Bastogne. By mid-December the battalion's enlisted ranks had swelled to 65 percent strength. The officer ranks exceeded 100 percent of the authorized strength, in anticipation of future casualties. Each platoon now contained a platoon leader and an assistant platoon leader. The hope was that they would have time to learn from the veterans before the 506th returned to combat. Hitler, however, had other plans.

In the predawn hours of December 16, Hitler launched his last great counteroffensive in the West in an attempt to seize Antwerp and disrupt Eisenhower's eastward advance. The attack struck Major General Troy Middletown's VIII Corps of Lieutenant General Courtney Hodges's First (U.S.) Army in the Ardennes. Both the scale and the scope of the German attack completely surprised Allied headquarters. That Hitler was able to amass twenty-five divisions for an offensive that exceeded his 1940 offensive and that resulted in the collapse of France went largely undetected by Allied intelligence. Several factors contributed to Ike's failure to decipher Hitler's intentions, beyond Allied overconfidence and the spirit of hubris that permeated Eisenhower's headquarters. First, abominable weather conditions prevented Allied aerial reconnaissance from identifying German assembly areas. Next, the enemy conducted all their concentrations on radio-listening silence to prevent interception of their signal traffic. Finally, Allied headquarters clearly underestimated Germany's military resources. In September Supreme Headquarters, Allied Expeditionary Force, had boastfully predicted the end of the war by Christmas. The failure of Market-Garden ended that hope, but Eisenhower's planners now forecasted that Hitler lacked the means to halt an Allied advance once the weather improved. The result of the German counteroffensive was the largest battle ever fought by the American army in its history. Until the fifty-mile German "bulge" was flattened in mid-January, Allied forces suffered in excess of 70,000 casualties. German casualties exceeded 120,000, including most of their armored reserves.

Of the senior Allied commanders, Eisenhower was first to recognize that the German thrust was more than a local counterattack. His immediate reaction was to halt Patton's Third Army in place and to rush all available reinforcements to stem the enemy's advance through the Ardennes. With his line stretched thin from the north German plain to Switzerland, Ike alerted the 82d and 101st Airborne Divisions to be prepared for truck movement within thirty-six hours. The destination for the 101st Airborne Division was the crossroad town of Bastogne, a town of 3,500 residents, nestled within a plain amid the Ardennes Forest. Eisenhower himself ordered Bastogne to be held at all costs since there were seven roads radiating from the center of town. In order to seize the port of Antwerp, the enemy would either have to bypass Bastogne and continue their advance on secondary roads or capture the town. They chose the latter course of action.

Word of the German offensive filtered down to 2d Battalion headquarters on the evening of December 17, and Colonel Sink immediately cancelled all leaves and began the process of assembling the battalions for immediate movement. Trucks from the Services of Supply forces arrived at Mourmelon the following morning, and by December 19, the entire 101st Airborne Division was heading toward Bastogne. The 506th conducted the movement in forty 10-ton trailers. The regiment made forty miles in the first two hours. Thereafter traffic became so congested that trucks moved bumper to bumper with long intervals of halting. Like most American units, our battalion was woefully under strength, inadequately clothed, and short on weapons and ammunition. Moreover, we were completely ignorant of the enemy's tactical dispositions. Nor could our senior commanders brief us, as they also had to develop the situation before they could issue the necessary orders to the combat battalions.

As battalion executive officer, my responsibility was to oversee the battalion's motor movement to Bastogne. As the convoy moved along, I brought up the rear of our section and made sure everyone kept the column closed and in the proper march order. When the convoy stopped, it was my custom to get out of the jeep and walk up and down the line. At one point in this long ride, Lieutenant Ben Stapelfeld, a replacement officer who had joined the battalion on December 10, approached me and asked if he should be doing anything. "Do you see what the men are doing?" I replied. "They are all sleeping. You do the same. When I need you, I'll let you know." Later Stapelfeld claimed that he never forgot his initial introduction to me. What I most vividly remember about this motor movement was that the drivers turned on the lights at night. We were in a terrible hurry and living dangerously. To illustrate how confused we were and how little time the battalion had had to prepare for movement, Colonel Strayer, who rushed back from England where he had been attending the wedding of Colonel Dobey of "The Rescue," was still adorned in his class "A" uniform as we moved out for Bastogne.

As 2d Battalion approached Bastogne, we could hear the sounds of a very sharp firefight to the north. Little did we realize that we were heading straight into the biggest, bloodiest battle in the history of the U.S. Army. Later we discovered that the sounds emanated from the town of Noville, where Easy Company would conduct one of the most desperate fights in its storied history. As the battalion disembarked from the trucks on the outskirts of Bastogne, additional vehicles arrived loaded with ammunition. As we marched down the road, the drivers drove through the files on each side of the road, while other soldiers literally dumped ammunition over the sides. It did not make any difference what one's rank was; everybody was on his hands and knees scrambling for ammunition. The sounds of that firefight told us that we were going to need it—and real soon. I can still recall the words of Brad Freeman, a paratrooper from E Company, as we moved toward the fight: "Here we go again!"

10

Surrounded Again

Ask any veteran of the campaign in northwest Europe to identify his toughest single engagement, and you might expect him to say D-Day or some other day when his unit underwent a significant emotional experience. October 5 was such a day for Easy Company, 2d Battalion, 506th PIR. Ask the veteran to identify his toughest campaign and the choices are less diverse. For a paratrooper in the 101st Airborne Division, the answer is simple: the Battle of the Bulge. The thirty days between our arrival at Bastogne and the conclusion of the regiment's attack on Noville on January 17 marked the most intense period of combat for the 506th PIR in World War II. Bastogne was undoubtedly the toughest campaign in which the regiment participated during the entire war. After Bastogne, the war was all downhill. Rushed into the line northeast of Bastogne, the 506th conducted large-scale defensive and offensive operations daily for an entire month. Defensive operations characterized the battalion's subsequent activities until January 1,

1945, when Sink's paratroopers transitioned to a series of attacks, culminating in 2d Battalion's offensive to seize the town of Noville, approximately ten miles northeast of Bastogne.

Immediately upon our arrival at Bastogne on December 19, 2d Battalion deployed into the line south of Foy as a part of the ring defense of Bastogne. Foy was a small village six miles northeast of Bastogne. Foy occupied the position in a valley to the south of which a hill sloped up to a very strong position some 300 to 400 yards in the rear. Initially Colonel Sink intended to hold Foy, but with the enemy in possession of high ground on three sides, such a position was untenable. The high ground to the south, however, offered a position from which we could dominate the approaches to Foy. Noville was situated four miles beyond Foy. Like Foy, Noville was the scene of intense enemy activity. The 101st Airborne Division's other battalions were deployed to positions surrounding Bastogne. Initially 2d Battalion, 506th PIR, constituted the regimental reserve as 1st and 3d Battalions moved into line at Noville and Foy, respectively. The next day we replaced 3d Battalion on the front line. Our left was anchored to 3d Battalion beyond the Bastogne-Noville Road by interlocking fields of fire. Our right flank extended to the railroad station at Halt and was supposedly connected to the 501st PIR. As 2d Battalion moved forward in route column, we encountered a scene unlike anything we had seen in the war. The U.S. Army was in full retreat. As American soldiers streamed to the rear, their faces told us this was sheer panic. Soldiers had abandoned their weapons, their packs, their equipment, and their overcoats. Their sunken eyes reflected the "thousand-yard stare" of men frozen in fear. As we passed them, they hollered, "Run, run! They've got everything: tanks, planes, everything!" I am proud to say that I do not remember any of our men saying a single word in reply. We afforded them no recognition. We just kept walking toward the firefight that lay somewhere up ahead.

As we approached a slight shoulder in the road in front of Foy, the battalion deployed to clear the woods on the right side of the road.

Somebody else had gone through the woods before we arrived and had fought a terrific battle. This section of the woods was literally covered with dead and dying men, German and American alike. Our men cleaned out a few pockets of enemy resistance and we were then ordered to establish a line of defense. We set up our forward positions just inside the woods, overlooking the plain southeast of Foy. The soldiers immediately prepared their foxholes and attempted to stay warm and catch a few hours sleep. I established battalion headquarters approximately seventy-five yards from the forward outposts. It is difficult to comprehend the confusion that characterized our first night at Bastogne. No one seemed to know where our boundaries lay, nor did anyone understand our precise mission. Since Colonel Strayer remained at regimental headquarters, I ordered Captain Nixon to locate Colonel Sink's command post and to coordinate with Major Hester, the regimental operations officer, to ensure we had our orders correct. Over the next few weeks, Nixon made many trips back to regiment to keep us informed and to ensure we understood our orders and our boundaries with adjacent units. This system worked well and kept 2d Battalion out of a lot of trouble. Nix's greatest contribution to the successful defense of Bastogne was serving as a liaison between battalion and regimental headquarters. No man contributed more to keeping the regiment together during the ensuing battle. Nixon performed exceedingly well in interpreting regimental orders and coordinating operational support while I positioned myself close to the forward edge of the battle area.

To give you an idea how dedicated Nixon was to the 506th PIR, at Bastogne he had his name drawn from a hat in a lottery that would have given him a thirty-day leave to the United States. Nix refused the offer, saying he wanted to stay with the outfit on the line. How do you explain that kind of dedication? Such devotion is never discussed by the men, but it is never forgotten. At the time, the 506th PIR was very short of men and officers, especially good, proven officers.

An incident that occurred the following morning demonstrates the mass confusion that existed during those initial days at Bastogne. A heavy mist or fog from the night before hung over the woods and fields at dawn on the second day. I was standing in a field at the edge of the woods to the rear of the battalion command post. All was quiet and peaceful when suddenly to my left out of the woods walked a German soldier in his long winter overcoat. He didn't carry a rifle or a pack, and he continued walking slowly toward the middle of the field. A couple of troopers next to me instinctively brought their rifles to their shoulders, but I signaled them to hold their fire. We watched in dismay as the soldier stopped, removed his overcoat, pulled down his pants, and relieved himself. After he finished, I hollered to him in my best German, *Kommen sie hier!* The soldier did as he was told and was immediately captured. All the poor fellow had in his pockets were a few pictures, trinkets, and the butt end of a loaf of stale black bread. To the best of my knowledge, he was the last German soldier to pass through our lines at Bastogne. Think of that: Here was a German soldier, who in the light of early dawn, got turned around in the woods, walked through our lines, past the company CP, and ended up behind the battalion command post. Nobody else penetrated our lines, but this kid just walked through it. That sure was some line of defense we had that first night! Now, think of the problem this lone soldier created for the poor German's first sergeant. How did he carry this guy on his morning report?

For the next several days, we sent out reconnaissance and combat patrols. The Germans did the same. Life on the front line was horrific. The winter of 1944–1945 was the coldest in thirty years. Until the weather permitted aerial resupply, our men lacked proper equipment, winter clothing, and enough ammunition to hold the line. American artillery ammunition was especially in short supply. Our division placed an artillery piece on our left flank beside the Bastogne-Noville Road. We were told that the gunners were down to three rounds, and that those last rounds would be used for anti-tank purposes in case of an armored attack. Nor did we receive much tactical air support due to the inclement weather that limited the visibility of the pilots. When we did receive air support, it was just as likely to fall within our lines as the enemy's. Not until December 23 did the first clear weather arrive and only then could the air force provide any tactical support. Until then, we were basically on our own. Being surrounded was nothing new for the 506th. At times we were outnumbered and surrounded on D-Day, outside Carentan, and at Eindhoven. At least in Bastogne we had the advantage of conducting an active defense. During the next three weeks we inflicted far more casualties than we incurred during the short period when we transitioned to the offensive at the end of the campaign. Had the enemy been able to organize their attacks and had their ranks been composed of seasoned veterans, they might have been able to penetrate our lines. Fortunately the Germans shifted their efforts to another part of the line during our first weeks at Bastogne.

Additional problems complicated our defense. Maintaining contact with the 501st PIR on our right flank remained a running problem. Sometimes we found their outposts; other times we failed to locate their forward positions. It appeared to me that our right flank was "in the air" and subject to envelopment if the enemy decided to attack our exposed flank. It was tough relying on another unit, even if they were paratroopers, to protect the right of our defensive line.

Sickness and trench foot remained recurring problems that reduced our rank and file. Fully one-third of our nonbattle casualties resulted from trench foot and frostbite. Some troopers attempted to remedy the situation by wrapping their feet with burlap sacks, but that merely exacerbated the problem. Trench foot results from extreme moisture and cold, which adversely affects the body's circulation. The use of burlap only increased the moisture surrounding the foot, causing the skin to become so tender that it was impossible for soldiers to lace their boots. Tech/5 Eugene Roe, one of Easy Company's medics, remembered the multiple cases of frostbite for the remainder of his life. The situation was so bad that Roe often took the morphine ampoules that every soldier carried and transferred the vials from dead soldiers to those who still manned the foxholes. Additionally, virtually every trooper suffered from some form of respiratory ailment, such as the soldier in 3d Battalion across the Bastogne-Noville Road from us. From a distance of about 150 yards, we could hear that poor fellow cough throughout the night. He was giving away our position. After several nights, his coughing stopped. He had either died or his squad leader sent him back to Bastogne.

Getting hot chow to the men presented me with a wide array of challenges. It seems everybody can remember exactly what he ate for Christmas dinner while in the army. I cannot. The only memory I have about food was the night we had bean soup. In the field, officers are the last men to go through the chow line. Naturally, all the enlisted men think this is one of the best rules in the officer manual. Chowhounds can finish off a canteen cup of beans in quick order, and in the dark on Christmas night they easily slipped back into line for a second cup. I made a tactical error in that I allowed several soldiers to return to the chow line for seconds before going through the line myself. That night I was the last man to get to the can of beans—I received about a half-canteen cup of bean soup. My entire meal consisted of five white beans and a cup of cold broth. I guess that is why I remember the bean soup, and I suppose that's why I've been trying to make up for that skimpy meal every Christmas since then.

Life on the front line defied description. The weather was bitterly cold and the ground was frozen solid. Digging foxholes was a job every trooper despised, but it was a necessary chore. Unfortunately, our motor movement to Bastogne had been so hurried that many soldiers lacked entrenching tools to dig textbook fighting positions. And the temperature was horribly cold. Cold is cold. You live in a foxhole. Your feet are wet and you're wiggling your toes to keep them from freezing. It is difficult to concentrate on preparing textbook fighting positions. As I walked the line, I observed the lousy positions the men had constructed. These positions were accompanied by equally lousy fields of fire. But what could I do? It was impossible to push the line forward and we could not drop back to improve the situation. Improving the foxholes with overhead cover was another matter. We did not have very good axes to cut trees of sufficient size for protection. Second Lieutenant Ed Thomas, a replacement officer who joined us in Holland, devised his own solution. Ed possessed a devil-may-care smile and a sense of humor different than most officers. He also liked to put on a show to demonstrate his toughness. His solution to the lack of overhead cover was that each night he placed two or three German "stiffs" over the top of his foxhole.

As the weather further deteriorated, physical exhaustion combined with mental fatigue to produce an unusually high number of casualties now classified as combat exhaustion or battle fatigue. In Normandy I had witnessed lots of stress; some in Holland; but much more at Bastogne due to the cold, lack of sleep, and constant artillery bombardment. I'm not sure that anybody who lived through Bastogne hasn't carried with him, in some hidden ways, the scars of fatigue. Perhaps that is a factor that keeps 101st paratroopers bonded so unusually close. In virtually every case, the men had been on the front line for extended periods since D-Day. They were now completely exhausted. They had no hot food, little sleep, no rest, constant tension, and the pressure of combat. The worst time was night, when temperatures plummeted and fog covered the battlefield until mid to late morning. The uncertainty of what lay just yards ahead in the next tree line was sufficient to break ordinary men. Not surprisingly, the men became physically exhausted.

Physical exhaustion leads to mental exhaustion, which in turn, causes men to lose discipline. Loss of self-discipline then produces combat fatigue. Self-discipline keeps a soldier doing his job. Without it, he loses his pride and he loses the importance of self-respect in the eyes of his fellow soldiers. It is pride that keeps a soldier going and keeps him in the fight. This is what I feared I would lose—the loss of will to measure up to my men. After seeing others break down, you wondered who was next and you started taking a hard look at yourself. I often wondered why I didn't break under the strain of combat. One factor undoubtedly lay in the fact that my battalion headquarters lay seventy-five yards behind the forward foxholes. No longer was I under enemy observation. Consequently, I was able to concentrate on my duties without fear of enemy small-arms fire. Another factor was undoubtedly my physical conditioning. I don't think there was a man in that battalion who was in better physical shape than I was. My responsibility to ensure the safety of the soldiers also hardened me to cope with the daily stress of combat.

One last observation on combat fatigue: When you see a man break, he usually slams his helmet down and messes up his hair. I don't know if it's conscious or unconscious, but a soldier goes to his head and massages his head, shakes it, and then he's gone. You can talk to him all you want, but he cannot hear you. When he reaches that point, the best thing for everybody is just to let him take a walk. Combat exhaustion occurs instantaneously. You don't plan to become a combat fatigue casualty.

How do you prevent combat fatigue? You talk to your troops and make some excuse to pull a soldier off the front line. Of course, pulling a soldier off the front line increases the stress of those who remain, but it is a necessary tradeoff. I often asked a soldier whom I saw on the verge of a breakdown, "How about coming back with me to the CP to help out for a couple of days?" In this manner, you invent a reason for pulling a guy from the line without damaging his psyche. T/5 Joseph D. Liebgott was a case in point. Liebgott was a very good combat soldier who had proven himself in Normandy and Holland. At Bastogne, the stress began to catch up to "The Barber," so I brought him back to my command post to be my runner for a few days, to let him rest up, to get away from the tension of being on the front. After a few days, he wanted to return to the line and join his buddies. Apparently he needed communication with his comrades more than he needed my company. The tension was still too much for him, so we sent him to division headquarters where he was assigned to the S-2 (intelligence) section to make use of his ability to speak German. This, in my judgment, was a huge mistake. Liebgott was Jewish and had an understandable hatred of Germans. He had also earned a reputation for demonstrating that hatred against prisoners, which created an entire new category of problems for Liebgott's commanders.

Though Colonel Strayer technically remained in command of the battalion, I operated the tactical command post approximately seventy-five yards behind the front line. This location facilitated daily contact with the forward elements of the battalion. Strayer was an exceptionally competent officer, but he always needed someone at his side. He ensured battlefield success by surrounding himself with equally exceptionally talented officers. Strayer and I had little conversation during the battle. The circumstances surrounding his absence were consistent with his performance in Normandy. As commander, Strayer delegated decisions to his operations officers: first Hester, and then Nixon. When I became executive officer, nothing changed. Colonel Strayer's express purpose in allowing me to direct combat operations was to give me the opportunity to operate a battalion in combat. Consequently, I automatically found myself making the tactical decisions. To find out what was required of 2d Battalion, Nixon traveled to regimental headquarters, then reported to me. He and I also took turns walking the line and checking on the men on a regular basis. Based on what we found, Nixon then ensured that we maintained the proper communications between regiment and the battalion. Since 2d Battalion was initially in defense, our task was not very complicated. Once we had established the main line of resistance, we merely maintained it.

My daily routine was to shave every morning and then to inspect the line. In retrospect, shaving in the bitter cold was pretty ridiculous, but the practice originated with one of my first meetings with Colonel Sink. At Toccoa, Sink had required us to shave every morning. He said, "You shave every morning for the men and if you want to shave every evening for the women, that is up to you. But I want you to set an example." He was absolutely right. I remember one morning when we prepared our attack on Foy, I got up in the middle of the night to shave before getting something to eat. In the process, I cut myself up pretty badly. I must have looked like hell. When Colonel Sink arrived to check on us before the attack commenced, he took one look at me and had a huge smile on his face. I realized later that he was laughing at me for shaving on that bitterly cold morning. But that was one of the things I did to set an example for the men—shave in the morning and once in a while I would strip to the waist and give myself a "French wash"—a routine that also caught everyone's attention. I did this for one reason and one reason only—to get the men's attention and to let them know that I was going to be around for a while and that this wasn't as bad as they thought it was going to be. Make the best of it.

Meanwhile 2d Battalion maintained their defensive positions and awaited yet another German attack. On the morning of December 24, the battalion received a small attack on our right flank, which we quickly repulsed. Later that morning the Germans aggressively patrolled our sector, but they withdrew after suffering four killed and four wounded. Christmas Day found 2d Battalion defending the line from the railroad underpass on the Foy Road-Bastogne-Bourcey Railroad to the south of Foy. Enemy contact remained relatively light the following day due to breaks in cloud cover that permitted tactical air support to disrupt German patrols and troop concentrations. In spite of the sunshine, life in the forward foxholes remained extremely uncomfortable. After a week in the snow and cold, all the while being constantly probed by the enemy, 2d Battalion held firm and denied the enemy any tactical advantage that they otherwise might have gained had the Germans pressed their attacks more vigorously.

One might ask how the men maintained their morale and their defensive positions. They held because they were paratroopers and because Dog, Easy, and Fox Companies contained men who refused to abandon their buddies for the comfort of the rear echelon ranks. If all the men who had a legitimate reason to go back to the aid station at

CLOCKWISE FROM TOP LEFT: My graduation picture from Lancaster High School in 1937. *Dick Winters's Private Collection.*

Working my way through Franklin & Marshall College by painting high-tension towers. *Dick Winters's Private Collection.*

Camp Toccoa, Georgia, 1942. In front of a hut with two guys who didn't make it. I am the officer on the left. *Dick Winters's Private Collection.*

Lieutenant Winters at Camp Toccoa, Georgia, 1942. I would serve in Easy Company, 506th PIR for the next two years. *Dick Winters's Private Collection.*

CLOCKWISE FROM TOP LEFT: End of training at Toccoa. Showing off my new leather jacket. *Dick Winters's Private Collection.*

Lieutenants Warren Roush, Lewis Nixon, Dick Winters (left to right) with Captain Herbert Sobel during field training exercises in the states, 1943. *Army Signal Corps Photograph.*

Captain Herbert Sobel, first commander of Easy Company, 506th PIR. Captain Sobel was a tough commander who court-martialed me in England for dereliction of duty. In a sense he "made" Easy Company by his rigorous training in the states. *Army Signal Corps Photograph.*

I rest at the end of a three day/night field exercise. *Dick Winters's Private Collection.*

LEFT: 2d Lieutenant Fred "Moose" Heylinger in center with pipe. Moose succeeded me in command of Easy Company before being wounded in Holland in October 1944. *Army Signal Corps Photograph.*

RIGHT: Lieutenant Winters before a demonstration jump for General Eisenhower in England. *Dick Winters's Private Collection. Photo by Forrest Guth.*

BOTTOM: Winters/Welsh quarters in room above Mr. and Mrs. Barnes's store in Aldbourne, England. Our window is on left. *Dick Winters's Private Collection.*

PROPOSED METHOD OF JUMPING WITH
BAZOOKA BUNDLE (OR ANY OTHER EQUIPMENT
BUNDLE) AT NIGHT - BY EMPLOYING A 'S CORD
GUIDE STRING BY THIS EXPEDIENT THE
N^o1 'CHUTIST STAYS IN "CONTACT" WITH HIS
BUNDLE UNTIL HE LANDS, AND THEN LOCATES
IT BY FEELING HIS WAY ALONG THE STRING.
(JUMPER SHOULD WEAR GLOVES TO AVOID BURNING
HIS HANDS ON THE CORD)

STATIC LINE

PARACHUTE

A5 PARAPACK

This end is tied to N^o1 jumper.

APPROXIMATELY
300 FEET OF 5 CORD
HELD LOOSELY BY
SUSPENSION LINE
RETAINING BAND.

NIGHT JUMP 12 March, 1944

Sergeant Burton Christenson drew this sketch to illustrate the proper way of jumping with a leg bag. On D-Day most of the paratroopers lost their leg bags due to the airplane's excessive speed.
Dick Winters's Private Collection.

5 June 1944-March to the Planes

TOP: On June 5, 1944, Easy Company walked to the C-47 transport planes that would carry them to Normandy and their rendezvous with destiny. *Dick Winters's Private Collection.*

BOTTOM: Photo depicting a disabled 105 mm gun outside Brecourt Manor on D-Day. Photo given by General Maxwell Taylor to Michel da Vallavieille in 1987, and is currently on display in the Museum at Utah Beach. *Army Signal Corps Photograph.*

TOP: Floyd Talbert (left) and Walter Gordon (right) visit with French farmers following D-Day. *Dick Winters's Private Collection. Photo by Forrest Guth.*

LEFT: Receiving the Distinguished Service Cross from Lieutenant General Omar N. Bradley in June 1944 during a lull in the fighting. Also receiving the DSC were Major General Maxwell Taylor, commanding general, 101st Airborne Division (left), Major Cassidy (502d PIR) (second from left), 1st Lieutenant Father John Maloney, our regimental chaplain (4th from left), Captain Lloyd Patch (1st Battalion) (fifth from left), and Major Hannah (S-3, 506th PIR) (sixth from left). I am seventh from the left. *Army Signal Corps Photograph.*

RIGHT: Publicity photo by Army Signal Corps on my return to Aldbourne in July 1944. I was told not to smile in order to project the proper warrior image. *Army Signal Corps Photograph.*

LEFT: German prisoners captured in Holland as part of Operation Market-Garden.
Army Signal Corps Photograph.

RIGHT: The British 43d Division took over two days to cover the forty miles to Nijmegen. This scene depicts the traffic on "Hell's Highway" between Veghel and Uden on September 21, 1944.
Army Signal Corps Photograph.

BOTTOM: The citizens of Eindhoven welcome their liberators on September 18, 1944. Later Eindhoven was subjected to an intense aerial and artillery bombardment by the Germans.
Army Signal Corps Photograph.

TOP: Two Easy Company paratroopers hold the line on the dike during fighting on "The Island" in October 1944. *Army Signal Corps Photograph.*

BOTTOM: On the dike on "The Island" after Easy Company destroyed two German infantry companies on October 5, 1944. *Army Signal Corps Photograph.*

LEFT: Captain Dick Winters, battalion executive officer, outside battalion headquarters at Schoonder-logt, Holland, after the battle on the dike on October 5, 1944. I hated leaving Easy Company to assume my staff duties on battalion staff. *Photograph by Al Kroachka / Army Signal Corps.*

RIGHT: Third Platoon, Easy Company, loads into 10-ton trailers at Mourmelon on December 18. The next day Easy Company and 2d Battalion took up defensive positions northeast of Bastogne to halt the German offensive through the Ardennes Forest. *Army Signal Corps Photograph.*

BOTTOM: Captain Winters (left) with Lewis Nixon (right). Note the absence of rank on the front of Nixon's helmet so the enemy could not identify us as officers. *Army Signal Corps Photograph.*

TOP: Entering Noville, Belgium, after 2d Battalion's attack to seize the high ground northeast of Bastogne on January 15, 1945. Shortly before the attack, I relieved 1st Lieutenant Norman S. Dike and appointed Captain Ronald C. Speirs commander of Easy Company. *Army Signal Corps Photographs.*

BOTTOM: In March 1945 at Mourmelon, France, General of the Army Dwight D. Eisenhower presented the Presidential Unit Citation to the 101st Airborne Division for their successful defense of Bastogne. This was the first time that an entire division was so recognized. *Army Signal Corps Photograph.*

En route to Berchtesgaden, 2d Battalion liberated the inmates at the Buchloe concentration camp outside Landsberg, Germany. As I observed the Nazi treachery firsthand, I told myself, "Now I know why I am here!" *Army Signal Corps Photographs.*

TOP: German troops walking along the autobahn towards Munich in late April 1945. Note the absence of American escorts. Even the Germans realized that the war was over.
Army Signal Corps Photograph.

MIDDLE: My battalion command post at Berchtesgaden, May 1945. Here I received the news that Germany surrendered uncond- itionally on May 7, 1945.
Army Signal Corps Photograph.

BOTTOM: Captain Lewis Nixon celebrates VE-Day courtesy of Reich Marshall Hermann Goering.
Photo by Al Kroachka / Army Signal Corps.

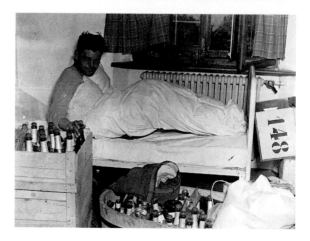

From left:
John Zielinski,---,---,---,---,Steve Mihok,Nixon,Henderson,Winters,Hattie,Cox,Welsh | BERCHTESGADEN - 2nd Bn. Hq.

TOP LEFT: 2d Battalion, 506th PIR headquarters at Berchtesgaden. Note the feeling of contentment that the war is over. From left to right are John Lielinski, –, –, –, –, Steve Mihok, Nixon, Henderson, Winters, Hattie, Cox, and Welsh.
Army Signal Corps Photographs

TOP RIGHT: First Sergeant Floyd Talbert on German limousine after testing if the windshields were bulletproof. They weren't. Talbert was the senior noncommissioned officer in Easy Company and the one paratrooper whom I considered the finest soldier in the company.
Photo by Al Kroachka / Army Signal Corps. Army Signal Corps Photograph.

MIDDLE: Hitler's Eagle Nest captured by 2d Battalion, 506th PIR in May 1945.
Photo by Al Kroachka / Army Signal Corps.

BOTTOM: We thought southern Germany was picturesque, but nothing compared to the natural beauty of Kaprun, Austria, where 2d Battalion took up the duties as an occupational army.
Army Signal Corps Photographs

TOP: Mission Accomplished! 2d Battalion officers at Kaprun, Austria. I am standing third from the right, front row. *Photo by Al Kroachka / Army Signal Corps.*

LEFT: Home at last. I had this photograph taken when I returned to Lancaster, Pennsylvania, in December 1945. *Dick Winters's Private Collection.*

RIGHT: Splitting stone for my home at the farm in the 1960s. I built the peace that I promised myself if I survived D-Day, one stone at a time. *Dick Winters's Private Collection.*

TOP: Two of the reasons that Hitler lost the war. Former Easy Company commanders Dick Winters and Ronald Speirs meet at Normandy, France, for the premiere of the HBO miniseries "Band of Brothers" on June 6, 2001.

Photo by Jake Powers, official historian for Easy Company, 506th PIR. Dick Winters Private Collection.

BOTTOM: Dick Winters and actor Damian Lewis, who portrayed Winters in the HBO miniseries, at my farm in 2001.

Photo setup by Kimberly Butler of People *magazine, actual photograph taken by Ethel Winters.*

TOP: President George Bush congratulates Major Dick Winters on a visit to Hershey, Pennsylvania, in 2004. *Official White House photograph, Dick Winters's Private Collection.*

BOTTOM: Dick Winters with Tom Brokaw at Hyde Park to receive Franklin D. Roosevelt Institute's Four Freedoms/Freedom from Fear Award as the representative from the U.S. Army in May 2001. *Photo by Matthew Gillis. Dick Winters's Private Collection.*

Bastogne had taken advantage of their position, there just would not have been a front line. Our forward positions would have been held by a series of outposts, not a main line of resistance. In recalling the tenacity of the American paratrooper, a number of soldiers immediately come to mind. I remember Don Malarkey trudging through the snow with blankets wrapped around his feet and legs in a futile attempt to ward off frostbite. After his buddy Sergeant Warren "Skip" Muck was killed by a direct hit by an artillery round on his foxhole, I offered to bring Malarkey back to the battalion command post for a couple days. He respectfully declined because he refused to leave his buddies in Easy Company.

First Sergeant Carwood Lipton was struck on the arm by shrapnel from a German 88. He had the medic bandage his wound and he stayed on the line. Later in February his commander and I recommended Lipton for a battlefield commission, which was immediately approved by Colonel Sink. Another noncommissioned officer, Staff Sergeant Steve Mihok from battalion headquarters company, was always first to volunteer. You always asked for volunteers before issuing the final orders. Mihok volunteered every night to go on a patrol. What a guy! If I live to be 100 years old, I'll never forget that little trooper standing there with his tommy gun slung over his shoulder, dark circles under his eyes which told me just how dead tired he was, answering, "I'll go." He later earned two Bronze Stars—it should have been a dozen.

Sergeant Joe Toye was wounded four times: in Normandy, Holland, and twice at Bastogne. On January 2, Toye was hit by a piece of shrapnel from a bomb during a German air raid. His platoon sergeant then sent Toye to the aid station in Bastogne for medical treatment. Later that same day, I looked across the field to our left flank, and there was Joe Toye walking up the road and across the field, his arm in a sling, heading back to the front line. I walked out to meet him and asked, "Where are you going? You don't have to go back to the line. Take a few days off." Not Joe Toye. He informed me that he had met another lieutenant at the aid station who was suspected of shooting himself in the hand to escape front-line duty. Joe would have none of that. He was a squad leader and his place was on the line. War had become old to Sergeant Joe Toye, and he was good at it. The lives of his squad depended on his ability to master his craft. In a sense, Toye and his platoon sergeant Bill Guarnere had become what Ernie Pyle termed "senior partners in the institution of killing" and caring for their men. Rather than remain in the rear, Toye hitched a ride with Father John Maloney and returned to the front. Toye told me, "I want to go back with the fellows." I knew he should not be on the line, but I so admired his devotion to his squad that I stepped aside. Sergeant Joe Toye was an American hero of the first order.

The next day Sergeants Toye and Guarnere were caught in an artillery barrage. They say that you never hear the shell that hits you. I'm not sure that's true, but the closer they hit, the less time you have to hear them. In the artillery bombardment that struck Easy Company at Bastogne, Guarnere lost a leg and Toye's right leg was so mangled that the doctors originally amputated it below the knee. Later, back in the States, they realized the knee was so badly damaged that he would never be able to use it again, so they amputated a second time, above the knee, at the England General Hospital in Atlantic City, New Jersey.

And then there was Corporal Walter Gordon, his head wrapped in a large towel, his helmet sitting on top. Walter sat on the edge of his foxhole behind his light machine gun. He looked like he was frozen stiff, blankly staring ahead at the woods. I remember walking by Gordon without any recognition from him. I stopped and looked back at him, and it suddenly struck me. "Damn! Gordon's matured! He's a man!" Walter was hit during the German attack at 0830 hours on Christmas Eve.

The grim determination that characterized the American paratrooper at Bastogne was not just confined to the enlisted ranks. Lieutenant Harry Welsh almost received his million-dollar wound while a group of us were standing around a fire at the battalion CP on Christmas Eve. We had decided to take a chance and start a fire in order to stay warm. Lo and behold, the Germans picked it up and fired a mortar round in our direction. I don't know if they were lucky or not or whether they were just that good, but the shell exploded in the middle of our group. As I picked myself up from the ground and looked over to Welsh, I could see that look of terror on Harry's face as he tore off his pants to see where he had been hit. He wasn't castrated, but it was too close for comfort. Sometimes the difference between life and death was a matter of centimeters. Welsh was immediately evacuated and operated on in Luxembourg, Paris, and England. No sooner had the doctors removed the stitches than Harry went AWOL and returned to 2d Battalion. After almost losing Welsh, the rest of us were scared to death. And that was Christmas Eve at Bastogne.

On December 22 the commander of German forces that had encircled Bastogne called upon Brigadier General Tony McAuliffe to surrender the 101st Airborne Division "to save the encircled U.S.A. troops from total annihilation." McAuliffe, a superb combat commander from the old army, was temporarily in command of the Screaming Eagles while General Taylor was in Washington, D.C., on official business. McAuliffe issued a monosyllabic reply: "Nuts!" to the enemy's demand for unconditional and immediate surrender. For those of us along the main line of resistance, we took quiet pride in McAuliffe's tough stance. I, for one, was happy that McAuliffe and not Taylor commanded the defense of Bastogne. While Taylor was always immaculately attired and had a regular retinue of aides and reporters in his wake, McAuliffe was a soldier's soldier who understood ground combat at the grunt level. As such, McAuliffe commanded my utmost respect.

The soldiers of 2d Battalion and Easy Company spent Christmas on the front line. Headquarters distributed a message from General McAuliffe, in which he extolled the virtues of the 101st Airborne Division and reminded us that we had held the line against impossible odds and that our tenacious defense was making headlines in the United

States. Colonel Sink also paid a personal visit to the battalion command post to give us an up-to-date report on the situation. We greatly appreciated that effort on his part.

Some of the men made an attempt to remember Christmas in their own way. Sergeant Bob Rader and Corporal Don Hoobler decided to man the forward outposts themselves rather than sending a couple of troopers or a squad to the forward positions. Hoobler and Rader, along with Shep Howell, had entered the army together and remained best friends. It was unconventional that two noncoms would man the same outpost, but their platoon sergeant approved this unorthodox arrangement considering the special circumstances. Hoobler and Rader then spent the next several hours whispering back and forth, talking about their families back home, what they were doing, and wondering if their families were going to church. Hoobler and Rader represented the best of Easy Company. On Christmas Eve, both risked their lives to give their comrades a little more peace. Regrettably, it was the last Christmas that they spent together. It wasn't long after that night that Hoobler died from a wound inflicted by a Luger that he was carrying and accidentally fired, severing an artery in his leg. Hoobler had jumped with me in Normandy and his loss was deeply felt throughout Easy Company.

The siege of Bastogne was finally broken on the afternoon of December 26 when Lieutenant Colonel Creighton Abrams, commanding the 37th Tank Battalion of Patton's Third Army, penetrated the German lines and marched into Bastogne. His arrival was a belated, albeit joyous, Christmas present. Behind Abrams was a large fleet of ambulances and supply vehicles. For the first time in a week, trucks rolled into Bastogne, bringing us food, ammunition, and other supplies. After unloading the supplies, the most critical of our wounded, including Easy Company's Walter Gordon, were the first to be evacuated. By the end of the day on December 27, 652 wounded had been moved back by the 64th Medical Group to army hospitals. By December 28, the last stretcher case of trench foot and walking wounded reached the rear. This brought the total of American wounded to over 1,000 troopers.

Now that the encirclement of Bastogne had been broken, 2d Battalion expected to return to Mourmelon. It didn't take too long before Allied headquarters dissuaded us of that notion. The Screaming Eagles would remain on the line and commence offensive operations at the first opportunity. A major component of the Allied attack would be the 101st Airborne Division's push toward Foy and Noville. The division's attack would be coordinated with a major offensive on the northern edge of the Bulge spearheaded by Montgomery's 21st Army Group.

December 31 was relatively quiet, but at 0001 on January 1, both sides welcomed the new year with artillery and mortar fire. New Year's Day brought the largest German air attack to date. Several hundred planes took part. It was in this attack that Joe Toye incurred his third wound. That same day, 2d Battalion, 506th PIR, received orders to attack and clear the Bois Jacques, the forested area that had served as home to Easy Company for the previous twelve days. Beyond the woods lay Foy, and beyond Foy lay the high ground in front of Noville. 2d Battalion attacked as part of a regimental advance on January 2 at 0930. Deep snow and thick woods impeded our advance and contact between the platoons and company was temporarily lost. Noncommissioned officers rapidly reestablished contact and the advance continued. The battalion encountered little resistance until we reached a line approximately 200 yards from the edge of the woods. Initial resistance was strong, but of short duration. By 1530 hours, 2d Battalion seized its objective. On January 3 we received orders to extend our front to cover 1st Battalion's sector because 1st Battalion reverted to Division reserve. That day it began to snow, and it snowed every day for the next week. Simultaneously, enemy artillery and mortar fire was on the upswing.

It is difficult to describe the effects of an artillery bombardment to someone who has not experienced combat. If you live through it, you will never forget it, nor will you ever be the same. Artillery doesn't only kill; it maims and tears the body apart, sending limbs in every direction. "Popeye" Wynn remembered that "we went through a couple of shellings that were earth-shattering." When a soldier is subjected to a concentrated bombardment, he often finds himself bouncing on the ground from the force of the concussion. The big problem for a leader is keeping his wits and not freezing in fear—being able to think and, as soon as possible, talking to the men, and getting them to get up and think. The intensity of artillery fire over a protracted period has a dramatic impact on a unit in combat. Just as soon as the last round falls, as a leader you must begin circulating among the men. "Is everybody okay? Let's get up. Let's move. Keep your eyes open for an attack." Get the men's attention. And moving among your men—the very fact that they see you and they are talking to you—they know that you are there and it makes all the difference in the world to realize that they are not in this by themselves. Even if a soldier remains fixed on his own feelings and his own fear, and if his leader is moving among the men, the soldier realizes that his leader is sharing the same hardship he himself is experiencing. Then and only then will the soldier be able to move. That is exactly what occurred on the afternoon of January 3 when Easy Company readjusted its lines and moved under the last vestiges of daylight to their new positions.

Just as the company entered the woods, the Germans commenced fire with a heavily concentrated artillery bombardment. Caught in a murderous fire, the men scurried to whatever cover they could find. Many jumped into shell holes and their former foxholes before the first artillery rounds exploded above the trees. Some of the men were lucky; others, like Sergeant Joe Toye, were not as fortunate. As squad leader, Toye refused to take refuge until he ensured all his men were accounted for. He never heard the round that hit him. Shrapnel tore off his right leg and embedded itself in his stomach and arms. Yelling for help, he lay there writhing in the snow. Bill Guarnere, his platoon sergeant and best friend, heard him. Like Toye, Guarnere's emotions were running extremely high. During a temporary lull in the shelling, Guarnere left the safety of his own foxhole and began pulling Toye to safety. Just then the shelling resumed. A shell burst above Guarnere and mangled his leg. The war was over for both Toye and Guarnere. Don Malarkey and Ed "Babe" Heffron helped pull them off the line and assisted the medics in placing both in an ambulance. To this day, neither can talk about the experience.

As quickly as the bombardment started, it ended, but the damage was already severe. First Sergeant Lipton supervised the evacuation of the wounded and visited each trooper. No sooner than Lipton moved forward did Lieutenant Dike instruct him to take charge of the company while he (Dike) returned to headquarters. You can imagine the men's feelings when they watched their commander walk off the line. For a company commander to abandon his men in the middle of an engagement when his men had already endured a number of casualties was inexcusable. No sooner had Dike left than the company lost another officer. Looking at Toye's and Guarnere's mangled legs, Lieutenant Buck Compton finally collapsed under the strain of combat. Taking off his helmet, he ran his fingers through his hair, dropped his helmet, and then, like Dike, he walked off the line. George Luz attempted to stop him, but to no avail. After months of combat and after seeing two of his closest friends horribly wounded, Buck had had enough. Within the span of several minutes, 2d Platoon had lost its most experienced squad leader, its platoon sergeant, and its platoon leader. Sergeants Guarnere and Toye were Toccoa men around whom the remainder of the platoon had rallied. And Compton had seen action with the company from D-Day, through Normandy and Holland, and now at Bastogne. Dike, of course, could be easily replaced, but the loss of so many key leaders severely affected the morale of my old company.

Easy Company was at the breaking point. Few units could sustain the number of casualties that Easy Company had suffered on January 3, particularly among its senior leadership. Its ranks were now at less than 50 percent capacity. The rest of 2d Battalion's companies were equally weak. Had 1st Sergeant Lipton and the other Toccoa veterans not stepped into the breach, Easy Company would have disintegrated. Lipton assumed command of the company in all but name, even though two other officers were present. Other noncommissioned officers filled in the gaps—men like Pat Christenson and Don Malarkey, who had been privates in Normandy, corporals in Holland, and now sergeants at Bastogne. They remained the backbone of Easy Company. Our line was now dangerously thin, but on January 4, the 501st PIR replaced us on the front line. Second Battalion assumed responsibility for 506th Regimental reserve.

Another odd memory of that night occurs to me. After sitting there for a while, I felt as though the foxhole was getting smaller. Then I noticed the ice frosting on the sides of the wall. So, I just stiffened my shoulders and rubbed along the sides, clearing off the frost.

The battlefront remained relatively quiet for the next week. Second Battalion patrolled the snow-covered woods to our front continuously. January 8 brought an extremely heavy snowstorm. Another heavy German artillery bombardment on the 506th's positions on January 10 inflicted 126 casualties. Two days later, 2d Battalion attached one company to 3d Battalion for an assault to take Foy. I selected Easy Company to lead the attack. The night before the attack I sat in my foxhole, reading the *Infantry Manual on Attack* by candlelight. When I think of that—lugging an infantry manual to Bastogne—I should have taken a Hershey chocolate bar instead. I had that manual memorized, but this time that manual wasn't advanced enough for the situation for which I was preparing. It just seemed too elementary. As I studied the manual, Sergeant Lipton arrived and asked to discuss a highly sensitive matter with me. Lipton expressed his concern that Lieutenant Dike was not up to the task to lead the following day's assault. I listened intently, but I had little choice other than to acknowledge his concerns and to tell him that I would investigate the matter. I then decided that I would stand on the line of departure and observe the attack when it began the following morning.

At early dawn, I personally briefed Lieutenant Dike on the conduct of the attack. I then ordered 1st Lieutenant Frank Reis to place two sections of light machine guns on the edge of the woods facing Foy. The guns would provide covering fire as Easy Company moved through the snow across approximately 250 yards of open field to the outskirts of the village. Easy Company crossed the line of departure at 0900 and proceeded to cross the field. The covering fire worked to perfection, but each time the assistant gunner changed the belt, I held my breath through that brief lull of fire. The Germans fired only a few random rifle shots from an outpost on the west end of the village. It was tough going for the men through that snow in a skirmisher formation, but Dike maintained a good formation as the company moved at a decent pace. Then suddenly, Lieutenant Dike halted the company about seventy-five yards from the edge of Foy. Everybody hunkered down in the snow and stayed there for no apparent reason. I called Lieutenant Dike on the radio, but I received no response. The company was like a bunch of sitting ducks out there in the snow. Colonel Sink, who was observing the attack, turned and hollered, "What are you going to do, Winters?"

"I'm going!" I yelled and I grabbed my M-1 and moved out to take command of Easy Company in order to get them moving again. I had only taken a few steps when I decided that my job was to lead the battalion, not a company. I turned around and walked back and there was Lieutenant Ronald C. Speirs, a natural killer, standing in front of me.

"Speirs!" I said. "Take over that company and relieve Dike and take that attack on in."

Why Speirs was standing next to me I had no idea. I just turned around and there he was. It was just a roll of the dice that he was standing there when I needed someone. I was glad it was Speirs. I respected him as a combat leader because he made good decisions in combat, though his decisions after the battle—off the line—were often flawed. On D-Day, Speirs and his men had disabled the fourth gun in the battery outside Brecourt Manor. Stories later circulated throughout 2d

Battalion that Speirs possessed a "killer's instinct" and that he had once shot one of his recalcitrant sergeants in Normandy on D+1. It was difficult to verify such a story, but the soldiers evidently believed it at face value. Naturally there was more to the story than initially met the eye. D Company had been fighting all night June 5–6, and all day on D-Day. The night of June 6 gave the men on outposts no more than two to three hours rest before starting the battle on June 7. D Company countermarched throughout the night as officers attempted to array the platoons in the proper alignment to cross the line of departure the following morning. The ensuing battle proved to be one of the most confused of the war. As the evening progressed, the tension of the upcoming battle, coupled with the fact that these men had been without rest since early morning on June 5, resulted in near exhaustion. A number of paratroopers and their leaders were actually sleepwalking and unable to comprehend orders. One observer noted that, "Officers and men had kept going too long and were now traveling on their nerve."

In spite of what rumors prevailed concerning Lieutenant Speirs's actions, what actually occurred that evening was D Company received orders to halt its attack toward Ste. Come du Mont in order for regimental headquarters to coordinate a rolling barrage in support of the ground assault. Regimental artillery had designated fifteen targets to be shelled in the vicinity of Ste. Come du Mont. To initiate the attack, regimental artillery fire was adjusted back toward American lines, before moving forward again in increments of 100 yards every four minutes. Colonel Strayer directed D Company to follow this "rolling barrage" toward the objective. Lieutenant Speirs then passed the word down the line to his squad leaders to hold their current position until the artillery fire was coordinated. One of his sergeants ignored the orders. Speirs repeated the order and the sergeant again refused to obey. Spears then shot the sergeant between the eyes. In doing so, Speirs probably saved the lives of the rest of the squad. To his credit, Speirs immediately reported the incident to his company commander, Captain Jerre S. Gross. Gross was killed the next day during the continued assault on Ste.

Come du Mont, so the incident was not pursued. Certainly none of Speirs's soldiers said anything to higher headquarters. I think the platoon members exercised sound judgment—they might have been next. Secondly, if anybody had taken it upon himself to return Speirs's fire, he would have had to pay an unknown price. I credit the men with a good instinct for survival.

Other rumors centered on Speirs's alleged killing of six German prisoners of war. My personal contact with Lieutenant Speirs after D-Day was somewhat limited until I relinquished command of Easy Company. As battalion executive officer, I knew each of the battalion's officers and could analyze each leader's strengths and weaknesses. My own assessment was that Lieutenant Speirs was one of the finest combat officers in 2d Battalion. His men respected him, but they also feared him because Speirs had clearly established the fact that he was a killer. He worked hard to earn a reputation as a killer and he often killed for shock value. The senior leadership of the battalion and regiment must have heard the allegations surrounding Speirs, but in their desperation to keep qualified officers who were not afraid of combat, they chose either to ignore or not to investigate the charges. When I first heard the stories, I was speechless. What he did in Normandy was unbelievable, inexcusable. In today's army, Speirs would have been court-martialed and charged with atrocities, but we desperately needed bodies, officers who led by example and were not afraid to engage the enemy. Speirs fit the bill.

In any event, Speirs ran forward at the double quick as soon as I directed him to take command of the company. Confronting Lieutenant Dike by a haystack behind which the command group had sought refuge, Speirs seized command of the company. Dike offered no resistance. Lieutenant Speirs then sprinted across the front to locate I Company, which was on E Company's flank. A German 88 opened up on him as he raced toward Foy. "Damn impressive," was how Lipton later described Speir's dash across the "no-man's land" that separated the German and American lines. After coordinating with I Company,

Speirs returned across the same field and led Easy Company into Foy. With support of Lieutenant Reis's machine guns that were laying down an effective base of fire, Easy Company captured Foy in house-to-house fighting. By 1100 Nixon reported that Foy was secure. In the process of taking the town, Easy Company had captured twenty prisoners, while suffering one man killed and several wounded. Without Speirs's intervention, however, the casualties would have been excessive.

In retrospect, what we had just witnessed during the attack on Foy was a classic case of combat fatigue at the worst possible time. We had observed indications of this earlier, but Dike had been sent to us as a favorite protégé of somebody from regimental headquarters. That evening Colonel Sink called for a meeting at regimental headquarters for all the principal parties involved in this attack. Lieutenant Colonel Strayer was present and Sink asked, "What are you going to do about Company E?"

Strayer turned to me and repeated the question, "What are you going to do about Company E, Winters?"

I gave no explanation, but just replied, "Relieve Lieutenant Dike and put Speirs in command." That settled it. End of meeting. Colonel Sink immediately approved my recommendation. Speirs was now in command and would remain in command of Easy Company until the end of the war. Of the six officers who commanded Easy Company since its activation at Toccoa—Sobel, Meehan, myself, Heyliger, Dike, and now Speirs—"Sparky" Speirs commanded the company longer than any of his predecessors. In spite of his alleged misconduct, his contribution to the unit's success cannot be underestimated. As far as Lieutenant Dike was concerned, he sure as hell did not return to my battalion. He just packed his bag and left. Later we discovered that he was transferred to regimental headquarters as an assistant operations officer.

One other memory of that day and that attack deserves special mention. It, too, left me in a foul mood. As the men were carrying the wounded back from Foy, I was suddenly aware of two photographers standing beside me, taking pictures of this detail. I was not sure where they came from or who they belonged to. I only know that I had never seen them before. When the casualty detail reached about twenty to twenty-five yards from the woods, well out of danger of any possible fire from Foy, one photographer put down his camera and dashed out to help carry one of the wounded soldiers. He grabbed the soldier in such a manner that he got as much blood on the sleeve and front of his new, clean, heavily fleeced jacket as possible. Then this photographer turned toward his buddy, who was still taking pictures, and put on a big act of being utterly exhausted as he struggled across those final yards to the woods. At that point, he immediately dropped out of the picture. What a phony! This just topped off my day for phonies.

The next day regiment directed 2d Battalion to continue the attack to seize the high ground around Noville. When word came down for this attack, it pissed me off. I could not believe that after what we had gone through and accomplished, after all the casualties we had suffered, that Colonel Sink was ordering us to lead another attack. H-Hour was scheduled for 1200. This was another point of not using good judgment by regiment or division command. Why would you send men across one and a half miles of wide-open fields to Recogne-Cobru-Noville, through snow almost knee-deep, in the middle of a bright sunny day? The Germans were sitting on the high ground with tanks concealed in hull-defilade under the cover of buildings. Why not attack in early morning, at the first light of day, so that we would have had the cover of darkness for at least part of the time?

That day I earned my pay. Before we crossed the line of departure, I recognized that our salvation just might be that there was a fairly deep shoulder in the terrain on the southwest side of Noville. If I sent the column straight for it, I could pick up more cover as we approached Noville. We were fortunate. The enemy did not have any strong points on the shoulder and the plan worked perfectly. I placed the entire battalion in single file to cut through the snow. It was a highly dangerous and not very tactical formation. As we approached Noville, 1st Battalion was about 400 yards to our left and slightly to the rear of our column. From time to time, I glanced over to see how they were doing. They were being cut up by direct fire from the German 88s from those tanks in Noville. The enemy fire was striking their line with devastating effect. Men were literally flying through the air. Years later in the movie *Dr. Zhivago*, I saw troops crossing snow-covered fields, being shot by cannons from the edge of the woods, and men flying through the air. Those scenes seemed very real to me; I could sure relate that experience with the attack on Noville.

We worked very hard getting across those fields and getting snuggled up to the underside of that shoulder by about 1530. By dark, I had worked the battalion around to a draw on the southeast corner of town. To do that, we advanced through fire from some machine guns in Noville that were covering the draw. To counter this fire, we set up a couple of light machine guns of our own. The Germans would fire; we would give them a return burst and at the same time, we sent a group of eight to ten men across the draw and a stream to the other side. It became a cat-and-mouse game. It took a lot of patience, but we accomplished it without any casualties. By dark, 2d Battalion was in position for the attack the next day. The night was the coldest night of my life and I think the same went for every other man in the outfit. We had worked hard all afternoon and we were dripping wet with sweat. After the sun went down, it grew bitterly cold. All we could do was shiver. At one point during the night, I attempted to rest on a little knoll of ground. In no time, I just shivered myself down that knoll to the bottom of the draw. I soon gave up trying to catch any sleep.

Without sharing this thought with anybody at the time, at one point I considered conducting a night attack rather than standing there all night freezing to death. For some reason I had the feeling that the Germans had pulled out. I quickly reconsidered my alternate plan, realizing that the chances were too great that we could end up shooting some of our own men in the dark. The next morning at first light, we jumped off the attack on Noville. Resistance was light. The enemy had evacuated Noville, leaving nothing more than a small rear guard to conduct a delaying action while the rest of the enemy retreated. We captured a few prisoners, among whom were two junior officers. Lieutenant Ed Thomas, my intelligence officer (S-2), tried to obtain some worthwhile information with no success. On January 16, 2d Battalion continued the attack and cleared the villages of Rachamps and Hardigny. This was our final attack in Belgium and marked an end to the major combat engagements of Easy Company and 2d Battalion, 506th PIR. Though we would routinely conduct combat patrols to establish contact with the enemy, never again would the battalion conduct large scale attacks against determined enemy resistance.

Apparently General Taylor was satisfied with our efforts. On the day following the capture of Noville, Taylor and members of his staff met with Brigadier General Gerry Higgins, his assistant division commander, and Colonel Sink to conduct an impromptu map reconnaissance adjacent to the Noville town hall to discuss future strategy. The next day the 17th Airborne Division relieved the 101st Airborne Division on the front line. Our division was ordered into Corps Reserve. The battle for Bastogne was finally over, but the Screaming Eagles of the 101st Airborne Division had written the brightest chapter in its combat history. It had been a costly campaign, but the American army learned valuable lessons in conducting winter warfare. One of the most valuable lessons was the importance of keeping your ears tuned to the noises of the night. A skilled soldier can recognize the sound of feet breaking the crust of the snow and the implications of a motor turning over in the distance. Radio operators learned not to talk directly into the microphone because the voice's condensation freezes the microphone and renders the radio inoperable. A light coat of oil on a weapon proved more effective than a thick layer of oil. The most important lesson lay in the reliance on common sense and field expediency, neither of which was covered in the elementary field manuals that addressed offensive and defensive operations.

I am not sure anyone who lived through Bastogne doesn't carry the scars of that ferocious campaign. I was extremely proud that 2d Battalion's lines were never broken. No enemy breakthrough or penetration occurred. Second Battalion held firm. Again, the performance of the American paratrooper in the war's deadliest campaign was the factor that kept Easy Company troopers, and by extension the remainder of the division, bonded so unusually close.

11

The Final Patrols

Unbeknownst to the 101st Airborne Division, which was fighting for its very survival at Bastogne, on New Year's Eve the Germans launched a diversionary attack in Alsace to divert Eisenhower's attention from the Ardennes. Code-named *Nordwind*, the offensive ran up against Alexander Patch's Seventh (U.S.) Army. Seventh Army had first landed in southern France in August 1944 and formed the southern terminus of Eisenhower's broad front approach to the Rhine. Once Allied headquarters directed Patton northward to relieve Bastogne, Patch's army extended its boundary to take over the portion of the line formerly held by Patton. The German attack initially made substantial headway, forcing Patch and his senior headquarters, Lieutenant General Jacob Devers's VI Army Group, to request reinforcements. With no available reserves at his disposal, Eisenhower dispatched the 101st Airborne Division. On January 19, Colonel Sink's 506th PIR was moving to the rear when new orders directed them to conduct a road movement 160 miles to Alsace along the German-French border. The thought of stopping another enemy breakthrough left me thinking, "My God, don't they have anybody else in this army to plug these gaps?"

The next day we boarded trucks and began the convoy over snow-covered, slippery highways. The route took us from Bastogne through Bellefontaine, Virton, Etain, Toul, Nancy, to Alsace. We arrived at Drulingen on January 22 and were immediately placed into a reserve position. This gave me the opportunity to write a short letter to my friend DeEtta Almon in the States in which I attempted to summarize the previous month's fighting and respond to a series of questions that she had posed. Rereading her previous letters, I noticed that she had again expressed disappointment at my lack of correspondence. That was understandable, but circumstances had been beyond my control. None of us would ever forget this past Christmas and New Year's Day. My friend said she was full of fight, so I responded in kind. I wrote, "If you want to fight, you might as well do it now while I don't have much zip left because I am a fighting man when I am strong. I might as well fight the Germans, the army, and you at the same time instead of individually. I feel like I can take care of the whole bunch and still not knock myself out. At least I am not really worried about a fight from you for all you can throw are strong words and right now they don't even faze me. The words just sort of bounce off." It was my first letter since we had departed Mourmelon for Bastogne. I then compared her letter to a close artillery shell—I just hit the dirt when I heard it coming, waited until the shrapnel stopped singing overhead, then I went about my way. Having endured a month on the line in freezing temperatures, nothing fazed me now. As I told my friend, "Sometimes a piece of spent shrapnel hits you, might leave your leg or arm stiff and a little black and blue, but you're not hurt enough to stop. So it goes in any kind of a fight. You get hit, sure, you are bound to; but that doesn't mean you're out or that you're even hurt, unless you want to think so." I still had a job to do.

From the perspective of sixty years, I am surprised how tired I was after the month at Bastogne. I added a footnote to my letter, in which I noted that between September 17, 1944 and January 22, 1945, I had jumped in Holland with the British 2d Army (73 days); been surrounded at Bastogne (30 days); and had been trucked to Alsace-Lorraine to stop the last German attack on January 1 (*Norwind*). This old war was mighty rough at times. For DeEtta to receive a letter written on January 22, 1945, she rated!

After several days in our initial encampment, 2d Battalion and the 506th PIR moved to Wilkersheim. Five days later the regiment returned to the line, taking over the villages Pfaffenoffen and Niedermodern. 2d Battalion remained in reserve at Grassendorf for the next two weeks. In early February the battalion moved to the forward edge of the battle area and established defensive positions along the Moder River. Since the Germans occupied the far bank, we conducted all our combat patrols under conditions of limited visibility. On February 4, Lieutenant Stapelfeld from Fox Company led a combat patrol across the river and ran into machine gun and mortar fire. In the process he lost one man killed and six men wounded. Life was still dangerous on the front and weather conditions remained abysmal. Fortunately the battalion received shoepacs, arctic socks, and felt insoles on February 4. How we could have used those items six weeks before at Bastogne!

The day following Stapelfeld's patrol, the 506th PIR relieved the 313th Infantry Regiment of the 79th Division, which had been holding Haguenau, a city of approximately 20,000 residents astride the Moder River. The width of the river varied from anywhere between 30 to 100 feet and contained a swift current that made crossing hazardous. To the rear of the town was a clear strip of fields for a distance of about one mile to the edge of the Forest de Haguenau. Colonel Sink deployed the regiment forward with 1st Battalion on the left, 2d Battalion on the right, and 3d Battalion in regimental reserve on the outskirts of town. By the time we relieved the 313th Infantry Regiment, the 79th Division was ready to leave the front. Combat had reduced its ranks to the point that they could no longer hold the line north of Haguenau. Having fought the German 21st Panzer Division from January 8 until January 21 in and around the village of Hatten, which was located just a few kilometers north of Haguenau, the 313th Regiment had broken off the engagement under cover of their artillery and withdrawn to the Moder River. Upon their withdrawal, Lieutenant Colonel Hans von Luck, a combat group commander in the 21st Panzer Division, celebrated his victory by playing Bach's chorale *"Nun danket alle Gott"* on the organ of the local church. As the sound reverberated through the ruins of the church to the outside, many of his men and the local residents flocked into the battered church and knelt on the ground. In his memoirs, von Luck said his men were not ashamed of their tears. As a side note, von Luck and I returned to this church in 1991 and he once again played *"Nun danket alle Gott"* for the residents of Hatten. Von Luck's capture of Hatten would be his last victory of the war. Within two weeks, his unit would be pulled from the line and redeployed to the Eastern Front in a futile attempt to halt a major Soviet offensive into the heart of Germany.

In mid-February General Maxwell Taylor adjusted the division front to ensure that all four regiments shared equally in the responsibility of frontline duty. Colonel Sink's 506th Regiment posted one battalion on line, one in regimental reserve, and one in division reserve. The 2d Battalion remained in position along the Moder River with H Company attached. To fill the officer ranks, we received three replacement officers recently graduated from West Point. One of these officers was 2d Lieutenant Larry Fitzpatrick, West Point Class of June 1943, who was assigned to Fox Company. On the evening of February 15, F Company conducted a patrol across the river. Without my knowledge or authorization, Fitzpatrick, too gung-ho and eager to prove himself in combat, volunteered to go along. After the patrol crossed the river, they climbed the north bank, where Fitzpatrick stepped on a mine and was instantly killed. I had always tried personally to interview and get to know each replacement officer and as many men as possible. Fitzpatrick was killed before I had had a chance to meet him. I can't remember or think of another instance where fate was so cruel to a replacement officer. Father John Maloney, who celebrated his last Mass, wrote Fitzpatrick's parents and informed them that, "The whole company was sad and gloomy for the next couple of days. . . . Without exception he [Fitzpatrick] was the most universally liked officer in the regiment." Fitzpatrick's premature death was yet another senseless tragedy of war.

At this stage in the war, my battalion staff consisted of an S-1 (personnel officer), Lieutenant Charles Bonning, and an S-4 (logistics officer), who seemed to have gotten himself lost about six weeks earlier while we were at Bastogne and who was still lost. In effect, I had no S-2 (intelligence officer), no S-3 (operations officer), and no S-4. My rank was still captain and for the past month, I had been dealing with commanding officers who were lieutenant colonels when coordinating with the other battalion commanders. Coordination with officers who were far senior in rank left me at a distinct disadvantage. The one advantage I did possess was my close relationship with Captain Nixon, who was Colonel Sink's operations officer. Nixon remained a close friend; however, when he needed a tough job done, he always came to 2d Battalion where he still had many good friends. Such was the case when he assigned 2d Battalion the mission of sending out a combat patrol to capture some prisoners.

Conducting a river crossing at night to capture prisoners is an extremely tough mission. How do you approach a soldier with a rifle, or a man behind a machine gun, who is in a defensive position and who has established clear fields of fire, and persuade him to come with you as your prisoner of war? Our target was a German outpost directly across the river from Easy Company. Due to my knowledge of Easy Company, the noncommissioned officer whom I suggested to lead the patrol was Sergeant Ken Mercier of 3d Platoon. I knew that Captain Speirs and the men would give me the support I needed to get the job accomplished. The plan was to cross the river upstream on Easy Company's right flank, then have the patrol sneak downstream on the German side of the river to the building where the enemy outpost was located in a cellar. This scheme of maneuver dictated that the patrol would be under the covering fire of E Company in the event of an emergency withdrawal. To accomplish the mission the patrol had to reach a point close enough to the outpost to lob a rifle grenade in the cellar window. Sergeant Mercier would take care of that job. The patrol would then charge to throw additional hand grenades in the cellar window. As soon as the grenades exploded, the patrol would move in to seize any prisoners while the Germans were still in a state of shock. Simultaneously, the patrol would plant and camouflage a satchel of explosives with a chemical fuse. Since I anticipated that the enemy would replace this outpost the next morning, I directed Mercier to set the delayed fuse to explode after ten hours. Sergeant Mercier would then blow a whistle to signal a withdrawal and to alert me in Easy Company's command post to initiate extracting fires to cover the patrol's withdrawal.

Every military operation, no matter how large or how small, has two components: a scheme of maneuver and a plan for fire support. To support Mercier's patrol, every known or suspected German position was covered by designated rifle fire, artillery, and mortar fire from 81mm and 60mm mortars, which were all zeroed on designated targets. Fifty-caliber and .30-caliber machine guns also had prearranged targets. The patrol would be able to withdraw under a blanket of supporting fire with no fear whatsoever that any German would be foolish enough to raise his head over the top of his foxhole.

Accompanying the patrol was 2d Lieutenant Hank Jones, one of our recent replacements. Like the ill-fated Lieutenant Fitzpatrick, Jones was eager to prove himself in combat. Though he outranked Sergeant Mercier, Mercier led the patrol. Any time a replacement officer joined the battalion in combat, I talked directly to the noncommissioned officers. I expected them to provide the leadership and to get the job done. The replacement officer would always be present, but, in my eyes, he was strictly an observer during "crunch times." In garrison, I respected the army chain of command and issued orders directly to the junior officer and expected him to complete the mission. But this was combat and I relied on my combat-hardened veterans to provide the necessary leadership. I considered it far too dangerous to place an unproven officer in command of a combat patrol when veteran noncoms were available. Consequently, Jones positioned himself in the rear of the patrol.

Due to Mercier's exemplary leadership, the conduct of the patrol was textbook in its execution. To this day I can still, very clearly, see Sergeant Mercier reporting into battalion headquarters with two German prisoners, whom I immediately passed to regiment. Mercier was proud, still excited, and wore a big smile on his face. The bad news was that we had lost Private Eugene Jackson, a replacement who had joined the company in Holland. Jackson was mortally wounded by grenade shrapnel in the forehead as the patrol closed in on the enemy outpost. He died before the medics could evacuate him to the battalion aid station. His death was highly regrettable, but the success of any raid to capture live prisoners depended upon a quick, hard charge immediately after the explosion of the grenades. The loss of a soldier was the price you sometimes paid. The following morning, we were pleased to see the satchel charge detonate on schedule. We never knew if any Germans returned to the outpost before the detonation, nor did we care. (Lieutenant Jones was later killed in Germany when his jeep hit a mine.)

The next day Colonel Sink was so elated with the results of the patrol that he paid me a personal visit with his friend Colonel Joseph H. Harper of the 327th Glider Infantry Regiment. Sink's visit was reminiscent of Normandy, when he had brought his colleague to company headquarters to hear how we had successfully silenced the battery at Brecourt Manor. Bob Sink was a magnificent commander, but this time he had had a little too much to drink and his order to dispatch another patrol to capture additional prisoners did not make sense. We had already captured sufficient prisoners for interrogation. A second patrol would only result in additional casualties for no apparent reason. Further exacerbating the situation was freshly fallen snow along the river that had quickly turned to ice during the day. If I followed Colonel Sink's order, the enemy would have heard us coming a long way off.

What to do? I responded, "Yes sir," and promptly ignored the order. To give the impression of compliance, however, I assembled the men in a building and told them we were not going to send out this patrol because I did not think it was feasible. I also informed them that my neck was in the noose if anyone ever said anything about it. With that the men lay down and caught some much-needed sleep as I took the radio and adjusted mortar and artillery fire on my supposed objective. On reflection I did exactly the right thing and I have never had any regrets. There was insufficient time for preparation, the field to our front was wide open, and I would have lost too many men for no purpose. I often wonder what I would have done had I been a career officer concerned about my own future. Would I have compromised my beliefs? The deliberate disobedience of a lawful order by my commanding officer presented an ethical dilemma of the first magnitude.

On February 20, 3d Battalion, 506th PIR, relieved 2d Battalion on the line. The battalion's combat days were nearly over. Two weeks later, on March 8, I received my promotion to the rank of major. Privately, I was thrilled to join the field-grade ranks, but my daily schedule was so hectic that I didn't have much time to think about it. With Colonel Strayer spending the majority of his time at regimental headquarters, I continued serving as acting battalion commander. I didn't expect the "acting" to last for long, but the job itself was pretty good. Regimental headquarters soon alerted us to return to Mourmelon. On the 23rd, the 36th Division finally replaced the 101st Airborne Division on the Moder River line. Within two days we boarded a train and made the eighteen-hour ride to Mourmelon-le-Petit. Casualties in the 506th PIR during February totaled far less than at Bastogne, but they remained significant for this stage of the war. In all, the month's combat had reduced the regiment's ranks by forty-four men. Of this total, 2d Battalion had suffered nineteen killed and wounded. We didn't realize it yet, but we all started walking with additional care, as if we had eyes in the backs of our heads, making sure we didn't get knocked off. Personally I never felt that my number was up, but I did feel that I was no longer invincible. Sometimes it scared me to think back on what I had done over the previous months of combat. Our attacks at Brecourt and at the crossroads in Holland had cost me two of those nine lives that a paratrooper was supposed to have. Somehow I had survived. I think it was safe to say that after Haguenau, each man had a gut feeling, "By God, I believe I am going to make it! I just might survive the war."

Prior to our departure from Alsace, I had the distinct privilege of presenting 1st Sergeant Carwood Lipton his honorable discharge from the U.S. Army, while simultaneously awarding him a battlefield commission as 2d lieutenant. No man was more deserving than Lipton. He had fought at Brecourt and Carentan with conspicuous gallantry. He had also performed commendably as Easy Company's senior noncommissioned officer since September. In Holland, at Bastogne, and at Haguenau, he was the glue that had held Easy Company together. Replacing Lipton as 1st Sergeant was Staff Sergeant Floyd Talbert, the noncom whom I have always felt was the best soldier in Easy Company. Both Lipton and Talbert were Toccoa men, two of the very few who still remained in Easy Company after three major campaigns.

Mourmelon seemed a pleasant reprieve after two months on the line, but there were drawbacks. Instead of being billeted in barracks, however, the men now lived in large, green, twelve-man tents. David Webster, a former Harvard English major and a Toccoa man who had rejoined the battalion just as we were loading the trucks on January 19 to go to Haguenau after recovering from his wounds in Holland, described the battalion's living quarters as worse than Fayetteville, North Carolina, the town outside the gates of Fort Bragg. Regardless of his assessment, Mourmelon presented the battalion the opportunity to take warm showers, clean up, and take care of the personal hygiene that had been so lacking at Bastogne and Haguenau.

Other changes were in store as well. On March 7, the senior officers in the division attended a demonstration of a new baseball-type concussion grenade. Unfortunately, one of the grenades exploded prematurely and injured eleven observers, including General Gerry Higgins, one of the 101st Airborne Division's assistant division commanders, and Colonel Harry W. O. Kinnard, the division operations officer. Their injuries created a snowball effect that led to a number of personnel changes within the 506th PIR. Lieutenant Colonel Charles Chase was elevated to division staff to replace the injured Kinnard. Replacing Chase as Sink's executive officer was Lieutenant Colonel Strayer, who relinquished command of 2d Battalion. Now that Strayer had been transferred to regimental headquarters company, Colonel Sink made permanent my assignment as battalion commander. It sure was an honor to receive command of 2d Battalion, for it meant that I had come straight up from junior second lieutenant to commanding officer in the same battalion in a period of two and a half years. To the best of my knowledge I was the only officer in the 506th PIR to advance from platoon leader in Normandy to battalion commander. I liked the job and responsibility that accompanied the promotion. I figured that if someone of senior rank didn't show up to take over and if my luck held, some day I might be a lieutenant colonel. But then again, I expected the war would be over within the next one hundred days. What my future held after that, I had no idea. In the interim I took the war one day at a time.

The remainder of March proved uneventful for 2d Battalion. From March until the end of the war, 2d Battalion sustained few battle casualties. As far as I can remember, Easy Company did not have another soldier either killed or wounded in action. With some time on my hands, I now selected my own staff. I appointed Captain Lloyd J. Cox as my executive officer; Captain Lewis Nixon joined the staff as operations officer; and Lieutenants Charles W. Bonning and Ralph D. Richey Jr. were assigned as battalion logistical officer and adjutant, respectively. Bonning was subsequently replaced by a Lieutenant Cowing. Harry Welsh served as my intelligence officer. Nixon's return to battalion staff was the result of his repeated drunkenness. Colonel Sink recognized Nixon's tactical brilliance, but he was fed up with his excessive drinking. One day Sink visited me and asked me point-blank, "Can you get along with Nixon?"

"Yes, sir, I can get along with him."

"Can you get something out of him?"

Again I responded, "Yes, sir, we work together very well."

"Would you like to have him back?"

"Yes, sir, I would."

"You've got him."

And that is how Nixon returned to battalion staff. From a personal perspective, it was nice being reunited with Nix. His reassignment to my staff created a domino effect on regimental staff. Colonel Sink now transferred Captain Salve Matheson to be his operations officer and backfilled Matheson with Captain Sobel. As regimental logistical officer, Sobel was now in close contact with the company that he had prepared for combat. Seeing so many of his old officers serving in positions of increased responsibility must have been bittersweet for Sobel. Former Easy Company officers now commanded two of the regiment's three battalions (Lieutenant Colonel Clarence Hester now commanded 1st Battalion) and they occupied two key positions at regiment (S-3 and S-4), as well as two positions on my staff (S-2 and S-3). Historian Ambrose is correct in stating that "Sobel must have been doing something right back in the summer of '42 at Toccoa."

As we prepared for our next operation, for example, I could not help but be impressed by the professionalism demonstrated by many of the German prisoners in our midst. After working at the Mourmelon hospital all day, the prisoners marched back to their stockade at dusk. As they passed their American captors, the prisoners sang their marching songs with the pride and vigor only found in units that had bonded in combat. It was absolutely beautiful. I always looked forward to that time of day and made it a point to stop and listen to a defeated foe still united in comradeship. Amid the chaos and butchery of war, I told myself that I would always remember this beautiful moment. By God, these men were soldiers! Though I despised what the Nazi regime represented, I clearly recognized that unit pride transcended nationality and political systems.

Recently promoted General of the Army Dwight D. Eisenhower visited the 101st Airborne Division on March 15 and decorated the Screaming Eagles with the Presidential Unit Citation for action in the defense of Bastogne. In congratulating the division, Ike noted that it was a "great personal honor" to acknowledge the bravery and heroism of the American paratrooper. He wished us good luck and asked for God's blessing as the war drew to a close. Amid much pomp and circumstance, General Taylor proudly received the award in an elaborate ceremony. At Taylor's side as his senior aide stood none other than Lieutenant Norman Dike, Easy Company's former commander. His presence hardly detracted from the ceremony since this was the first time in the history of the army that a full division had received this prestigious award. War Department regulations established the criteria that a unit was to receive the Presidential Unit Citation only if it had distinguished itself by conspicuous battle action of a character that would merit the award to an individual of the Distinguished Service Cross, the army's second-highest award for valor. Ike's normal policy was to limit unit citations to the smaller formations except in most unusual circumstances. Prior to his departure from the European Theater of Operations at the conclusion of the war, however, Eisenhower reconsidered his position and wrote General George C. Marshall that "the Army esprit de corps centers around a division much more than it does any other echelon. Consequently, the citation of particular battalions within a division does not mean as much to the soldier as a commendation to the division itself." After the war, Eisenhower also recommended eight other divisions for the Presidential Unit Citation, but the 101st Airborne Division was the only one of four airborne divisions cited in the European Theater.

A week prior to the Supreme Commander's visit, General Omar Bradley telephoned Eisenhower that General John Millikin's III Corps had captured an intact bridge over the Rhine River at Remagen. Eisenhower exploited the opportunity and quickly established a bridgehead over Germany's last natural barrier. As the remainder of the Allied Expeditionary Force advanced to the Rhine, General George S. Patton, using the leading elements of the U.S. 5th Infantry Division, pushed his 3d U.S. Army across the Rhine near the small town of Oppenheim, midway between Worms and Mainz on the evening of March 22. The next evening, March 23, Field Marshal Montgomery launched Operation Varsity, a massive attack across the Rhine at Wesel with his entire 2d British Army. Though Ridgway's XVIII Airborne Corps, of which the 101st Airborne Division was an integral part, had originally been slated to participate in the offensive, changes in the troop list resulted in William (Bud) Miley's 17th Airborne Division being the only American airborne division participating in Montgomery's highly touted offensive. The 101st was allowed to send observers, so I dispatched Captain Lewis Nixon.

Fortunately for Nixon, he was assigned to be jumpmaster of his aircraft. As he approached the drop zone, his plane was struck by heavy antiaircraft fire. Nixon and three other men made it out of the plane, but the rest were lost when the plane crashed. Nix remained with the 17th Airborne Division for one night and was then returned to 2d Battalion at Mourmelon on a special plane. Nix's brush with death left him visibly shaken, particularly when at this stage in the war, no one intentionally put himself in danger now that victory was at hand. Captain Nixon found his usual retreat in alcohol that evening, but I was glad to see him safe. On a side note, Nixon's jump with the 17th Airborne Division qualified him as one of two men in the 506th PIR eligible to wear three stars on his jump wings: Normandy, Holland, and Operation Varsity. The other trooper was a pathfinder by the name of Wright who had served in Easy Company at Toccoa.

Rumors abounded within the United States as to what the now-famous Screaming Eagles were doing. One day after Varsity had bridged the Rhine River, we heard on the radio that the 101st Airborne

Division had also jumped east of the Rhine. Mighty interesting! Wish they would have told me, so I could have taken the battalion along for the show.

As we waited for word on our next combat mission, battalion duties kept me busy. I corresponded with my friend DeEtta Almon in the States and expressed my concerns and my observations of how the war had changed a young man from Lancaster, Pennsylvania, who had enlisted in the summer of 1941 to rid himself of a military commitment in as rapid a time as possible. In a photograph I had sent home, she noted that my hair was darker and that my forehead was wrinkled by "worry muscles." I responded somewhat caustically that my hair was darker because I hadn't had an opportunity to wash it but a couple times a year. As to the worry muscles covering my face, the longer this war continued, the deeper they would grow "for I now had over 600 individual worries plus myself when I got time to think about my future." Nor did I have much tolerance for garrison soldiers who had not served in combat or soldiers who bragged about their wartime exploits to impress women. When DeEtta informed me that she had met a trooper from a rival regiment, my sarcasm reached new heights of intolerance. I wrote that, "It must have been interesting to hear what the lad had to say about what the paratroopers must go through. Terrible, I imagine. I'll just bet that they run him to death . . . did he tell you about the time he killed three Germans with his bare hands? Or about the time he received a letter from his girl and he was so inspired that he went out and killed ten more of those dirty old krauts?" I guarantee I had heard all the stories.

I certainly didn't feel like writing anymore. I couldn't explain why, but the only emotion that I could arouse were feelings of anger and after staying mad all day and half the night, I was just plain tired. Mad at what? Just about everything, for just about everything was done wrong or it wasn't done perfectly. Since nothing but perfection was acceptable, I stayed mad. What struck me most was how damn tired I became by the end of each day and how difficult it was to concentrate. I now had people asking me questions about weapons, targets, harassing fire, grazing fire, chow, transportation, and base of fire. It never ended. I had no time to consider a person's feelings or devotion to the point, or incidental matters. Combat required that my thoughts and feelings remain hard, cold, indifferent, and effective. As to any tender thoughts I might have possessed before the war, I had left them behind in the marshalling area in England. There was no room for trivialities. I did, occasionally, think about death. Sure, I thought long and hard about the paratroopers who had paid the ultimate price, but there was no time to mourn them. Whether on the front line or in a rear area, I refused to lower my guard. Commanding a battalion required every ounce of energy that remained—no time to let up now that the war was drawing to a close.

12

Victory

On April 1, Colonel Sink alerted 2d Battalion that the regiment had received another defensive mission, this time along the Rhine River to assist in sealing the Ruhr "pocket." Our job was to hold the west bank of the Rhine opposite Dusseldorf and the area south to Worringen, while General Omar Bradley's armies encircled and pinched off the pocket to the east. Second Battalion's sector extended from Sturzelberg on the north to Worringen on our south flank, where we linked up with the 82d Airborne Division. The 82d Division's paratroopers' area extended ten or twelve miles north and south of Cologne, from Worringen on the north to Bonn on the south. Both airborne divisions were basically occupation troops, sending only harassing patrols and artillery fire across the river, and receiving occasional artillery fire in return. This occupation duty continued until the pocket collapsed on April 18. In the interim, we patrolled across the Rhine, although not with the intensity that characterized our combat at Bastogne. Occupation duty also produced our first real contact with the native German population and with the problems associated with fraternization. Eisenhower's Supreme Headquarters Allied Expeditionary Force (SHAEF) was adamant on the point of no association between American GI's and the German populace. With so many camps populated with displaced persons (DP) of various nationalities who had been brought into the Fatherland for slave labor, nonfraternization proved a pipe dream. None of our soldiers performed much manual labor since the DP did most of the menial tasks and irritating duties like KP associated with soldiering. The orders prohibiting personal contact were well-intentioned, but totally unrealistic, particularly to soldiers who had spent months on the line with no female contact. As battalion commander, I strove to enforce the regulation, but was never so naïve to think that my paratroopers didn't develop innovative ways to circumvent SHAEF's policy.

As we waited for the Germans encircled in the Ruhr pocket to capitulate, my battalion received orders to send a patrol across the Rhine. The area I selected lay directly across the river from Sturzelberg. This was the safest area in our sector. On the German side of the river, we had observed no activity and the farmland on the opposite shore was covered by an extensive orchard. Lieutenant Harry Welsh, Battalion S-2, was given the job of leading the patrol and I personally set the objectives and controlled the covering artillery concentrations as I accompanied the patrol step by step up the east bank of the river toward the industrial center of Benrath. Welsh was thoroughly disgusted with the safety limits I purposely imposed on the patrol, but I had no intention of losing any more soldiers. Actually we went through the motions of a combat patrol, found nothing, and everybody returned safely. The most dangerous part of the patrol was crossing the Rhine and returning since the river was 350 yards wide and flowing very swiftly.

I also toured a small town named Zons on our side of the river. Zons was a typical German village, founded in the early fifteenth century. All of the buildings, the castle, and walls were constructed of stone, and a moat surrounded the castle. I wondered how many times this town had been under attack over the past 550 years. After all the destruction that I had witnessed, I was elated that Zons had not been destroyed by the air corps or by artillery fire. In contrast to the small villages that dotted the German countryside, Allied bombers had obliterated the large cities like Cologne. Months of bombardment left only a few houses standing in the entire city. Much of the population fled to the countryside and the few who remained in the large urban areas wandered around in the rubble in search of food and personal possessions. Cities that I had read about in travel journals when I was young simply no longer existed. During the early stages of the war, German residents could scarcely imagine how terrible war could be. They now appreciated the horrors of modern warfare as they witnessed their own cities crumble around them.

In the countryside the Germans fared far better than their urban counterparts and much better than the inhabitants in the countries in which we had fought since D-Day. The rural Germans weren't hurting for much during this war, but who would expect them to with France, Poland, and a handful of other countries supplying them with silk stockings, raw materials, and other amenities. What a contrast to the English, who rationed virtually every commodity since early in the war. In my estimation, the people in Germany had not suffered nearly as much as our newspapers had led us to believe. German towns and villages were really something to behold. I never had seen anything like them in England, France, or Belgium. On the whole, military duty in Germany wasn't half bad. The battalion moved into a town, picked the best house, told the folks, "I'll give you a reasonable time to move— fifteen minutes. Leave the beds, silverware, and cooking utensils." At the end of the reasonable length of time, 2d Battalion had a nice command post and if time permitted a good meal, bed, and bath. What a great way to fight a war! Occupation duty was much better than Normandy, Holland, or Bastogne, where we lived in foxholes most of the time. Now that we were playing ball in their backyard, a fellow gained a degree of satisfaction in knowing that these people were going to pay for bringing on the war. They knew it, too. After seeing what others had endured at the hands of German occupiers, I was hardly sympathetic to the plight of the German people.

On April 10, the majority of the battalion received a seven-day furlough to Nice, France. While they enjoyed the amenities of the French countryside, the 506th continued sending out periodic patrols. On one of these patrols, Lieutenant Purdue from Fox Company was wounded by a booby trap and was immediately evacuated. That same day, Major William Leach, 506th Regimental S-2, led his first combat patrol. In preparation for the patrol, Leach persuaded my friend Sergeant Al Krochka, a photographer from division headquarters, to fly a small Piper cub over the Rhine for photos of a suspected machine gun emplacement. The plane was hit and Krochka was wounded in the arm by fire from the machine gun. That night, Major Leach and four men attempted to cross the river. Unfortunately they failed to notify friendly forces that they would be crossing the Rhine. Midstream, Leach and his patrol were fired upon by an American machine gun crew and all were killed. Their bodies were recovered on April 18 in front of Fox Company's position at Sturzelberg.

Leach was a good staff officer who made his way up the ladder of success on the strength of his personality and social expertise. During the crunch times—this Ruhr pocket duty was nothing more than police duty—Leach had never led a patrol. Like Lieutenant Hank Jones at Haguenau, he had not yet earned a battlefield decoration, and like Jones, Major Leach planned to make the army a career. Jones survived his initial brush with combat and was immediately transferred out of the company, but Leach was not as fortunate. The common feeling after his death was that this was a foolish patrol, and that Leach was on an "ego trip," trying to earn a stupid decoration. In the process he got his entire patrol killed. Six days later, German resistance in the Ruhr pocket came to an end when 325,000 German soldiers surrendered on April 18. This was the largest bag of enemy prisoners in the war to date.

By mid-April, the war in Western Europe neared a rapid conclusion. Even the Germans realized that the war was over. They battled on only because they were professional soldiers. As we prepared for the final push, the battalion received word that President Roosevelt had died on April 12. Roosevelt was more than a fixture in our lives. He was the only president most of us could remember. Every American soldier in the U.S. Army held the commander-in-chief in utmost respect. Few were familiar with his successor, Harry S. Truman, but none doubted that the new president would see the war to a successful conclusion. By General Eisenhower's orders, each command conducted a simple memorial service for our fallen commander-in-chief. In the interim, 2d Battalion received badly needed supplies. April 19 marked an important day as each paratrooper received a new pair of socks, three bottles of Coca-Cola, and two bottles of beer. Life now was a far cry from what the men had experienced at Bastogne and Haguenau. For the most part the farther that we traveled into Germany, the better we lived. One trooper noted that for the past month, he had never eaten better, kept cleaner, or slept in more comfortable beds than at any other time in the twenty months that he had been overseas. Rations also improved. Instead of eating K-rations, the men enjoyed fresh eggs for breakfast six days in a row. Staff Sergeant Robert Smith joked that if living conditions continued like this for the remainder of the war, he "might sign up to be a thirty-year man." On careful reflection, he then wrote, "What am I saying? Someone must have jabbed a morphine needle in me."

Three days later, the entire 101st Airborne Division was en route to Bavaria as Allied headquarters attached the division to Lieutenant General Alexander Patch's Seventh (U.S.) Army in southern Germany in its advance to secure Hitler's "Alpine Redoubt." Whether Hitler ever intended to fortify the Bavarian Alps was anyone's guess, but Eisenhower wasn't taking any chances. We left our defensive positions along the Rhine and boarded 40' x 8' (cars designed to carry either forty men or eight horses) railroad cars. Supply also issued five K-rations per man. Due to the conditions of the German railroad system at the time, the rail convoy trip of 145 miles traversed four countries: Holland, Belgium, Luxembourg, and France, to reach Widden, Germany. On April 25, we switched modes of transportation and climbed aboard big, amphibious vehicles called DUKWs: D (1942), U (amphibian), K (all-wheel drive), W (dual-rear axles), to carry us to the vicinity of Miesbach southeast of Munich. We traveled through the German countryside, continuing our journey through Mannheim and Heidelberg until we reached Ulm. At Ulm astride the Danube River, we stopped to gas the DUKWs and then proceeded to Buchloe, which lay at the foothills of the Bavarian Alps. There we halted for the night because once again the convoy was low on fuel. Our standard operating procedure was to dispatch reconnaissance patrols whenever we halted. Earlier in the day, Frank Perconte, one of the original Toccoa men from Easy Company, reported that he and his patrol had discovered a German concentration camp. The 10th Armored Division had entered Landsberg the previous day and had also come across several concentration camps in the Landsberg-Buchloe area. Later we discovered Hitler had constructed six large "work camps" in the vicinity.

By now the men and I were seasoned combat veterans, but the sights we witnessed when we arrived at the camp defied description. The horror of what we observed remains with each paratrooper to this day. You could not explain it; you could not describe it; and you could not exaggerate it. It did not take long to realize that the Nazis were intent on eliminating all the Jews, gypsies, and anyone who disagreed with Hitler's regime. The memory of starved, dazed men who dropped their eyes and heads when we looked at them through the chain-link fence, in the same manner that a beaten, mistreated dog would cringe, left a mark on all of us forever. Nor could you underestimate the barbarity of the Nazi regime, even during the latter stages of the war. I immediately directed Nixon to take all the local inhabitants to clean up the camp, including the crematorium and the burial pits.

As I went through the war, it was natural to ask myself, *Why am I here? Why am I putting up with the freezing cold, the constant rain, and the loss of so many comrades? Does anybody care?* A soldier faces death on a daily basis and his life is one of misery and deprivation. He is cold; he suffers from hunger, frequently bordering on starvation. The impact of seeing those people behind that fence left me saying, if only to myself, *Now I know why I am here! For the first time I understand what this war is all about.*

That night, I selected a large home in Buchloe for my battalion headquarters. In the cellar and in the adjoining buildings, we discovered stacks and stacks of huge wheels of cheese. I did not know if the Germans had a factory in the village or not, but I knew what had to be done. We immediately distributed cheese to the internees at the camp and to our troops. I then radioed our problem of the concentration camp to regiment and requested help. Within hours Major Louis Kent, the brigade medical officer, arrived and cautioned us against overfeeding the former inmates. Under his supervision, we halted the distribution of the cheese because the ingestion of so many calories would have produced a detrimental effect on the emaciated prisoners. A more difficult task was forcing the liberated internees to return to the camp so that medical personnel could care for them.

In spite of the horror associated with our initial contact with the Holocaust, it is difficult to exaggerate the natural beauty of the Bavarian countryside. Spring flowers covered verdant fields watered by crystal-clear mountain brooks. One Easy Company trooper, Staff Sergeant Robert T. Smith, couldn't believe "that he had ever seen countryside so nice to look at as here in Germany . . . since they prohibit the lining of the roadways with signboards and such. When we ride down a highway you can take in all the scenery instead of having to read all about 'Burma-shave.' " The most beautiful region in Germany heralded the coming spring. It was an enchanting time, watching Hitler's Third Reich crumble before our eyes.

Munich fell to the Seventh Army on April 30, prompting congratulations from SHAEF for the destruction of "the cradle of the Nazi beast." The 101st Airborne Division, however, sought a bigger prize—the capture of Hitler's Alpine retreat of Berchtesgaden. On May 3, 2d Battalion was located at Thalham, Germany. The past few days had been spent moving through streams of German soldiers, who were slowly walking toward Munich, or just lying along the sides of the autobahn. Once in a while we encountered scattered rifle shots, a token resistance by a dying regime. At other times there were more German soldiers with weapons marching north than there were 506th paratroopers heading south. Literally thousands of Germans choked the autobahns as we raced into Bavaria. American and German soldiers exchanged glances with great curiosity. I am sure both armies shared one thought—*just let me alone. All I want is to get this war over and go home.* That night we received the word that at 0930 the next morning, we would be moving out to seize Berchtesgaden. Regiment directed us to draw additional ammo and rations.

Bright and early on May 4, the convoy started down the German autobahn toward Salzburg. We passed Rosenheim and the Chiem-See to Siegsdorf, a distance of forty miles from Thalham. At Siegsdorf, we turned right on Route 30, the direct route to Berchtesgaden. About eight miles down the road we ran into the stalled French 2d Armored Division under General Jacques Philippe de Leclerc. This outfit had supposedly been on our right flank for the past week, but we had not been able to maintain contact with them. They had been there, and then they would disappear. We had a gut feeling that they were looting their way through Germany, but we had no proof. Here the convoy halted because the Germans had destroyed another bridge over a deep ravine. Moreover, the enemy covered that blown-out bridge and the ravine from the sides of the mountains with plunging fire from their machine guns. Under these circumstances, Colonel Sink could not move the regiment's bridging equipment into position. Up front the French exchanged long-distance fire with the Germans, but since the enemy was out of range of the machine guns, nobody was hurt on either side.

The 101st had been briefed on the new 57mm and 75mm recoilless rifles while we were back in Mourmelon. While at Thalham, we were issued four 75mm recoilless rifles. This morning 2d Battalion had our first opportunity to employ them on a long-range target. While this firing was going on, the French 2d Armored Division and the 506th PIR headquarters staffs assembled in one group and enjoyed a rare meeting under combat conditions where there was no pressure. It was a festive mood, a time for international fellowship. Before too long, I grew bored with this party and I approached Colonel Sink to request permission to dispatch a platoon to outflank the German roadblock. His answer was correct for this stage of the war: "No, I don't want anybody to get hurt."

Later he reconsidered and ordered me, "Take 2d Battalion back to the autobahn and see if you can outflank this roadblock and get to Berchtesgaden." We immediately backtracked to the highway and went down to Bad Reichenhall, only to be halted by another blown bridge. Consequently, we had to stop by the roadside that evening, still thirty-five kilometers from our objective. Standard operating procedures dictated that all squads were to be quartered in houses, so the men enjoyed a restful night. Early the next morning, we resumed our march and by 1230 we entered Berchtesgaden.

Berchtesgaden was a town unlike any that we had encountered in Germany. Set against the Bavarian Alps, the town had served as a magnet for Nazi officialdom ever since Hitler had constructed a home called the *Berghof* in the vicinity. His villa contained a large picture window from which he could look into Germany and neighboring Austria. Overlooking the Austrian city of Salzburg, the last home of Wolfgang Amadeus Mozart, was the *Obersalzburg*, a mountain that was the site of Hitler's personal chalet, the homes of most senior-ranking Nazi officials, and an SS barracks. The residences of the German officials were located along the hillside, widely spaced so that each home enjoyed the luxury of privacy. All homes were well constructed and elaborately furnished. Five miles from the Berghof was Hitler's private diplomatic house, a mountain retreat called the *Adlerhorst* (Eagle's Nest), atop the Kehlstein. It had been designed by Hitler's henchman Martin Bormann as a present for Hitler's fiftieth birthday. Bormann used over 3,500 laborers to construct the Eagle's Nest before it was finished in summer 1938. The views from glassed-in circular hall and the adjacent veranda were some of the most picturesque in all of Germany.

My only orders from Colonel Sink were to put a guard on the Berchtesgaden Hof "because Division wants to make this their headquarters." Naturally, the first place I headed when we reached the center of town was the Berchtesgaden Hof. Accompanying me was Lieutenant Harry Welsh, my S-2. As we entered the front door, we could see the hotel's staff disappear around the corner. We walked into the main dining room where we encountered one very brave waiter gathering a very large set of silverware in a velvet-lined case. The case must have been four feet long. Obviously, he was preparing to hide this last set of silverware, but he was just a little late in getting the job done. Harry and I simply walked toward the man. There was no need for orders; he took off. I glanced at the silverware and thought to myself, *Hell, this is more than I can carry in my musette bag.* So, I said to Harry, "Why don't we split the set?" He agreed, so we divided the set right down the middle. Today we are both still using the silverware from the Berchtesgaden Hof in our homes. I then placed a double guard on the Berchtesgaden Hof to prevent further looting. When regiment and division headquarters arrived, they finished the job, looting everything of value that remained—what a fool I had been not to complete the job with 2d Battalion. I also placed additional guards on various strategic points around the town, at the ammunition dump, the railroad tunnel, the P.O.W. enclosure and Hermann Goering's house. We moved into Berchtesgaden so fast and had taken over the hotel, the key buildings, and the homes for billeting so quickly, that if there were any serious problems or resistance from the German soldiers or civilians, I was not aware of them.

Now that we were in *Der Fuhrer*'s backyard, we simply seized what we wanted. I selected a private home on the outskirts of Berchtesgaden for my battalion headquarters. The surrounding homes were taken over by the companies, one home per platoon. Seizing German property was a simple matter. Take for example, the house that served as my battalion command post. I told Lieutenant Cowing, my logistics officer, that I wanted this particular house as my CP. "Tell the people they have fifteen minutes to move out." Cowing was a replacement officer who had joined us at Haguenau. He was a very nice, polite, and efficient officer, who had never been hardened by battle. In a few minutes, he returned to report, "The people said no. They will not move out."

"Follow me," I said. I went to the front door, followed by the rest of the battalion staff. I knocked and when the lady answered, I simply announced, "We are moving in. Now!"

We did, and the family disappeared. Where they went, I don't know, but there was no further problem.

Did I feel guilty about this? Did my conscience bother me about taking over this beautiful home? No! We had been living in foxholes in Normandy; we had been in the mud at Holland; and we had suffered in the freezing cold at Bastogne. Just a few days earlier I had seen a concentration camp not 100 miles from here. These people were the reason for all this suffering. I felt no sympathy for their problems. I did not feel that I owed them an explanation. This is about the way I think it went as each of the platoons took over a home and got themselves settled throughout the community. Billeting the troops—no problem whatsoever!

How did the troops react to the liberation of Berchtesgaden? You could see the smiles on their faces. They simply enjoyed themselves; they were at peace with the world. There was no breakdown in organization. We maintained our guards on the key points in order to pro-

tect vital installations. Mostly, the 506th PIR relaxed and simply enjoyed a little sight-seeing. We confiscated a wide assortment of German
cars, and we seized a lot of German army trucks. We were in total control of the situation and of ourselves.

While conducting a private reconnaissance on May 6, I found my
way to Goering's private compound, including a set of officers' quarters and club. It was rather foolish to be walking around, exploring by
myself, at this stage of the game, but I felt no danger. I found a dead
German general in full dress uniform in Goering's private quarters. In
his hand was a Luger. He had committed suicide, putting a bullet
through his head. Later, I learned that corpse was General Kastner.

Just as I exited the dining room of the officers' club, I noticed another door in the corner of the room. Somewhat apprehensively, I
walked down a stone staircase, which led to a darkened basement.
Lord, I had never seen anything like it before. This high room, about
fifty feet long and thirty feet wide, contained rack upon rack of liquor,
wines, champagne, all the way to the ten-foot-high ceiling. Brand
names covered virtually every wine-producing region in the world. A
conservative estimate was that the wine cellar housed nearly 10,000
bottles of the world's finest liquor. I deemed it prudent to put a double
guard on the officers' club, especially the wine cellar.

Captain Nixon was always my finest combat officer. My only
problem with Nixon was keeping him sober. That afternoon I told him,
"Nix, you sober up and I'll show you something you have never seen
before in your life." Then I promptly forgot about the wine cellar.
There were too many other important points and places to cover. It was
obvious that the excessive drinking could get out of hand, so I issued
an order—everybody on the wagon for seven days. Now, I was no fool,
and I didn't expect an order like that to be carried out 100 percent. But
the message was clear—keep the situation under control. I didn't want
a drunken brawl.

The following morning a sober Nixon approached me and asked,
"What was that you said yesterday that you were going to show me?"

"Follow me," I responded.

We then took a jeep and drove directly to Goering's officers' club. Nixon thought that he had died and gone to heaven. I told him, "This is yours. Take what you want, then have each company and battalion headquarters bring around a truck and take a truckload. You are in charge." I have of picture of Nixon with his stash of liquor next to his bed as he awoke on VE-Day as proof that he did a good job in distributing the liquor, but only after he collected his personal spoils of war.

Private David Kenyon Webster penned a different account of Goering's wine cellar. Webster was shocked to find that "Hitler's champagne in the cellar was new and mediocre, no Napoleon brandy, no fine liqueurs." Webster was a Harvard man, a self-styled connoisseur of liquors. So was Nixon, who prided himself on being a Yale man. Before Webster reached the wine cellar, Nixon had already absconded with his personal booty and supervised the distribution of five truckloads for the troops. Once the troops had their share of the liquor, Nixon lifted the guards. On this occasion the Yale man pulled rank on the Harvard boy. Small wonder that Webster was disappointed in what remained. Nixon would have been first to attest that in the army, rank still had its privileges.

Another of my favorite memories of Berchtesgaden is that of 1st Sergeant Floyd Talbert on the hood of one of Hitler's staff cars, a Mercedes-Benz. The men found eight or nine of those cars around Berchtesgaden. I know that Captain Speirs commandeered one. The windows were supposed to be bulletproof. When we received orders on VE-Day that we were to leave for Zell-am-See, Sink's headquarters issued orders that we must leave the cars behind for 101st Airborne Division senior officers. Until that time, nobody in headquarters had the nerve to commandeer the cars from the men who had found them. From what I understand, that last day some of the cars ran off cliffs. Nobody was injured for no one was in the cars at the time of the "accidents." Talbert later reported to me that the windows on the cars really were bulletproof, but if you used armor-piercing ammunition that would get the job done. This was very interesting. You never knew when you might need this kind of information.

Other places of interest in Berchtesgaden were Hitler's Eagle Nest and Konig-See. To reach the Eagle's Nest, troops had to climb a spiraling road that Hitler's engineers had constructed up the sheer mountainside. The Eagle's Nest had been constructed at a height of nearly 2,000 meters above the valley floor, some 800 meters higher than Hitler's private residence at the Berghof. Hitler himself was not fond of the Eagle's Nest and rarely went there except to impress foreign diplomats because at that height, the air was very thin and bad for his blood pressure. I assigned Easy Company the mission of securing the Eagle's Nest, where Alton More discovered two of Hitler's private photograph albums. More confiscated the albums, keeping the books hidden when a French officer, supposedly speaking on behalf of a high-ranking French general, demanded that More turn over the albums. In Kaprun he slept on the books and guarded them constantly. When an American officer threatened to court-martial More if he didn't relinquish the photograph albums, I solved the problem by transferring More from Easy Company to Headquarters Company, where he served as my driver and where I protected him until he returned to the States with his treasured souvenirs. After the war, Alton More died tragically in a 1958 automobile accident.

Berchtesgaden remained full of surprises. In addition to the chalets around the Konig-See, Nixon and I came across a group of German civilians guarding several railroad cars. They were a pathetic-looking group, but something about that scene told us to use common sense and leave them alone. We understood later that the cars contained a cache of artwork, which was later taken over by division.

In recent years, controversy has surrounded the identity as to which unit captured Berchtesgaden. Was it the French 2d Armored Division, the 7th Infantry Regiment's "Cottonbalers" of the U.S. 3d Infantry Division, or Sink's paratroopers from the 506th PIR? Major General John W. "Iron Mike" O'Daniel's 3d Infantry Division certainly seized neighboring Salzburg without opposition and may have had their lead elements enter Berchtesgaden before we arrived in force, but let the facts speak for themselves. If the 3d Division was first into Berchtesgaden, where did they go? Berchtesgaden is a relatively small community. When I walked into the Berchtesgaden Hof with Lieutenant Welsh, neither of us saw anyone except the hotel staff. Goering's officers' club and wine cellar certainly would have drawn the attention of a Frenchman from LeClerc's 2d Armored Division or a rifleman from the 3d Division. I find it inconceivable to imagine that if the 3d Division were there first, they left those beautiful Mercedes staff cars untouched for our men. Regimental and divisional histories provide contradictory accounts. In *Rendezvous with Destiny*, the 101st Airborne Division's official history, the 506th PIR are latecomers, but I assure you, members of 2d Battalion have different memories and photographs to prove that we didn't do too badly in getting our share of the loot at Berchtesgaden during the final days of the European war.

World War II ended about as gloriously as I had ever hoped. Berchtesgaden was really the heart of Germany, not Berlin, and it was quite an honor to be in on the final drama. Reich Marshal Goering, Field Marshal Albert Kesselring, generals by the dozen, and Germans by the thousands hurried to surrender and escape capture by the Russians. I had never seen anything like it, nor could I have imagined it. The enemy was backed up right into the mountains with no place to go. Then they threw in the towel and started coming out of the hills. Days before the final surrender, everyone knew it was over. Thank God, there just wasn't any fighting!

It was at Berchtesgaden on May 6 that the 506th PIR received the following communiqué from division headquarters: "Effective immediately all troops will stand fast on present positions. German Army Group G in this sector has surrendered. No firing on Germans unless fired upon. Full details, to be broadcast, will be issued by SHAEF." For all intents, combat operations ceased with the receipt of this message. At 0241 hours, local time, May 7, General Eisenhower received the unconditional surrender of Germany at his headquarters at Reims. The Nazi surrender became effective at midnight. Word of the German capitulation immediately filtered down the echelons of command to my headquarters. VE-Day was officially proclaimed on May 8. Outside my command post, the sun climbed into a clear sky over Berchtesgaden. It was D-Day plus 335. The war in Europe was finally over.

PART FOUR

Finding Peace
After a Lifetime of War

We have won this war because our men are brave . . .
not because destiny created us better than all other
peoples. I hope that in victory we are more grateful
than we are proud. I hope we can rejoice in victory—
but humbly. The dead men would not want us to
gloat.

ERNIE PYLE, *Brave Men*

13

Occupation

May 8, 1945—Victory in Europe—a day for which we had been fighting for over three years. War's end brought little inner emotion, only a tired sense of relief. We held no formal victory celebrations, but the men conducted their private celebrations, courtesy of Reich Marshal Goering. Photographs of 2d Battalion's paratroopers at Berchtesgaden give a good idea how happy the men were to have survived the carnage of war. Ernie Pyle, who perished in the war's final campaign in the Pacific, had penned a final column to cover the end of the Nazi regime before he departed France in 1944. Like many of us, Pyle had had enough of war and needed a respite. As usual he summed up our collective emotions when he wrote: "Somehow it would seem sacrilegious to sing and dance—there were so many who would never sing and dance again. Far too many American boys have come to join the thousands who already had slept in France for a quarter of a century." Aboard a naval ship enroute to Okinawa in late March 1945, Pyle penned his final thoughts on the war in northwest Europe, when he freely admitted that his "heart is still in Europe, and that's why I am writing this column. It is to the boys who were my friends for so long. My one regret of the war is that I was not with them when it ended." He later added, "In the joyousness of high spirits it is easy for us to forget the dead. . . . But here are many of the living who have had burned into their brains forever the unnatural sight of cold dead men scattered over the hillsides and in the ditches along the high rows of hedge throughout the world." I numbered a good many of my men, all good paratroopers, among them. I thanked God that the killing had come to an end.

Leave it to General Eisenhower to place the war in perspective. Ike distributed his "Victory Order of the Day" as soon as he announced the unconditional surrender of Nazi Germany. As usual, he paid tribute to the American G.I., whose "route through hundreds of miles was marked by graves of former comrades. Each of the fallen died as a member of a team to which you belong, bound together by a common love of liberty and a refusal to submit to enslavement." The Supreme Commander urged each member of the Allied Expeditionary Force to "revere each honored grave, and to send comfort to the loved ones of comrades who could not live to see this day." Forty-eight members of Easy Company, 506th PIR, alone had paid the last full measure of their devotion so that others could live in a world without tyranny. The war indeed had been a great crusade against the forces of totalitarianism. A steep price had been paid to liberate Europe. I was merely one survivor of the greatest war in the twentieth century. I wasn't sure how to feel other than to express my gratitude that somehow I had emerged from this great struggle. I found it difficult to summarize my emotions.

When I realized that the war was over, I felt like a retired fire horse. *It's over,* I thought. *I'm finished.* I did not know what to do with myself, nor did I have much time to think about it. While Americans celebrated the end of the European war in Times Square, the war was sure as hell not over for me. Second Battalion was in the middle of thousands and thousands of German prisoners of war and recently liberated displaced persons, all waiting for someone to tell them what to do. After leaving Berchtesgaden, the 101st Airborne Division began the unenviable task of military occupation. The division's area of responsibility was a fifty-mile square region just across the border in Austria. On May 8, Colonel Sink ordered 2d Battalion to move out that night at 2200 for Zell-am-See, some thirty miles south of Berchtesgaden. Our convoy consisted of all U.S. Army trucks available, plus any captured German trucks that remained in working order. Each company gave top priority to its truckload of booze from Goering's officers' club. Captured German limousines were left behind in Berchtesgaden, though few remained in working order. The convoy moved out with the headlights on full beam. There was no longer need for security. In the back of the trucks the men remained in a party mood. For the past year the normal practice for the troops in a night convoy had been to catch as much sleep as possible since they never knew what was expected of them when they reached their destination. The evening of VE-Day, however, was different. That night was a happy night: a night to celebrate, a night to remember.

Without realizing it, during the night we bypassed Field Marshal Albert Kesselring, the commander-in-chief of the German armies in Italy and his staff, who were four miles back toward Berchtesgaden as we drove through Saalfelden. He would later turn himself in to General Taylor on May 10. One by one the bigwigs of the Nazi Party were rounded up. Colonel Sink accepted the surrender of General Tolsdorf on May 7. The 101st Airborne also bagged Julius Streicher, the famous Jew-baiter, and Franz Xavier Schwarz, treasurer of the Nazi Party, along with Frau Goering. Streicher would later be condemned to death during the Nuremberg trials and executed on October 16, 1946.

At dawn on May 9, our ragtag convoy arrived at Zell-am-See. This part of Austria was a popular resort region containing beautiful country, picturesque scenery, and clear mountain lakes. Around the lakes stood numerous mansions that Nazi officials had enjoyed since the *An-*

schluss incorporated Austria into Hitler's Third Reich in 1938. As we drove into town, Austrian civilians and the German soldiers stared in amazement and utter disbelief at the sight of our invading army. I can't imagine what must have gone through their minds as we rolled into town. They certainly could not have been impressed with our military appearance. Unlike the highly immaculate German army in which equipment and appearance were maintained at a high state of readiness, Sink's paratroopers arrived in nondescript trucks. We had no big tanks, no large artillery, and our uniforms were old, beat-up army fatigue pants and blouses. The German soldiers outnumbered us many times, and their dress and military appearance was far more impressive than ours. Had I been an Austrian or German soldier that morning, I would have asked myself, *This is the army that beat us? Impossible!*

Impossible or not, we were the victors. Military occupation was the spoils of war, the price of defeat for the loser, the payment for the victor. Second Battalion was ordered to continue across the valley and take over the villages of Kaprun and Bruck. Kaprun lay at the foot of the Austrian Alps, which had halted the German retreat south. The few passes available through the Alps to Italy were still closed by snow. I established my headquarters in the hotel located in the center of Kaprun. The companies were scattered throughout the villages, wherever the company commanders could find good housing.

Our first priority was to establish order and to maintain discipline. Consequently, the first thing I did was to contact the local German military commander. My instructions to him were threefold: first, I wanted all weapons in the valley and the villages around Kaprun-Bruck collected and deposited at the airport, the school, and the church; second, all officers could keep their personal sidearms and enough weapons for their military police; and third, I would inspect the enemy army's camps, troops, and kitchens the following day. The German commander nodded his concurrence, saluted smartly, and left to execute my orders.

Let me point out that at this time, I was twenty-seven years old, only a few years out of college, and like all the troops, I was wearing a dirty, well-worn combat fatigue jacket and pants. I felt a little ridiculous giving orders to a professional Prussian-born German colonel, twenty years my senior, who, while I was attending college from 1939 to 1941, had been invading Poland, Holland, Belgium, France, and the Soviet Union, and who was dressed in a clean field uniform with an array of medals covering his chest. The picture was analogous to what Robert E. Lee experienced when, dressed in his finest uniform, he surrendered the Army of Northern Virginia at Appomattox Courthouse to Ulysses S. Grant, who wore a private's tunic covered with mud.

On the first night in Kaprun, I established a curfew and passed the word through the local *burgomaster* (mayor) to the townspeople that everybody would be required to be off the streets and in their homes by 1800 hours until 0600 the following day. By 1800 the streets were empty. In the center of the village around the hotel where the battalion command post was located, all the townspeople and soldiers were standing in the doorways of their homes or leaning from the windows. Everybody was cooperating with this new army of occupation, when, suddenly, one old, bald-headed Austrian, in his leather Alpine-style short pants, marched to the middle of the square and very defiantly, with his hands on his hips, took a belligerent stand. Along with the rest of the battalion staff, I was taking all this in from an upstairs balcony overlooking the square. Lieutenant Ralph D. Richey, a gung-ho replacement officer, one of the very best replacement officers we received, came over to me and asked if I would like him to take some men and arrest the old man. I answered, "No, let him alone. Let's just watch for a while."

The old man stood there, chin out, challenging us. All the townfolk and troops in the area had nothing else to do or look at but him. After about five minutes it started to strike everyone as silly, and after an additional ten minutes, everybody was giggling and laughing so the old man went back to his house, embarrassed. We never had additional trouble with the people of Kaprun again, so I lifted the curfew after one week.

The next morning, accompanied by Captain Nixon, I took off in my jeep to inspect the sites where I had ordered the weapons to be deposited. I was shocked at the mountain of weapons that had been assembled at each site. Then I realized that I was looking at the result of the famous German reputation for efficiency. I had stipulated yesterday "all weapons," meaning all military weapons. No one had questioned my order or sought clarification, so they gathered "all weapons." Before us now lay stacks of hunting rifles, target rifles, hunting knives, antiques, and of course, military weapons.

After I made arrangements to collect the weapons, I inspected the camps and kitchens. I found everything well organized and functioning. Some of the German troops were lined up for review. They were clean, well-dressed, and in good condition. The kitchens themselves were in good order and that day, the German troops served from a large kettle of potato soup cooking over the fire.

The inspection of a few camps and troops was nothing more than a means of establishing a line of communications and a relationship between our headquarters and their headquarters. We left them alone; they respected us; there was no trouble. After the initial inspection, each day the German commander sent a staff officer who spoke English to my headquarters in the morning. After we got to know each other, he recalled stories about the horrific conditions on the Eastern Front. He told us how in the winter the tanks became so cold that if your bare skin touched the metal of the tank, the skin's surface literally stuck and tore as you pulled away. He also related his experiences fighting the 101st Airborne Division at Bastogne. Reflecting a common belief that circulated many Allied camps at the time, our new friend suggested that "our armies should join hands and wipe out the Russian army." I can also remember my answer to that invitation: "No thanks, all I want to do is get out of the army and go home."

Until we arrived at Kaprun, none of the officers, me included, fully comprehended the scope of occupational duties. I had graduated from OCS, fought in four major campaigns, and conducted two combat jumps, but no one had ever taken the time to tell me how to handle a surrender. My region of responsibility literally contained thousands of former Allied prisoners of war, thousands of displaced persons brought here to work from other countries, and now thousands of German soldiers. They all wanted something. They needed help, food, medical care, everything. I looked at these people and thought how lucky they were to be alive since so many had died and so many others were crippled. Here they were, all wishing to return home. Charming as the Austrian countryside was, occupation duty was one hell of a mess. Despite the fact that I had 25,000 Germans under my charge, there seemed like nothing to do, no reason to work.

There was little alternative but to address the problems, one issue at a time. We went to work. As soon as possible, in an orderly manner, German prisoners were moved out of the area via truck convoys and by train to stockades in Nuremberg and Munich. On May 10, Lieutenant Stapelfeld escorted a trainload of German soldiers, women, and horses to Nuremberg, before hitching a ride back to 2d Battalion two days later. There were certainly no shortages of prisoners. We had no idea how many German soldiers remained in those hillside forests. Some were in small groups, some were solo. Each day, we sent jeeps to patrol secondary roads and trails, trying to locate and direct these troops to our airport compound. Today, I still find it amazing that we did not suffer casualties from these patrols, for we were sitting targets for any die-hard Germans who weren't prepared to surrender. Apparently they wanted to return home as much as my men. I estimated that my battalion of 600 men had been surrounded by approximately 25,000 German soldiers and almost as many displaced persons when we moved into the area on May 9.

There was one German prisoner who caught my personal attention. He was a major from a German panzer unit—a true German and one hell of a good soldier. We talked over tactics, soldiering in general, and were pleased to discover that at Bastogne we had fought each other tooth and nail. Quite a coincidence! The major had been wounded six times during the war, but he had kept soldiering to the very end. The day following our revelations, he presented me his pistol as a token of friendship between us and as a formal surrender to his captor. He did so of his own volition rather than leaving his pistol on a desk in some office. When he handed me his sidearm, I noticed that the pistol had never been fired. There was no blood on it. It remains one of the few mementos I have kept from the war. The pistol still has not been fired— and it never will be. This is the way wars ought to end. Let the generals and politicians participate in elaborate ceremonies. At the soldier level, a peaceful transfer of weapons, a smart salute or some other gesture of respect—that's the way it should be for soldiers who had faced the bullets.

The growing number of displaced persons continued to present a special problem. I thought I had seen a lot of DPs before, but this area was jammed! Feeding these people was a problem. We were in no position to handle the feeding of so many people. As quickly as possible, we assembled them in groups according to their nationality: Hungarians, Poles, Czechs, and other eastern European nations. Once organized, we next shipped them by truck convoy to major holding areas throughout southern Germany.

Regimental headquarters now directed me to consolidate the mounds of captured German equipment and the excess U.S. Army equipment that we no longer needed for combat. Convoys of trucks were organized and all excess equipment was shipped to depots in France. Supply officers made ridiculous demands on subordinate headquarters, which culminated in the height of absurdity when senior headquarters directed all officers who had received a silk escape map before the jump into Normandy to turn them in or be fined $75. I had kept my escape map sewn in the belt lining of my pants all through the war. After four campaigns, that map had sentimental value. There are times that the army comes up with some rules and orders that defy common sense and are meant to be disobeyed. This time I took a firm stand and I borrowed a punch line from General McAuliffe at Bastogne. Writing a short note to Captain Sobel, still serving as regimental S-4, I wrote, "Nuts!" To add salt into Sobel's wound, I signed the message, "Richard D. Winters, Major, Commanding." That ended it. I kept my map and it currently occupies a place of honor in my private office. Nor did I pay the $75 fine. Memories of this type of military inefficiency made it easy to decide not to make the army a career.

Sobel suffered one additional mishap before returning to the States. In late May, Charles Lindbergh and the chief of staff of the Strategic Bomber Survey visited the 506th Regiment in Zell-am-See. Close to Colonel Sink's headquarters was a senior officer from the *Luftwaffe* with the unusual name of Martini. Lindbergh wanted to interview Martini's chief signal officer concerning German attempts to improve their communications and radar facilities. No one could find Martini until Sobel sounded off after hearing his name. According to Major Salve Matheson, Sink's operations officer, Sobel said, "Oh, I threw him in the pokey a couple hours ago for violating curfew." Matheson retrieved the German officer in time for Lindbergh to complete his interview.

Now that the prisoners and displaced persons had been cleared from the area, it seemed to me that I had relaxed a bit during the past week. Keeping the troops occupied now became my biggest challenge, so I let the men concentrate chiefly on resting. In fact, I took a few afternoons off myself for mountain climbing and sunning. How lovely it was just to look at those snow-capped peaks and watch a cloud or two bump into an Alp. I had nothing more than my own men to worry about. They were such nice, quiet lads that they were really no trouble at all.

As troop duty changed from combat to occupation, we reorganized from our former way of life as frontline soldiers and returned to a garrison style of life and training. We could not ignore training, however, particularly since replacements now comprised the vast majority of 2d Battalion. Since rumors abounded that the 101st might deploy to the Pacific, I constructed rifle ranges to sharpen the men's marksmanship.

Close order drills and troop reviews once again appeared on the weekly training schedule. The largest review occurred on July 4, complete with a parade and the release of hundreds of pigeons.

The next thing we organized was a highly competitive organized athletic and calisthenics program. During the ballgames when the men were stripped to their waists, or wearing only shorts, the sight of all those battle scars made me conscious of the fact that other than a handful of men in the battalion who had survived all four campaigns, only a few were lucky enough to be without at least one scar. Some men had two, three, even four scars on their chests, backs, arms, or legs. Keep in mind that at Kaprun, I was looking only at the men who were not seriously wounded. This type of atmosphere created an unspoken bond of mutual respect between the men and a fierce pride in their unit.

The story of Private First Class Joe Hogan spoke for all of us on the subject of pride in Company E. During an argument with a soldier from another company about whose company was better, Hogan proclaimed, "My Company E will lick your company in fifteen minutes, and if you wait until the guys who are AWOL come back, we'll do it in five minutes."

My staff and I devised other means to occupy the troops as they awaited their discharges or next assignment. High in the Alps behind Kaprun was a beautiful ski lodge that overlooked the valley. The lift to the lodge was not in working order, but it could be reached by climbing the mountain trail. I established a program where we rotated one platoon every seventy-two hours to the ski lodge to learn how to ski and to hunt. These men were on their own—no officers, nobody but a cook, a few servants, and two instructors. They could really relax since they were so far away, nobody would think of bothering them. This alpine retreat allowed the men to escape the monotony of a daily military routine. Snow was present year-round so the men could ski, hunt mountain goats, or if they were so inclined, they could climb the adjacent mountains in search of edelweiss. To carry edelweiss in your cap was the mark of a true alpine climber. As with most of the troops, I climbed high in the mountains and found my edelweiss. I treasure that alpine flower to this day. After four campaigns and the loss of so many comrades, it reminded me that beauty and peace could once again settle over a troubled land.

The enemy had surrendered, but our men were still dying. A ticket to the States required eighty-five points. Soldiers accumulated points based on length of service, the number of campaigns in which they had fought, medals earned, wounds incurred, and whether or not a trooper was married. Those with eighty-five points were eligible for immediate transfer home and discharge. Most of the men had not accrued that total. What they did have was too much booze and too much time on their hands. Soldiers not involved in strenuous activity inevitably get into trouble. In a letter to Sergeant Forrest Guth, who was in England recuperating from a wound, Captain Speirs summarized the misfortunes that befell Easy Company in the first month of occupational duty. George Luz had fallen off a motorcycle and injured his arm. Sergeant Jim Alley was busted because of repeated drunkenness. Sergeant Darrell "Shifty" Powers was en route home to the States when the truck in which he was riding overturned. Powers, who had won a lottery ticket home, was hospitalized for the next year. Sergeant "Chuck" Grant caught a bullet in the head from a drunken American soldier and would have died had he not received immediate medical attention from an Austrian surgeon. To replace Grant as platoon sergeant, Speirs assigned Staff Sergeant Floyd Talbert, who had asked to be relieved from his duties as 1st Sergeant due to a personality conflict with Speirs. Staff Sergeant John C. Lynch from 2d Platoon replaced Talbert as company first sergeant.

Despite the amenities of occupational duty, there were two things that 2d Battalion didn't have: the first was enough food. The 506th PIR was at the far end of the pipeline in terms of distribution. Everybody from the ports of Cherbourg and Antwerp right on down the pipeline had a crack at the food for themselves, their civilian girlfriends, and the black market before we were taken care of. The battalion particularly suffered during the first three weeks following the German capitulation. It did no good to complain to regimental headquarters. Dried potatoes and dried tomatoes simply did not maintain body mass for young men, so we all lost a considerable amount of weight. To compensate for our lack of rations, we shot a few cattle and, once in a while, a mountain elk, but this hardly provided sufficient meat to feed all the troops.

I decided to do my part, so one day I went to the ski lodge and talked a local Austrian guide into taking me up the mountain to hunt mountain goat. We climbed high above the clouds, above the tree line, above the grass line. We finally discovered a family of four goats resting on a ledge below us to our right, just out of range of my 1903 Springfield rifle. We stalked the goats, getting closer, but just about the time that I was within range, I slipped in the snow and tumbled over a ledge. I slid farther down the mountain and tumbled over a second ledge. I thought I was a goner, but after the second tumble, I was on my back and able to stop my slide by jamming my rifle butt into the snow and ice. After surviving so many battles, I couldn't help but think that this would have been a hell of a way to die.

I turned around, looked back up the mountain, and there was that mountain goat that had been below me before I fell. Now, he was looking down at me. I opened the bolt of the rifle, blew the snow from the rifle barrel, closed the bolt, and shot the goat. The goat tumbled down the mountain, stopping about 100 yards past me in another snowbank. I sat down, my knees shaking. I was weak from shock. When I had fallen over that first ledge, my field glasses had bounced up, hit me in the mouth, and broken my front tooth at the gum line, leaving the nerve of the tooth hanging free. My guide came down to check me out. I told him, "I'm okay. If you want that goat, you can have him. All I want are the horns." He was delighted with the deal. Very carefully, I climbed back up the mountain and made my way back to the ski lodge. On the way I promised God and myself that never, ever, was I going to go mountain climbing again. And I still have the horns of that mountain goat.

The hunting incident brought to my immediate attention the second major thing we were lacking—a good dentist. I was in desperate need of one, and I sure as hell was not going to see "Shifty" Feiler again. We had troops quartered in the home of a civilian dentist, so I went to see him with my problem. He, too, had a problem—American soldiers living in his nice home. We soon arranged a deal. He would take care of my front tooth and my cavities if I would find another home for the troops. This would take care of my problem, but what about the men? We were all in need of dental care and attention. We soon agreed that each day he would take care of twelve men. From that day forward, he had a steady stream of customers, including Colonel Robert Strayer from regimental headquarters.

In mid-June, Sergeant Al Krochka, the photographer from division headquarters, visited me at Kaprun. Al had a very sad story. He claimed that he had never been in a position where he could obtain a good German Luger pistol. Could I help him out? If I did, he would provide me a series of photographs that he had taken from Normandy to Berchtesgaden, many of them taken while he visited the 2d Battalion along the way. Having never owned a camera, I had never taken a single picture, and I sure wanted a set of those photographs to take home. We made a trade—Al got his Luger and I received the photographs. Later, I discovered the truth behind his "sad" story. Al had made quite a few sets of photographs and he was negotiating for pistols to sell in Paris to finance a good furlough.

Aside from the natural beauty of Kaprun and its surroundings, perhaps the most rewarding activity was taking the opportunity for personal reflection after eleven months of sustained combat. My initial thoughts encompassed the pride I felt in being a paratrooper and being associated with so many fine young soldiers. The significance of the role paratroopers played in the war can never be fully explained. They had proven beyond all doubt to be practicable. Even the ever-present threat of our employment was of major importance in the general picture. And when we dropped, it was proven that the enemy often just took off, plain scared. That was not the case in Normandy, of course, because we encountered German paratroopers in our approach to Carentan. You could always determine the discipline of your enemy by how ferociously and tenaciously they fought. German paratroopers had always proved our most dangerous adversaries.

Occupation duty was about as exciting as my first months on battalion staff. After commanding Easy Company in Normandy and Holland, sedentary duty on the battalion staff had been a huge letdown. The same was true now that the actual fighting was over. A typical day followed a schedule something like this: Up around 0700, breakfast, paperwork, inspect guards, quarters, and kitchens the remainder of the morning. After a little lunch, fool around for a while, and then take a sunbath for a few hours while I read or just lay and think. That's what I really enjoyed, just drifting around and thinking of nothing in particular. In the evenings we played volleyball, after which I took a run, did some exercises, and then a group of us would shoot the bull, maybe try and write a letter or read, but it was really just a lot of foolish talk. Life wasn't really that bad.

Late evenings usually consisted of sitting around the table and shooting the bull with Lewis Nixon and Harry Welsh. The conversation usually centered on old battles, transferring to another outfit in the South Pacific, talking about snafu (a military acronym depicting complete chaos) officers we knew and had known. It's a funny thing: The first thing soldiers talk about is old battle experiences. It doesn't matter what topics you plan to discuss, it isn't long until the conversation turns to combat. You would think the conversations would become boring, but not to us. We talked about the same battles over and over, about how we destroyed the battery at Brecourt and how we survived the cold at Bastogne.

Next, we talked about putting on some flashy review for the top brass, with pigeons being released as the colors passed the reviewing stand, and buglers blasting from the top of the Alps and letting the music reverberate around the valleys. Of course, we laughed about the loot that we had confiscated at Berchtesgaden and about lesser, more mundane matters. I recalled how one officer had discovered a large supply of silver coins, which he duly reported to me. I took the matter directly to Colonel Sink, who contacted a silversmith in neighboring Innsbruck. The silversmith melted the coins and then made individual silver cups for each officer in the 506th. Across the base of the cup was inscribed the name of the four campaigns in which Sink's commissioned officers had participated as officers. Most bull sessions ended with Nixon and me saying to hell with going home, we were volunteering for the China-Burma-India (C.B.I.) Theater. We tried to convince Harry Welsh into going along, but he had an Irish lass named Kitty Grogan back home who was waiting for him.

In mid-May SHAEF lifted its restrictions and its censorship of military mail. Most of us took the opportunity to write home in a futile attempt to put into words what we had gone through since D-Day. Writing to DeEtta Almon, I summarized the war from my personal perspective, but I found it impossible to convey my innermost thoughts to someone who had not experienced combat. I had grown frigid mentally and couldn't think of anything to write. Instead I outlined my plan to volunteer for combat duty against the Japanese. Now that the war in Europe was over, I had been wondering what was the use of sitting around here for six months or so of occupational duty when I could utilize my talents in the Pacific Theater. Call it professional pride or simply a desire for additional action, but I decided to volunteer for duty with some parachute unit or infantry unit in the C.B.I. Theater. My desire for additional combat had nothing to do with earning medals. I had never cared about public recognition—my reward had always been the look of respect in the eyes of my men. After eleven months of war, I understood fire and maneuver, planning, and leading soldiers in combat. In garrison, I enjoyed the soldiering part, but as far as social activities were concerned, I was a class-A flop. Volunteering for Japan would relieve me of the monotony of occupation. I reckoned that I had to die sometime, so what was the use of sitting in Kaprun? I discussed my options with Colonel Sink, who asked me point-blank, "Why are you leaving me?" He reluctantly agreed to arrange an interview with Major General Elbridge G. "Gerry" Chapman, commanding general of the 13th Airborne Division. Selected for the invasion of Japan, the 13th Airborne Division was scheduled to sail from France on August 15 to participate in the assault on Kyushu scheduled for November.

I reported to General Chapman on May 26 and informed him of my desire to transfer to his outfit. I figured that since the 13th Airborne Division had been alerted for duty in the South Pacific, combat duty beat the heck out of occupational duty. I repeated much of the rationale that I had expressed to my mother when she first heard that I intended to transfer to fight in the Pacific. I felt that God had been good enough to let me live through the European war. As a result, I was combat-wise and in a position to do some good to help a lot of men. I knew that I could do the job, better than, or as well as, any of the rest. How could I sit back and see others take men out and get them killed because they didn't understand? These new officers just didn't have "it." Maybe I would get hurt or killed for my trouble, but so what, if it meant I could make it possible for many others to go home. Their mothers wanted them alive, too, the same as me. So what else could I do and still hold my own self-respect as an officer and as a man?

General Chapman listened graciously and told me that he would welcome me to his outfit, but—just as my mother had expressed—that I had done enough. Let the other fellows have a chance. Well, I had given it the old college try. I thanked him for his time, saluted, and departed. On returning to my headquarters, I couldn't help but think that Colonel Sink had greased the skids for my interview, but he had also asked General Chapman to disapprove my request. The 13th Airborne Division had its own officers and they didn't need me.

So, I was staying put, but apparently not for long. In mid-June General Maxwell Taylor announced that the 101st Airborne Division was earmarked to go to the Pacific at some unspecified time and that the Screaming Eagles should plan and train accordingly. The announcement did not sit well with the troops, particularly the remaining Toccoa men. My best estimate was that I would remain awhile in Europe and would see the States in January. Following a month's leave, I expected to be training around Fort Bragg or Mackall until we deployed overseas. After such a long rest, going into combat again would be tough. I found myself changing as the weeks went by. As the frustration of occupation duty increased, I was really bitter and put out with everybody and everything. Becoming more or less resigned to the fact of returning to combat with inexperienced troops, I yearned to return home. I figured I had been lucky, mighty lucky, from the very first day, but I'd seen so many get it and go out feetfirst. I just knew if I stuck around long enough, I'd have my turn sometime because I had taken too many chances. I had to lead from the front, with my position, prestige, and job on the line. Consequently I was no longer too keen on going to the Pacific after being rejected by General Chapman, but orders were orders.

On June 28, all "eighty-five-point" men departed Kaprun. To my great satisfaction, most of the Toccoa men stopped by to say goodbye before returning home. As I told my Stateside friend DeEtta Almon, "It was a good thing you weren't around to see that one. You'd think we were a bunch of schoolgirls. If you'd heard some of the things they had to tell me, you'd understand why I want to stick around and see the end of this war out on the front line. They sure appreciate . . . everything."

I had accrued 100 points as of May 12 and should have been en route to the United States under ordinary conditions, but my services were "needed" in Austria by Colonel Sink. Regrettably many of our men remained longer in Europe than they should have because General Taylor had been notoriously stingy in awarding combat medals to the frontline soldiers. Over the course of the war, only two troopers from the 101st Airborne Division received the Medal of Honor. One was Lieutenant Colonel Robert G. Cole, a battalion commander, who was killed on September 18, 1944, by a sniper at Best, Holland, near the bridges over the Wilhelmina Canal as we were attacking Eindhoven.

Just a few days earlier, Cole had been notified that he would receive the Medal of Honor for leading a bayonet charge in Normandy. The second recipient was Private First Class Joe E. Mann, who hurled himself on a grenade to save the lives of his squad near the Wilhelmina Canal outside Eindhoven on September 19, 1944. Officers from West Point received an unusually high number of awards, including General Taylor, who received the Distinguished Service Cross in Normandy, but for those at the grunt level, higher headquarters downgraded far too many recommendations.

And so, many of the Toccoa veterans returned home, yet all would be forever connected by their shared experiences in combat. Over the course of the war, Easy Company alone lost forty-eight men killed and over 100 wounded, incurring 150 percent casualties. This percentage was not uncommon among similar units who had fought in the campaign of northwest Europe. "At the peak of its effectiveness, in Holland in October 1944 and in the Ardennes in January 1945, it was as good a rifle company as there was in the world," according to author Stephen E. Ambrose. How so many men survived the campaigns in Normandy, Holland, Bastogne, and Germany was a true testament to their courage, their training, and their discipline under fire.

14
Coming Home

In late July occupation duty came to an end. Second Battalion, 506th PIR, now bore little resemblance to the organization that had fought through Bastogne, Alsace, and Berchtesgaden. With few exceptions, the Toccoa men were gone, having rotated to the States. To escape the boredom, I traveled up and down the Continent three times inside of two weeks. I was bored, tired, sore, and looking for constructive ways to bide my time. On one occasion I supervised a large convoy of trucks to Paris for redeployment to the Pacific. It was a mess. Everybody turned in their worst trucks and tires. There were no tools to change tires and the drivers were a bunch of "8-balls." Many of the soldiers were replacements with little or no combat experience. Since most of the battle-hardened NCOs had already returned to the States, discipline became a major challenge. I worked my head off keeping that mob together, and at the same time I drove them into the ground. By the time I returned those soldiers to Austria, they knew just what an officer in the paratroops was like—dominating as hell!

Colonel Sink was quite pleased with the job though, and he allowed me a couple of days to recuperate and then let me come up in a special chartered plane while the 506th PIR departed the Zell-am-See–Kaprun-Bruck area and traveled by train to Joigny, France. Joigny is an old town of narrow, cobblestoned streets situated eighty miles southeast of Paris. Like any other French town, it was hot, dirty, and, being French, I could not say much good about it. We moved into living quarters formerly occupied by the 13th Airborne Division. The conditions in the camp were absolutely terrible for the men. Latrine facilities were nonexistent, so I procured lumber and equipment to build several latrines. Washing facilities consisted of two little faucets about 100 yards from their quarters. The men were forced to live like pigs. Apparently nobody gave a damn, so the battalion began building washstands and coverings so the men could wash and shave with hot water. Evidently this facility once served as a Nazi work camp and the 13th Airborne Division seemed content to live like that for seven months.

Nonfraternization remained a problem, just as it had in Germany and Austria. The nonfraternization policy stipulated that all German, Austrian, Hungarian, and Romanian women were out of bounds. That left Poles, Russians, and French foreign laborers, and it was quite a problem to tell the difference between the nationalities. I did the best I could to defuse potential problems and just said, "No messing around at all." That covered it altogether, as far as I was concerned. However, I was army-wise enough to know that what went on behind my back was more than just a little fraternization, but what I didn't know didn't hurt me. As far as I was concerned, the results were 100 percent okay, at least on the surface. I just made myself heard, but nothing happened. I asked for 100 percent, received maybe 40 percent, but to all appearances, the results were as I wished. After about three months of being in charge of these men, they sort of snapped to when they saw me coming. I was not exactly a grizzly bear, but if something was not right, somebody heard about it pronto. The entire process of dealing with the fraternization issue was the sort of thing that convinced me that I did not belong in the army after all.

To escape the boredom, I took a week's leave and visited England. Captain Nixon accompanied me and through a little creative collaboration, we stretched a seven-day leave into fourteen days. I had a wonderful time—went straight to Aldbourne to visit the Barnes family and I spent ten beautiful days right there. Mr. Barnes had passed away in October 1944, shortly after we left to jump into Holland, leaving only Mother Barnes and her store. I knew she had saved my room and bed for me, just as I left it, and there would be a cup of tea. I went to town once to a show, but the rest of the time I just puttered around the garden, cut the grass, or slept. It was my way of thanking the Barneses for being my second parents. After ten days in Aldbourne, I traveled to London and spent four days just watching shows. The day I was supposed to leave, the plane didn't show up, so I returned to London for one last fling. That evening was the most lonesome night I had spent in years. The city was full of air corps men, not a man or soldier in the bunch. I couldn't talk to any of them; they were mere boys, kids, no depth. Hell, I quit and found a corner in the lounge to myself and read. Get me back to my battalion!

When I returned to my unit, everyone wanted to know what kind of time I had, and how I had spent my leave. Most were surprised when I mentioned that I had spent the majority of my leave in Aldbourne until I told them that going to Aldbourne was like going home. What these men had forgotten was what home was like, what a real home was. Oh, they wrote home to their folks and friends, and they talked and planned about coming home, but you can't actually be away from home three or four years and remember what home is like. That was precisely why "my home" in Aldbourne meant so much to me. As I wrote Mrs. Barnes, "I was still walking around on that cloud that you had put me on during my recent visit. I really enjoyed those songs and hymns that were so dear to you, as well as those Bible readings and prayers." That was just the way things should be, and it was so soothing to me to find a small niche in this mad world that was still sane, quiet, peaceful, and in order.

Later, I attempted to tell Mrs. Barnes, albeit inadequately, what she had meant to me during the war. Now that the fighting was over, I needed time to relax. Physically I always was fully prepared even in the hottest combat, but mentally I was strung tight as a fiddle. I knew when something was wrong and I could tell exactly what it was, but responsibility, work, the accumulation of past problems, and present and future challenges had placed me in such a mental state that I began functioning more like a military machine than an understanding officer and a human being. After seven day's under Mother Barnes's care, I regained a lot of the caring that I had forgotten existed. As I told her, "There were times when your influence on me permitted me to pass my thoughts and feelings along to other officers and men." I addressed my letter, "Dearest Mother." After I finally returned to the States, I maintained my friendship with Mrs. Barnes through a warm correspondence and exchange of gifts until her death in the 1970s.

On August 11, Colonel Sink received a well-deserved promotion, and he was assigned as assistant division commander of the Screaming Eagles. During the war many officers had accepted promotions and moved up the chain of command, but Sink always elected to remain with the 506th. I had thought about that as the war went on. Sink was very proud of the regiment and was very dedicated to it. With the fighting now over, I was happy that he finally received (and accepted) just recognition for his services. In recommending Colonel Sink for promotion to brigadier general, General Taylor stated that our regimental commander was "temperamentally quiet, resolute, and cool under the most trying conditions of battle. He possesses all the qualities desired of an Airborne General Officer." In short, Bob Sink was an extraordinarily talented officer who was the heart and soul of the 506th. He did things with a personal flair, and his southern drawl was full of home-

spun sayings that endeared him to the regiment he led so gallantly beginning in July 1942. He always talked to his soldiers on a man-to-man
basis. He gave us all a sense of "we." The 506th PIR was going to fight
the war together, not as a series of independent battalions. To have
been a member of the "Five-Oh-Sink" had been a badge of honor.

How Colonel Sink welded a disparate group of citizen soldiers into
a first-class fighting unit is a topic that merits a book of its own. The
army had given him kids fresh off the streets. Many were undernour-
ished and poorly educated. The officers were not much better—and I
include myself in that group. I was a year out of college. I had gone
through Officer Candidate School, so I was a newly minted second lieutenant, a ninety-day wonder. This was the kind of officer Sink was assigned and told to turn the group into a crack airborne unit. Colonel
Sink straightened us out. He was the one who put it all together. I was
highly skeptical of his ability at first, but he proved me wrong. In my
opinion, our regimental commander was one of the finest West Point
officers of the war. Colonel Sink remained in the army after the war
and retired with the rank of lieutenant general.

With Sink transferred, his executive officer, Lieutenant Colonel
Charles Chase, became commander of the 506th PIR. Three days later,
on August 14, Japan surrendered. Apparently the atomic bomb carried
as much punch as a regiment of paratroopers. It seemed inhumane for
our national leaders to employ either weapon on the human race.
Within weeks of Japan's surrender, General Taylor left the 101st to assume duties as superintendent of the U.S. Military Academy at West
Point. Colonel Sink followed Taylor to West Point in December. Now
everyone was going home, regardless of points.

With the war finally over, my time in Europe drew to a close. On
September 2, the day Japanese officials signed the documents of surrender aboard the U.S.S. *Missouri* in Tokyo Bay, a number of officers
with the necessary points departed for the States by plane. Though
Colonel Sink had declared me essential, as of the 15th of the month, all
officers were now allowed to leave if they desired. Naturally, I wished

to go. In May I had contemplated transferring to the Pacific, but after four months of occupation and "make work," I was ready to return to civilian life. I could see in the wind just how the army was changing, or at least close enough so that I could appreciate the fact that I did not wish to be associated with it in any way. In the paratroops, the money looked good. That was the end of it though, for it was a big party after that, with troopers growing lazy, both mentally and physically and going to hell fast. They could have it all; I'd dig ditches first.

It would have been an honor to leave for home with the 101st Airborne Division, for I was a bit sentimental about my outfit. The thing was, however, there were only about half a dozen officers and men left who were worth saying hello or goodbye to. Late one evening, Speirs, Welsh, and Nixon—my remaining buddies—dropped in and spent a few hours reminiscing about the good times we had shared. Nixon departed Joigny the next week, making me about as lonesome as a lovesick sailor who married a Wave on an eight-hour pass. As for Harry Welsh, he became my constant companion, but drinking remained his outlet to pass the time. During one of his spells, he told off some soldiers from another command. Being a good friend, I smoothed things over by sending Welsh off and explaining that Harry was just a bit "off": too many mortar shells and artillery barrages—just feeling the reaction since the war was over.

Other memories of Joigny are few. Each day I would go for a run, play football, or join the men for a baseball game. On September 20, I made my final parachute jump, which was my first since we had jumped into Holland the previous September. Exactly one year earlier, we had hit Holland and attempted to hold open fifty miles of road so the British 2d Army could make an end run. I'm not sure why I scheduled this jump other than to break the monotony of things around Joigny. It was a voluntary exercise and those who did not wish to jump just had to say so. Quite a few of the men came up with flimsy excuses to miss the jump, feigning illness when the real reason was nothing more than to avoid injury. Others, like Staff Sergeant Robert T. Smith, participated just to see if he still "had the guts to do so after not jump-ing for a year and three days." Yet even Smith agreed that he experi-enced the worst three minutes that he had ever spent on a jump since he was among the four "high pointers" who weren't sure that they were doing the smart thing. Having survived the war, Smith and the veterans who had jumped into Normandy no longer desired taking un-necessary chances with regard to their physical safety.

As the paratroopers put on their chutes and boarded the aircraft, more than a few suddenly got very serious. In combat, these same para-troopers usually horsed around before climbing aboard the plane. Things seemed different now, but as soon as the veterans buckled up, they started to play around and to rib the replacements. After the air-craft took off, Staff Sergeant Smith reconsidered the wisdom of risking his life on an unnecessary jump. In his own words, he "couldn't talk, he couldn't move, he felt stiff all over, and he had sweat pouring from his eyes." Once out the door, however, the panic left him as he felt that friendly jerk that signaled that his canopy was fully deployed. Person-ally, I would jump for $10, and for $100, I'd land on my head. During the war if a man refused, it was standard operating procedure (S.O.P.) to send him to the guardhouse, no pay, and at least six months' hard labor. My, how things had changed! Now, they just said, not today, thank you. Oh well, I didn't hold anything against them, provided that they were old combat men.

Four days before my last parachute jump, I reflected on where I had been one year earlier when we jumped into Holland. I wished that I could relive some of those thrills and glows of satisfaction that filled a man when he outmaneuvered, outfought, and outguessed the enemy. Great sport! Then there was the day that a lieutenant in the company (Lieutenant Brewer) was shot. I had told him a hundred times in train-ing not to walk around in front like that or he would get it, sure as hell. That day I walked up front with Brewer, demonstrating just how I wanted his platoon to cross this open field to the suburbs of Eind-hoven. He took off, but he didn't think—which was why most people got shot. As I walked two hundred yards behind him, I remarked to some of the men, "He's going to get it." He did, seconds later, right through the neck. Brewer went down like he had been hit with a baseball bat. Then I was forced to make one of my better decisions. I took over the platoon and pushed them forward to the town and sent back for another lieutenant to replace him. It ended up that I had to remain with the lead platoon until we secured the town. By pushing forward, we saved a lot more men and the medics were able to save Brewer's life.

Though I yearned for the days when I commanded Easy Company, I didn't long for the Dutch weather, which had produced such misery. For one thing, I would never spend another night like that one a year earlier: I was wet through and through, and naturally being a paratrooper, I did not have a change of clothes—no blanket, nothing. And it was cold as a son-of-a-gun. Things were all "snafued," walking around in the black of night, not knowing where we were exactly, where anybody else was, and houses burning, people crying, shaking hands, and every bush a prospective enemy.

By the final week in September 1945, preparations were made to send the remaining members of the 101st Airborne Division back to the States. Rumors circulated throughout the camp that all remaining "eighty-five-pointers" and a quota of high-point officers would leave soon. I immediately went to see Colonel Chase and presented my case for my early departure. All I wanted to do was to get out of the army, to return home, and to start my new life. If I stayed, I would have sat around every night with old soldiers and fought the war over and over through stories and memories. I couldn't live like that. There was far too much chickenshit in this man's army, now that the fighting was over. In fifteen minutes Chase vowed that I was okay, that I had done right by him, and now in my hour of need, he'd do okay by me. He did just that. Regiment issued orders on October 1 to transfer me to the 75th Infantry Division, which was to be filled with high-point men and was scheduled to return home with the 16th Corps Headquarters in the early part of October. For my last Saturday night with the 506th PIR, I attended a regimental party. Actually I made only a token appearance, having delegated my work to junior officers with considerably more social experience than I possessed.

When I received the news that I would be going home, I could hardly believe it. I had been lucky enough to live through this whole damn mess and get a round-trip ticket home. Home! My gosh, would my folks even know me? Would I know them? My sister? Chow? Water—hot water. And milk, I really had not had any in over two years at that point, not real milk with calcium in it. Returning home, however, proved to be a more difficult task than I expected. Originally the enlisted soldiers were going to Reims while the 75th Division and the officers were scheduled to depart from Marseilles in southern France. A strike by transportation handlers, coupled with the army's usual red tape and bureaucracy, delayed our redeployment. Two weeks after I was scheduled to leave, I was still in Camp Pittsburgh, France, where I was now serving as 2d Battalion executive officer of the 290th Infantry Regiment, 75th Infantry Division. Naturally I had daily contact with the other officers in the battalion, few of whom had spent much time in combat. What little contact I had with these officers was reserved for them telling me how the 75th Infantry Division had won the war. Their first action had been in the Ardennes on Christmas Day, 1944. Seemed that I remembered that day as well.

To compensate for our delay, headquarters issued us three-day passes which were supposed to soothe our ruffled feathers about being confined in Europe when all we wanted was to return to the United States. I for one had joined the 75th Division to return home, not to go on pass. What's more, headquarters rescinded the order that stated all field-grade officers with less than 100 points could not go home. I now had 108 points and was about as rare as a man in a Wave barracks.

On November 1, I finally arrived at the staging area following a two-day ride through the French countryside. I was now commanding the battalion since the commanding officer had been transferred because he didn't have sufficient points. Watching a bunch of low-point officers trying to make the ship was a sight to behold. As the train transited the country, my chief concern was keeping 1,150 G.I.s from riding on the top of the cars and jumping off the train to kiss the girls. The experience certainly kept a fellow from becoming despondent. Our staging area at Marseilles was a hill so hard that in order to pitch tents, the soldiers used iron stakes. I spent my last afternoon in France driving a jeep through the streets of Marseilles. The port was mighty big and in relatively fair shape, but the Germans had sunk a lot of ships and destroyed a number of piers and warehouses when evacuating southern France during the summer of 1944. As for the town itself, Marseilles was rough, tough, and ugly, a typical port town.

On November 4, I climbed aboard the *Wooster Victory* en route to Hampton Roads, Virginia. As the ship left the harbor, I couldn't help but remember a similar voyage when the S.S. *Samaria* had departed the United States. In the interim between both voyages, two years had passed, but I had aged two decades, seemingly a lifetime of war encapsulated in twenty-two months. Like most soldiers, I would never be the same, but I would adjust, just as we had done when we arrived in England in September 1943, and as we had done following our baptism of fire on D-Day. The U.S. Army processed me for separation on November 29, 1945, at Indiantown Gap, Pennsylvania, only a few miles from my home in Lancaster.

The next day, the 101st Airborne Division was officially deactivated. Easy Company, 506th Parachute Infantry Regiment, no longer existed. When I received the news, I was saddened because the division had been my home for the better part of three years. Originally the 101st was the airborne division scheduled to remain in the postwar army, but with the departure of General Maxwell Taylor to West Point and a highly publicized public relations campaign engineered by Major General James Gavin, the commanding general of the 82d Airborne Division, Army Chief of Staff General George C. Marshall personally intervened to save the 82d. Since the peacetime military force only fielded a single airborne division, the Screaming Eagles passed into history. The whole thing, to me, felt like an insult.

When I reached home, one of the first things I did was to go directly to the post office, where the Internal Revenue Service office was located, and insist that I pay the income tax on my income as an officer. The IRS man looked at me incredulously and said, "Son, you don't have to do this even though the regulations say you must. We will waive this return."

I responded, "Sir, I want to pay my part of the bill. I am proud to be an American!"

He bowed his head and we figured out my bill, which I immediately paid in full.

My expectations upon returning to civilian life were no different than most servicemen lucky enough to come home. I was ready to change my army fatigues for civilian attire. My priorities consisted of finding a decent job so I could make a comfortable living, finding a wife, beginning a family, and finding peace and happiness. I remained on terminal leave until my official discharge on January 22, 1946. At long last I was Mr. R. D. Winters again. Proud as I was of my wartime rank, I never used it in my postwar life. I enjoyed my civilian status after four years of war.

While I was extremely happy to put the army behind me, I realized that I was a different man than I was when I joined the army over four years earlier. The war changed me in many ways, as it does all who experience combat. Having witnessed so much mass suffering and the unparalleled barbarism that mankind is capable of inflicting upon itself, I don't see how any survivor can ever be cruel to anything again. In addition, I was a far better judge of character than I had been in 1941. That feeling remains with me today, a full sixty years after the war. When I meet people for the first time and get to know them, I can't help but judge them and size them up. Do they have leadership? Would they be good in combat? Do they pass the test?

I was also more disciplined than I remembered being before I deployed to Europe. This discipline helped me adapt to civilian life once I returned to Pennsylvania. Like all veterans, I had to adjust to society, the life that you are going to share with others in order to make a living. I certainly never confused the challenges in the workplace with what I had experienced in combat. There would be no life-and-death struggles in the corporate world. Business hardly equates to war. Such comparisons demean the word.

Within two weeks of returning home, I accepted Lewis Nixon's invitation to travel to New York City and meet his parents. His father offered me a job and in January 1946, I became personnel manager for the Nixon Nitration Works in Nixon, New Jersey, for $75 a week. While working, I took advantage of the G.I. Bill and attended refresher courses in business and personnel management at Rutgers University. The G.I. Bill provided me the opportunity to adjust my frame of mind from military to business. I married Ethel in 1948 and was later promoted to general manager of Nixon Nitration Works, where I remained until my recall to service for the Korean conflict.

Now a family man, I had been briefly recalled to active duty for the Korean War in June 1951, with orders to join the 11th Airborne Division at Fort Campbell, Kentucky. I had seen enough of war, so when the army in its infinite wisdom granted reservist officers a delay of six months to report for active duty, I traveled to Washington, D.C. to see General Tony McAuliffe, who was the U.S. Army's personnel chief. I asked if he remembered me and he certainly did. After a few minutes of informal conversation, I told him that I would like to be excused from going to Korea. McAuliffe sat there, nodding his head understandingly, and he asked me point-blank if he could make battalion commanders out of the officers currently graduating from West Point and from the universities around the country. From what I had seen of the peacetime army in Europe and the United States, I responded, "No, sir, I don't think you can."

"Well, that's your answer," he said, "So, there isn't a whole lot more to say."

I thanked him for his time and left, went back home and packed—not for overseas, but for Fort Dix, New Jersey. There, the army assigned me as a regimental plans and training officer. Compared to my wartime experience, training at Fort Dix was simply terrible. I had always prided myself on my ability to adjust to any situation, but training new officers who couldn't care less about attending classes exceeded my patience. I couldn't wait to get out, so I volunteered for ranger school. Before long, I received orders for overseas deployment. I traveled to Seattle, the port of debarkation, and was going through the indoctrination and preparation when an administrative officer walked into a room full of officers and announced, "There is a new order. Any officer who has been recalled involuntarily does not have to continue to Korea. He can resign. If there are any officers here who would care to take advantage of this, please step forward." I stepped forward and that's how my military career came to an end.

Deciding not to return to Nixon Nitration Works, I became a production supervisor of an adhesive plaster mill for Johnson & Johnson in New Brunswick, New Jersey. In 1951, I had purchased a 106-acre farm in Pennsylvania along the foothills of the Blue Mountains, east of Indiantown Gap. I rented the old farmhouse to a young family and eventually started building a new home for our family, stone by stone. Wanting to return to Pennsylvania to be closer to the farm, in 1955 we rented a home near Gettysburg and I found employment in the agricultural field with Whitmoyer Laboratories and then several other companies. During this time we continued to spend all possible weekends at the farm, and our home was finally well enough along for us to move into in 1960 when our second child was ready for first grade. Here, I finally felt I had found the peace and quiet that I had promised myself on D-Day.

In 1972 I formed my own corporation and for the next twenty-five years, I distributed animal health products and basic vitamin premixes to feed mills in Pennsylvania and Maryland. In 1979, when the push for recycling had begun, I was asked by Hershey Chocolate Company if it was possible to sell their waste candy by-products for animal feed. Planning to use the contacts that I had developed over many years, I agreed to a contract with them to manage a warehouse to store and process the material. With my two employees, and Ethel as office manager and secretary, we went to work cleaning up the abandoned plant and putting it back in working order. We hired more men and as we found that cattle and hogs loved chocolate as much as humans, we soon became a thriving business selling to feed mills and large farmers. With experience and a little imagination, I found new uses and new combinations for the products and we finally were shipping material to new customers in other parts of the country and overseas. With the business prospering, Hershey Chocolate Company decided to take over the running of the warehouse. I continued as a distributor of nutritional premixes until I finally retired in 1997.

By 1980, with employees and office staff to help me at work, I had been able to attend the Company E reunion. Life before that had been too hectic to think much about my wartime experiences and like most veterans, I was too busy earning a living, but I had always maintained contact with the men by phone, letters, and occasional visits from the closest ones or any men passing through the local area.

The 1988 reunion in New Orleans and the contact with author Stephen Ambrose sparked a new interest in recalling my war experiences, and I dedicated myself to putting my memories as well as the letters from the men in order. Our second home in Hershey became the central repository for private correspondence and official records of the company and the battalion in which I had served. Telling the story of Easy Company not only became my motivation, but also my passion. Hence, when Ambrose wrote *Band of Brothers*, the records that I had compiled over the years became his primary source.

Beginning in 1946, former Sergeant Mike Ranney, Sergeant Bob Rader, and Corporal Walter Gordon began organizing Easy Company reunions. Later, Bill Guarnere took up the torch and encouraged the members of the company to stay in touch, but it was Ranney, who had earned a journalistic degree at the University of North Dakota, who served as the principal organizer of the initial reunions. He had hoped to write his memoirs and a history of Easy Company that he intended to entitle *Easy Does It!*, but his premature death in 1988 at the age of sixty-five halted his efforts. It was a shame that Easy Company lost Mike Ranney before we found Steve Ambrose and before we started to get organized to write *Band of Brothers*. Mike was a natural journalist who would have added immeasurably to the project.

At first only a few veterans attended the reunions, but as the years went by, more Toccoa veterans and their subsequent replacements assembled on an annual basis. Few officers attended the initial reunions, but in 1980, I called Moose Heyliger and Harry Welsh and convinced them to join the men in Nashville. Buck Compton, Clarence Hester, Bob Strayer, and Lewis Nixon completed the officer contingent that attended the Nashville reunion. Few had changed, and "Blackbeard" Nixon still tried to convince everyone, albeit unsuccessfully, that he really did shave every day. In total, thirty members of Easy Company attended the reunion in Nashville. Since it was my first reunion, I was overwhelmed when the men presented me a gold-plated mess kit with an accompanying poem.

In September 1987 I returned to Europe for the first time since the war. Accompanied by Walter and Betty Gordon, Ethel and I dined with Louis de Vallavieille in Paris. The next day Louis and Michel, the brother who had been shot on D-Day, escorted us to Normandy. I was anxious for a tour of the field that had played such an important role in my life and that of Easy Company. Michel, who never harbored any ill feelings at being shot by American paratroopers on June 6, gave me a test to ensure I was who I claimed to be. Taking me to a field near Le Grand Chemin, he inquired if it looked familiar. "No," I said, "this doesn't look familiar."

We then went to another field and he repeated the question. I gave him the same response.

After several hours he brought me to the field outside Brecourt Manor and asked again, "Does this look familiar?"

"Now, this is familiar. Number one gun was there, number two gun was here, and so on down the line."

Dormant memories returned after a half century. Walking across the field that housed the German 105mm howitzer battery created an eerie feeling. In the recesses of my mind, I could see "Popeye" Wynn, "Buck" Compton, Bill Guarnere, Joe Toye, Don Malarkey, Carwood Lipton, and the other members of our small band who had conducted an assault against overwhelming odds. Words simply escaped me as I traversed the area from every conceivable direction. The hedgerows and drainage trenches had largely disappeared, but the tree lines and the locations of each gun remained very distinguishable.

I returned to Brecourt and the other battlefields several times over the next decade, the last time in June 2001 for the premiere of the HBO series *Band of Brothers*. I chose not to participate in the preliminary tour and party in Paris. I didn't want to be part of that—it just wasn't in my nature. I preferred quiet reflection to reminisce about Easy Company's baptism of fire fifty-seven years earlier. Though I always considered Easy Company's performance on the dike in Holland on October 5, 1944, as my apogee as a company commander, Brecourt remained more special to me. Nothing has ever equaled our baptism of fire on D-Day. Ernie Pyle wrote that the first pioneering days of anything are always the best days. That is the way I feel about Brecourt. There was something special about silencing those guns that never was repeated. Brecourt was Easy Company's initial trial by combat and the place where I demonstrated to myself that I measured up to my personal standard of leadership. That is what made it special. Consequently, rather than joining the other veterans in a large hotel, Ethel and I spent eight days and nights at a Norman château near Brecourt so I could return to the battlefield each morning to walk the fields and to study the battle. My wife and I were warmly welcomed by Charles de Vallavieille, the grandson of the French colonel who owned Brecourt in 1944. Nearly six decades earlier, I had been the first American soldier to trespass on the de Vallavieille farm without Charles's grandfather's permission. This time I asked and received permission to return to Brecourt Manor. Special memories vividly returned as I stood in the remnants of the trench, gazing at the hedgerow across the field from where we received the machine gun fire as we assaulted the artillery pieces. The sapling from which Sergeant Lipton fired on the enemy was still there, though the tree had long since died. One morning I retraced my steps from Le Grand Chemin through the fields and ditches that now presented far greater obstacles than the hedgerows on D-Day. After the formal ceremony on June 6, we returned to Paris in time for the farewell banquet with the other men.

Charles de Vallavieille cordially invited me to return for the sixtieth anniversary celebration, but considering my advanced age, I felt it in my best interest to live within my limitations and watch the celebration at home. Even though I could not return, Charles continues to preserve the memory of the soldiers who liberated his grandfather's farm. "It's like when a friend asks you to watch over his grave," he says, "You can't ignore the sacrifice."

Returning to Hershey was bittersweet since I realized that I would never return to the battlefield. Still, I had a lifetime of memories and I remained determined to pass on the "untold stories" from all the men to future generations. Simply tell the stories of the men; the rest will take care of itself. Personal rewards, profits, recognition, and enumeration have never been important to me. Even when the Franklin D. Roosevelt Foundation selected me to represent the U.S. Army veterans of World War II when it presented its 2001 Franklin D. Roosevelt Four Freedoms/Freedom from Fear Award, I did so only as a representative of the American G.I.s who won the war. At the ceremony, news anchor Tom Brokaw said that the courage and service demonstrated by the five representatives of the military services "made possible a world of peace and justice and dreams that we continue to fulfill today."

Brokaw also called us "heroes," but I have always been uncomfortable with that term. Only a few heroes came back from the war. The real heroes lie under white crosses in North Africa, Europe, and across the Pacific. I still cannot visit the American cemetery overlooking Omaha Beach without crying for the men who never had the opportunity of achieving the peace that many of us have enjoyed. I know plenty of heroes, but I am certainly not one. Bill Guarnere is a hero for leaving the safety of his foxhole to help his buddy who had been severely wounded. Floyd Talbert and Joe Toye are heroes of the first order—so are Popeye Wynn, Babe Heffron, and scores of others who carry the wounds of war as badges of honor.

Perhaps the best characterization of what a true hero consists is found in a letter Sergeant Mike Ranney sent me in January 1982 shortly before he went back into the hospital for a series of tests. Historian Stephen Ambrose used the passage to conclude *Band of Brothers* because Ranney encapsulated the cohesion that became the hallmark of Easy Company. "In thinking back on the days of Easy Company, I'm treasuring my remark to a grandson who asked, 'Grandpa, were you a hero in the war?'

"No," I answered, "but I served in a company of heroes."

Mike Ranney then signed the letter "Your Easy Company Comrade."

15

Steve Ambrose Slept Here

Stephen Ambrose, the leading historian of our time, changed my life forever through his friendship and through his writing of *Band of Brothers*. Steve wrote *Band of Brothers* to fill his time as he prepared to write his book on D-Day. To give you an idea of what kind of man Steve Ambrose was, on Christmas morning 1995, he got up early and wrote me a letter that read, "Thanks for teaching me the duties and the responsibilities of a company commander." Later he gave Easy Company the recognition for what they had done in World War II. I appreciate the recognition and I appreciate the fact that he never forgot me. To make sure that I never forgot him and his friendship, I placed a brass plaque over the door at the house and at the farm that reads: STEVE AMBROSE SLEPT HERE.

I first met Steve Ambrose on February 26, 1990. The meeting, which Ambrose hosted in his home in Bay St. Louis, Mississippi, included Easy Company veterans Carwood Lipton, Walter Gordon, and

Forrest Guth. Two years earlier, Easy Company had held its reunion in New Orleans. Ambrose took the opportunity to tape-record a group interview to support the Eisenhower Center at the University of New Orleans' project of collecting oral histories from World War II veterans. I decided not to join the meeting in order to let the men speak out without deference to my role in the war. It was a wild interview session. I later mailed my written account to Ambrose. When I read the transcript from the group session, I believed that some important details were missing. I asked Walter Gordon, who was Ambrose's neighbor, to arrange a follow-up interview to set the record straight. Ambrose graciously consented and invited us to his home. Over the course of that afternoon, we discussed Easy Company's attack at Brecourt Manor. I then suggested that Steve consider writing a history of Easy Company, which might prove a nice complement to *Pegasus Bridge*, a book Ambrose wrote detailing a British light infantry company that seized important bridges over the Orne River and Orne Canal on D-Day. Steve jumped at the opportunity and asked us to obtain copies of wartime letters, photographs, newspaper clippings—anything we had on E Company.

The following month Gordon wrote "the intrepid trio" of Lipton, Guth, and myself to discuss a letter that he had recently received from Ambrose. Steve thought we had "a hell of an idea and he was ready to run with it." I provided copies of my diary and the letters that I had accumulated over the previous two decades. Later that summer, Ambrose came to my farm outside Hershey, where we spent several days discussing leadership and combat fatigue. Ambrose was an accomplished historian in his own right, and he seemed fascinated by Paul Fussell's depiction of the "slowly dawning and dreadful realization" that each soldier experiences three phases of combat depending on the length of his time on the front line. "Two steps of rationalization and one of accurate perception," is how Fussell describes the factors contributing to combat fatigue. The initial stage is, "This can't possibly happen to me. I'm not going to get wounded; I'm too smart; I'm too young. Quickly following is the second stage where the soldier rationalizes, "Jesus, this could happen to me if I'm not more careful." The third stage is, "This is going to happen to me unless I get out of here." Ambrose seemed surprised when I informed him that I had reached the third stage in Bastogne. Sooner or later, I felt that I was going to get it. I just prayed to God that it would not be too bad. I felt that I was going to be hit sooner or later, but I never felt that I was going to break. I had prepared myself physically and emotionally not to reach the breaking point. Nor did I feel that my judgment was ever too impaired to make the correct decision.

Following three days of one-on-one questioning, Harry Welsh, Joe Toye, Rod Strohl, and Forrest Guth joined us for a group interview. A few months later, Ambrose visited Carwood Lipton, Bill Guarnere, Don Malarkey, and a group of Easy Company West Coast residents. A quick tour of the European battlefield completed his initial research. That is the origin of *Band of Brothers* that hit the book shelves in 1992, in enough time to mark the fiftieth anniversary of the formation of Easy Company at Camp Toccoa, Georgia. Initial sales were modest, but they increased dramatically when Ambrose published *D-Day: June 6, 1944: The Climactic Battle of World War II* to coincide with the fiftieth anniversary of the invasion of Europe. The exploits of Easy Company made national headlines and a number of veterans were invited to relate their wartime experiences to local audiences. Each of us was grateful that Ambrose did such a masterful job in telling our story in his inimitable style.

After the publication of *Band of Brothers*, Steve returned my diary and the stories that I had collected since the war. I immediately made a file for each soldier in Easy Company and I spent the entire next year going through everything. Friends familiar with the official records from the War Department added the operational reports from 2d Battalion and the 506th PIR. I now had the complete story of Easy Company from start to finish in my possession.

Steve Ambrose changed my life even more drastically when he sold the rights of *Band of Brothers* to Steven Spielberg and Tom Hanks. The night he negotiated the deal, Ambrose took time to call me and to advise me that Tom Hanks was interested in the project and that he assumed that Hanks wanted to play Dick Winters. The conversation went something like this: "This is Steve Ambrose. I have a letter from Tom Hanks and he wants to buy *Band of Brothers*. He sent me the Home Box Office (HBO) series he did entitled *From the Earth to the Moon*. Hanks wants to produce a twelve-part series along these lines. He feels that *Band of Brothers* will make a magnificently, richly textured story that needs many hours to tell. I presume he wants to play Dick Winters, but I told him that Herbert Sobel was closer to the mark (kidding). Anyway, I just wanted to share the good news with you."

Just prior to HBO's release of *Band of Brothers* in September 2001, commentator Charlie Rose interviewed Ambrose and asked him directly, "Knowing as much as you do, if you had to serve in World War II, and I know that you would have served, where would you have wanted to be? With the pilots? With the soldiers? With the men of the Navy?"

Ambrose instantly responded, "With Easy Company, 506th Parachute Infantry Regiment, 101st Airborne Division."

When asked why, Ambrose elaborated: "Because the commander of that company, Dick Winters, was almost a Meriwether Lewis. He was that good. If Dick told me then, and if he told me now, to do something, I wouldn't ask why. I would just do it. He has character, of course, but he is honest, he has a firmness of purpose, and a direction. He knows so much: how to lay down a base of fire, what are the strengths and weaknesses of every man, how to lead an attack. He knows what a good company commander should be."

Needless to say, I was and continue to be flattered by all the attention and the recognition. But just as I said at the Emmy Awards in September 2002 when Spielberg and Hanks received the Emmy for best miniseries, I merely represented all the men of Company E who were present and all who had passed on before us. Spielberg summed up what we were all thinking when the award was handed to him: "Easy Company won this award back in 1944." In a sense we have all become celebrities since the release of the series, but I caution myself at the end of the day to remain humble and not to let it go to my head. Ours was merely a story that had to be told.

None of us anticipated the flood of correspondence that followed the release of Easy Company's story. Most correspondents write to express their appreciation for the sacrifices of the World War II generation. Others seek an easy solution to what constitutes effective leadership. Our lives are no longer private, but such is the price of fame. It is now impossible to keep a low profile, as everyone wants a little piece of you, striving to glean a sense of what made Easy Company such a remarkable combat unit. The attention is flattering, but nobody really knows me. The neighbors, the people whom I have known most of my life, now see a different part of me as a result of the television series. Still, it is impossible to convey the horrors of war to someone who has not experienced the crucible of combat. It is not their fault; like most veterans, I have only recently spoken about the war. World War II was, and remains, an intensely personal experience. When I have discussed the events that so shaped my life, I have talked about the war, never about myself. I prefer to keep it that way, but the letters keep arriving.

Voices:

From Sister Marie Andre Campbell and Sister Marie St. Paul, two cloistered members of the Poor Clare Nuns of Perpetual Adoration at Our Lady of the Angels Monastery:

> When we read about you, we said to each other: "Ah, here is a good and God-fearing man!" Goodness and beauty lead to truth after all, and no matter what state of life we live, everyone is searching for truth, and maybe that is why so many people are drawn to you after reading about the heroic deeds you and your men performed in France, Holland, Belgium, and Germany during World War II.

I visited Normandy with Mom and Dad when we lived in France. The cemeteries were open when we went. . . . It was an experience I will never forget. . . . One last item: I was particularly moved by the story of Floyd Talbert. He reminded me a lot of some Vietnam vets who came to speak to my class in college. They were "bikers": black leather jackets, long beards, rather intimidating, but they were some of the nicest men I ever met. The war deeply affected them in ways that I could never comprehend. Just like you said in one article, it's one thing to read and hear about it, but it's quite another to experience combat.

From Michael Nastasi, a police officer in the New York Police Department, who wrote to me in the aftermath of the World Trade Center attack on September 11, 2001:

. . . At the time, things were pretty bad and all of us were pretty distraught and confused about the whole scene, but we were also determined to do whatever we could to facilitate the recovery effort. By watching the series and reading the book about you and your men, it gave us all inspiration to carry out our duties no matter what the circumstances, and also for me personally, I realized that as in any situation, it could have been a whole lot worse. Reading about your experiences at Bastogne has humbled me and made me realize the true meaning of dedication and courage in the face of almost-insurmountable odds.

From Candace W. McKinley, "Popeye" Wynn's daughter, who gained a greater appreciation of what her father had experienced during the war:

Knowing little about the time all of you spent during the war, watching the miniseries made me wish Daddy had talked more about it. Not the horror you all witnessed, nor the cold and isolation you suffered, but the camaraderie shared by the men . . . To think of Daddy so young, so fit and so disciplined was a sharp contrast to the way he had begun to fail physically the last two years of his life . . . When he was being interviewed by a crew from Playtone, I heard more about his time in the service than I'd heard my whole life. What he said at the end of the interview has stayed with me . . . when asked if he ever thinks about what you guys did over there, his answer was, "No, I don't think about that. But the guys . . . I think about them every day." . . . I am thankful that you were a part of my daddy's life, and I truly feel the same respect for you that he did until the day he died.

From Josephine Bruster, an elderly woman from Oklahoma, who recalls watching the 101st Airborne Division land in Holland in 1944:

I want to thank you for saving my life and family. September 17, 1944, in Veghel—a Sunday afternoon the planes came and all the parachutes started opening up. It was the most beautiful sight. I shall never forget. I was a young girl of ten years old and we lived in Veghel. We were so excited and thankful to see all those American soldiers coming to free us from that awful war. Such brave men! It is because of soldiers like you that I am here today. I came to the United States in 1955, married an American, and now live in a small town in Oklahoma. I have two sons and two daughters, eleven grandchildren, and I am so proud to be an American . . . I just want to let you know what your soldiers meant to me, a ten-year-old girl.

From Linda B. Canzona, a lady in North Carolina, who wrote about her greater appreciation of her grandfather:

. . . I cannot express the gratitude I felt for you and your company while watching the series. As a result of the sacrifices made by men like you, my generation was able to grow up and live in freedom. . . . Because you were willing to tell your story, it not only gave me a greater appreciation for what your generation did for mine, but also a greater appreciation for the actions of my grandfather, who received two Bronze Stars and a Purple Heart at the Battle of the Bulge. I have asked him, as has my brother, what he did to earn those medals and his response is, "It was nothing. It was just another day." I have truly come to appreciate the contributions (of my uncles and grandfather who fought in World War II and Vietnam) . . . and now realize what freedom really means and how very blessed my generation is because of sacrifices made by others.

When I was young my family went to the beaches of Normandy. My father hoisted me up on his shoulder and as we looked out across the field of crosses, he told my brother and me that all those men died for us.

From Maggie Blouch, a junior at Palmyra Area High School, who wrote an essay for her advanced placement European History class after attending a presentation on "Leadership in the Band of Brothers":

What or who do you think of when the phrase Veterans' Day is mentioned? . . . This year, I was deeply touched by the story of not just any veteran, but a man who is indeed an American hero and an example of outstanding leadership, honest, direction, and knowledge . . . As [Major Winters] began to share with us, his eyes sparkled with passion and love for his "buddies," his mission, the events he encountered, and his version of the true band of brothers . . . He also discussed superior leadership and dedication of other men in his Company. These men included Sergeant Hall, Wynn, Nixon, Blithe, Lesniewski, Lieutenant Speirs, and Joe Toye. These many examples of selfless service, leadership, and true dedication were precisely the elements of what Easy Company was all about.

. . . Major Winters's story transformed my interpretation of this special holiday, made me further appreciate soldiers past and present while showing gratitude for our freedom that's often too simply taken for granted, and essentially taught me some of life's greatest lessons: the importance of faith in yourself, faith in your cause, and faith in the people around you.

Perhaps the most succinct testimonial came from Bryce E. Reiman who wrote, "[Easy Company] has made me want to be a better human being."

And it goes on, thousands of voices reflecting on the extraordinary achievements of ordinary men placed in extraordinary circumstances. Thank you, the men of Easy Company and thank you, Steve Ambrose.

The most frequently asked question to any member of Easy Company is, "What made your company so special?" Ambrose did his best to answer that question, but a soldier's perspective explains what really brought us together. Major Clarence Hester, who began the war as Easy Company's executive officer and ended the war as a battalion commander, shamelessly proclaimed that he used Easy Company when the "chips were down and they never let me down." So close were the men that Hester freely admitted that he "knew how they looked in front, in back, dark, or light. *We could call each other by name on a moonless night just by seeing the way we moved.*"

Sergeant "Burr" Smith, who was yanked out of the company headquarters' plane and moved to another aircraft on June 5, thereby escaping the fate of Lieutenant Meehan, left the army after the war, but was recalled to duty in 1952. Accepting a reserve commission, he eventually went on to become a lieutenant colonel in the postwar army, where he was in a unique position to observe the evolution of the modern military force. He served in Laos as a civilian advisor to a large, irregular force and remained on jump status until 1974. Toward the end of his career, he served as special assistant to the commander of the U.S. Army's counterterror task force, then known only as Delta Force. In 1979, he wrote me, "Funny thing about 'the Modern Army,' Dick. I am assigned to what is reputed to be the best unit in the U.S. Army . . . and I believe that it is. Still, on a man-for-man basis, I'd choose my wartime paratroop company *any time*! We had something there for three-plus years that will never be equaled . . . not in our lifetime, anyway."

Ronald Speirs concurred. "I was scared to death and never thought I would survive the war," wrote the officer who commanded Easy Company for the longest period of time. "But my best days were as platoon leader and company commander with you guys." Speirs provided another insight, this time on unit cohesion. Soldiers risk their lives for the small unit, the squad, or the platoon. The "infantry soldier is aware of the regiment, the division, and the democracy he belongs to, but his fighting spirit and good morale are caused and nurtured by his buddies, the guys in the foxholes alongside him. That is the reason men persevere in battle. Combat fatigue, the desire to flee, is stopped by small-unit morale." I could not agree more.

I have always been proud to have been a member of Easy Company, 506th Parachute Infantry Regiment. The 101st Airborne Division was comprised of hundreds of good, solid, infantry companies. We were special, but you could probably say the same thing about Companies A, B, and C. Every soldier thinks his company is special and unique. E Company, 506th PIR, stands out due to a very special bond that brought the men together in the summer of 1942. That cohesion began with Captain Herbert Sobel at Camp Toccoa. During Sobel's tenure of command, the only way the men survived was to bond together. Eventually, the noncommissioned officers bonded further in a mutiny against his tyrannical rule and their fear to go into combat with a leader in whom they had no confidence. Good as they were prior to the invasion, it took battle experience to make Easy Company complete soldiers. The stress in training was followed by the stress in Normandy of drawing the key combat mission for gaining control of Utah Beach. In combat, your reward for a job well done is that you get the next tough mission. Easy Company kept right on getting the job done through Carentan, Holland, Bastogne, and Germany. I was partially responsible for repeatedly selecting Easy Company for difficult missions. E Company had every reason to be irritated with me. Whenever the battalion received a tough mission, I selected Easy Company because I knew I could count on them. The net result of sharing all that stress throughout training and combat has created a bond between the men of Easy Company that will last forever. Easy Company was the most special group of warriors and men with whom I have had the pleasure to serve.

As the years increasingly take a toll on the survivors, I take a quiet pride that so many of my wartime comrades have voiced their opinions that I have in some way contributed to their success. Floyd Talbert wrote shortly before his death, "Dick, you are loved and will never be forgotten by any soldier who ever served under you. You are the best friend I ever had . . . you were my ideal, and motor in combat . . . you are to me the greatest soldier I could ever hope to meet." I also treasure a letter I received from the son of Staff Sergeant Leo Boyle after his father died in December 1997 from the effects of Parkinson's disease. Boyle's son said his father spoke of very few people from the war, but, "You are the one. It is clear that his admiration of, and the respect for you, is beyond anything I know. He literally would have followed Dick Winters into Hell"—his words, not mine. Former Easy Company comrades Don Malarkey and Bill Wingett served as Boyle's honorary pallbearers. And that is yet another reason that makes Easy Company special—they remain comrades in life and comrades in death.

Ambrose did a marvelous job summarizing the postwar lives of the men who had served in Easy Company and his efforts need little recounting in these pages. Since the publication of *Band of Brothers*, however, a number of Easy Company men and their commanders have passed from the scene.

Colonel Robert Sink left Germany to serve on the staff of General Maxwell Taylor at West Point in December 1945. Sink was a model officer whose charisma and leadership played a profound effect on my personal development as a combat commander. He later served as commander of both Fort Bragg, North Carolina, and its 18th Airborne Corps. He was best known for helping form the Strategic Army Corps Forces (STRAC) in the 1950s. STRAC consisted of 125,000 troopers, including two airborne divisions. Under Sink's dynamic leadership, the Strategic Army Corps became an alert, well-trained, combat-ready striking force capable of performing worldwide operational missions on call. General Sink's last major assignment was as commander of U.S. forces in Panama. Lieutenant General Sink died of complications from chronic emphysema at age sixty in 1965. His place remains forever fixed in the history of the 101st Airborne Division. The Robert F. Sink Memorial Library is located on Screaming Eagle Boulevard at Fort Campbell, Kentucky.

Lieutenant Colonel Robert Strayer, commander of 2d Battalion, 506th PIR, assumed command of the 507th PIR in July 1945 and remained its commanding officer until its deactivation in December. He was promoted to full colonel in December 1945. After he left active duty, he organized 2d Eastern Pennsylvania Airborne Combat Command, which was the first reserve outfit to actually function as a reception center in processing civilians into the military. Later he served as chief of Training Division in the Pentagon. Strayer's last command was as the commanding officer of the 157th Infantry Brigade. "Colonel Bob" was a frequent attendee at Easy Company reunions until his death in December 2002.

Lieutenant Colonel Clarence Hester, Captain Sobel's first executive officer, left the army in 1946 and worked for a friend for twenty-six years who promised to take him in as a stockholder. When he asked for his share, Hester was turned down for the boss's son, so he established Hester Roofing Company in Sacramento, California. He became very successful while his former employer went broke after a few years. He visited Herbert Sobel once after the war while attending a convention in Chicago. Sobel appeared to be the same unsure person he had been in the army. Sobel and Hester enjoyed an uneasy lunch and both said the usual, "Nice to see you," but neither had a desire to see each other again. In a letter to Carwood Lipton, Hester stated that "as an ex–G.I., I have always felt Easy Company was my home." Easy Company had given Hester a sense of purpose and responsibility that led to his self-confidence. In five short years, Hester had been promoted from private to lieutenant colonel and appointed commander of a battalion in the 101st Airborne Division. He wasn't sure how much Easy Company had helped, but "they must have, as they are the ones I always return to." Hester hoped that Ambrose's book would "capture the spirit of America and the willingness of our young people to fight for a cause and go far beyond the normal effort and risks." Clarence Hester died in 2000 at the age of eighty-four from complications due to kidney failure.

Moose Heyliger temporarily assumed command of Easy Company when I was transferred to battalion headquarters in October 1944. Following his accidental shooting by a member of his own command, Moose remained in the hospital until his discharge in 1947. He spent the next forty years as a leading horticulturalist and a landscaping consultant. Before his death, an interviewer asked Moose if he was proud to have been a member of Easy Company. "Am I proud? You bet your life I am," my successor-in-command instantly replied. Moose Heyliger died on November 4, 2001, shortly after the release of the initial episodes of the HBO series. His passing was a deep personal loss to all who knew him.

Captain Lewis Nixon and I were together every step of the way from D-Day to Berchtesgaden, May 8, 1945—VE-Day. I still regard Lewis Nixon as the best combat officer who I had the opportunity to work with under fire. He never showed fear, and during the toughest times he could always think clearly and quickly. Very few men can remain poised under an artillery concentration. Nixon was one of those officers. He always trusted me, from the time we met at Officer Candidate School. While we were in training before we shipped overseas, Nixon hid his entire inventory of Vat 69 in my footlocker, under the tray holding my socks, underwear, and sweaters. What greater trust, what greater honor could I ask for than to be trusted with his precious inventory of Vat 69? Following the war Nix went through tough times and several failed marriages until in 1956, he married a woman named Grace and everything finally came together. Until Lewis met and married Grace, he had never found or experienced true love. It was only after his marriage to Grace that he found true happiness, peace within himself. Together they traveled to just about every corner of the world and shared many wonderful experiences together. Nix and I corresponded over the years and always shared some laughs. We told more than our share of lies at Easy Company's reunions. My friend Nixon died in January 1995, and Grace asked me to give the eulogy at his funeral, which I did. Also in attendance were Clarence Hester and Bob Brewer. In my remarks, I made a point of quoting Grace, whose love and care had kept Nix alive for many years. In her many letters and Christmas cards, Grace's message was always the same: "Lewis is so brave; he never complains; he always has a smile for me whenever I come into his room—and that just makes it all worthwhile." Seven years later, Grace Nixon joined us in Los Angeles for the presentation of the Emmy for Best Documentary.

Next to Nixon, Harry Welsh was my best friend during the war. During the war he was awarded two Bronze Stars and two Purple Hearts. Following the cessation of hostilities, Harry remained on my staff throughout the summer of 1945. Together with Nixon, he and I contemplated volunteering for duty in the Pacific. Although he had accrued the necessary points to return home to get married, I convinced Harry to stick around for a while. He was an excellent soldier, the kind of man who made an outfit click and the type of leader who won battles. Harry finally returned home to Wilkes-Barre, Pennsylvania, and married his childhood sweetheart, Kitty Grogan. He went to Wilkes College and graduated with honors in 1957. Three years later, he earned his master's degree. Welsh taught political science at the college for nine years and then served as an administrator in the Wilkes-Barre

School District for several decades until his retirement at age sixty-five in 1983. Harry Welsh died in 1995 from heart failure. His beloved Kitty followed three years later.

Other Toccoa men have passed since the publication of *Band of Brothers* in 1992. George Luz, for one, returned home to Providence, Rhode Island, where he became a handyman. His first job was in a used furniture store where he earned seventy-five cents an hour. After four months, Luz had had enough and he became a painter for a dollar an hour. "Things were looking up," he claimed. A few odd jobs later, he finally obtained a job with the federal government. George Luz raised a wonderful family and lived long enough to enjoy his grandchildren. "It's been a wonderful life," he stated in one of his last letters. When George Luz died in 1998, over 1,600 people attended his funeral—a testament to his character and community involvement. At no time was his character more evident than in the funeral home when his pastor noticed two medals placed on George's chest: a Purple Heart for being wounded in combat, and the Bronze Star for valor. When the pastor mentioned to a family member about how proud George must have been at being awarded the medals, the response was, "We didn't even know he received them." That is the stuff real heroes are made of. Nobody really needed to know. George Luz typified the average soldier in Easy Company—he was tough as nails, had a wonderful sense of humor, and possessed a fierce loyalty to Company E that was second to none.

Carwood Lipton, whom many considered the best noncommissioned officer in the company, returned to civilian life after the war where he received an engineering degree from Marshall University in Huntington, West Virginia. He remained active in the Army Reserves as commanding officer of Headquarters Company, 3d Battalion, 398th PIR, until after the Korean war, but his unit was not called to active duty. Carwood Lipton proved as adept in the corporate world as he had been in leading soldiers in combat. After a career as an executive with Owens-Illinois, a manufacturer of glass products and plastics packaging, Lipton retired in 1983. In the last two decades of his life, he traveled throughout the world and enjoyed his hobbies of golf and reading. On the fiftieth anniversary of D-Day, Lipton said what most of us had felt as we boarded the aircraft destined to carry us to Normandy on June 5, 1944: "If we were afraid of anything, it was that we wouldn't measure up. We wanted to be heroes: not to the American public or in books, but to each other." His words proved to be a fitting epitaph. Carwood Lipton died at the age of eighty-one in Southern Pines, North Carolina, from pulmonary fibrosis in December 2001.

Denver "Bull" Randleman followed Lipton in June 2003. Bull was one of the finest noncoms in Easy Company. Like most of the men, he became a highly successful businessman and served for years as the superintendent of a heavy-construction contractor in Louisiana. He spent his last years in Texarkana, Arkansas, where he succumbed to a staph infection at the age of eighty-two in June 2003.

David Webster, a veteran of Easy Company, always said that Sergeant Johnny Martin was the sharpest soldier in the company. After the war Johnny Martin used his G.I. Bill at The Ohio State University before returning to his old job with the railroad. In 1981 he decided to start a new career as housing contractor. Within years he became a millionaire. A frequent attendee at Easy Company reunions, he usually arrived in a fancy car that flaunted his high financial status. With each passing year, he expressed his desire: "to stay alive—that's all." Johnny Martin passed away in late January 2005, which left only one survivor from 1st Platoon from Toccoa days. When I received a call that he had passed on, I could not help but think had I not always placed 1st Platoon in the lead, that more of Martin's platoon members would be alive today.

Next to Floyd Talbert, Sergeant Joe Toye was the best soldier in Easy Company. Among his numerous awards were four Purple Hearts and two Bronze Stars. After several operations as a result of losing his leg at Bastogne, Joe was discharged from the army in February 1946. He always respected Bill Guarnere for risking his own life to save him from being hit with more shrapnel. That was the way it was in Easy Company, said Toye, "One Screaming Eagle helping another Screaming Eagle." Despite his physical handicap, Joe faced the responsibilities of raising a family with the same dedication he demonstrated in serving his country during the war. He worked for Bethlehem Steel for twenty years before retirement. Every man in the company would tell you that when the chips were down in combat, he would like to have Toye protecting his flank. Joe Toye died in 1995, and I was honored to be asked by the family to deliver the eulogy and to serve as a pallbearer. His tombstone said it all: SERGEANT JOE TOYE, 506TH PIR, 101ST AIRBORNE DIVISION. His time in service meant that much to him.

Gone too are "Popeye" Wynn, who apologized to me after being wounded during our attack on the artillery battery on D-Day, and T/Sergeant "Burt" Christenson, whose sketches of D-Day delighted Easy Company veterans for years. T/Sergeant Amos "Buck" Taylor, who replaced Carwood Lipton as platoon sergeant of 3d Platoon after Lipton was wounded at Carentan, remembered Popeye Wynn and Shifty Powers as two of the best infantrymen in Easy Company, always dependable to take the point when the platoon moved out. No history of Easy Company would be complete without the meticulous research of Burt Christenson, who maintained complete rosters of every man who served in the company over the course of the war. Ambrose relied extensively on Christenson to compile a list of casualties, addresses, and rosters in writing *Band of Brothers*. Christenson passed away in December 1999. Wynn followed three months later. Neither lived long enough to witness the accolades showered by an adoring public following the release of the HBO series.

No veteran who served in Easy Company had a more distinguished military career than Salve "Matt" Matheson, who stayed in the army and rose to the rank of major general. One of the original platoon leaders in Easy Company, Matheson was born in Seattle, Washington, on August 11, 1920. Graduating from the University of California at Los Angeles, he accepted a commission in the U.S. Army and joined Easy

Company at Toccoa. Colonel Strayer and Colonel Sink rapidly recognized Matt's talents and transferred him first to battalion and then to regimental staff, where he served from Normandy through Berchtesgaden. After the war, he served in various command and staff positions in the 82d Airborne Division and fought in both the Korean and Vietnam Wars. During the Korean War, Matt participated in the Inchon and Wonson landings and the amphibious withdrawal from Hungnam. In Vietnam, he commanded 1st Brigade, 101st Airborne Division (Separate) and served on General William Westmoreland's staff during the Tet Offensive. Later he commanded the 2d Infantry Division in Korea along the Demilitarized Zone and Army Readiness Region IV before his retirement in the early 1970s. He always took immense pride in being appointed as the Honorary Colonel of the 506th Regiment. General Matheson passed away at his home in California on January 8, 2005, leaving me as the sole surviving officer from Easy Company's Toccoa days.

My life would certainly have been very different without Company E. I think I would have done a good job in any outfit, but Easy Company made me who I was. They brought out the best in me. If you had anything good in you, they brought it out. That is why as I look back over the six decades since the war, I find that as I meet, interact, and talk to literally thousands of people, I am always measuring them against and hoping to find men like those who served in Easy Company. They are truly my "other" family.

As I look back on the men of Easy Company and the closeness we have enjoyed over the years, I am reminded of the dialogue attributed to a senior German officer bidding farewell to his men in the HBO miniseries. Paraphrasing his words, I would say to Easy Company and the officers and men of the 506th PIR: "It has been a long war; it's been a hard war. You have fought bravely, proudly for your country. You are a special group of men connected by a bond that only exists in combat. You've shared the incommunicable experience of war and have been tested under extreme adversity. You've shared foxholes and held each other in dire moments. You've seen death and have suffered together. You've lived in an environment totally incomprehensible to those who do not know war. I am proud and deeply honored to have served with every one of you. You all deserve long and happy lives in peace. I bid each of you godspeed and ask the Almighty to shower His blessings on you and your families now and for generations to come."

16 Reflections

One of the last things Steve Ambrose told me before his death in 2003 was, "From now on, Winters, if you are going to talk about anything, talk about leadership." Leadership is an interesting concept and somewhat difficult to define. General George Patton once said, "Leadership is the thing that wins battles. I have it, but I'll be damned if I can define it." Like Patton, I have been fascinated with leadership. It is something that you have within you that gets the job done.

Was I a successful leader? They tell me I was and modesty prevents me from disagreeing with them. I am not so naïve that I don't realize that the wide appeal of Dick Winters today is based on leadership in combat. I may not have been the best combat commander, but I always strove to be. My men depended on me to carefully analyze every tactical situation, to maximize the resources that I had at my disposal, to think under pressure, and then to lead them by personal example. I always felt that my position was where the critical decision had to be made. Nor am I ashamed to admit that fear was a principal factor that contributed to my success as a leader. I was always afraid of letting my men down and I was always afraid of dying. It was a combination of these fears that drove me to learn everything I could about my profession so I could bring as many of my men home from war as possible.

Having said that, I am not sure there is such a thing as a natural-born leader. Some leaders are born with special aptitudes or talents, but any success I might have had was the product of good upbringing, intense study and preparation, and physical conditioning that set me apart from many of my peers. I was also surrounded by a group of men who were disciplined and highly trained to accomplish any mission. Add luck to the equation and you can understand that the secret to my success was that somehow I always managed to survive another day.

In recent years, I have been asked to address an increasing number of civic groups, corporate seminars, and governmental agencies on the subject of leadership. Most are looking for cookie-cutter solutions as to what constitutes a successful leader. What is the recipe for success? In truth there are no simple solutions, just as there is no average day in combat. Each situation is different and each requires a leader to be flexible in adapting his or her particular leadership style to the specific circumstances required to accomplish any mission. It's a matter of adjusting to the individual, and you do this every day. You don't have just one way of treating people. You adjust yourself to whom you are talking.

If I were to give advice to a young leader going to war, based on my observation of what had constituted the success of the outstanding leaders who comprised the American parachute infantry regiments of World War II, I would offer a series of principles that I am certain would result in great success, regardless of the field of endeavor in which the individual was participating.

First and foremost, a leader should strive to be an individual of flawless character, technical competence, and moral courage. In Anton

Myrer's bestselling novel *Once an Eagle* (which is on the required reading list of many senior military officers), the protagonist Sam Damon says, "You can't help where you were born and you may not have much to say about where you die, but you can and you should try to pass the days in between as a good man." How do you become a good man? You start with a cornerstone—honesty—and from there you build character. If you have character, that means the guy you are dealing with can trust you. When you get into combat, and you get in a situation such as we were in along the dike in Holland, when I gave the orders, "Ready, aim, fire," nobody else was thinking about anything except what he had been told to do. The men trust in you, have faith in you, and they obey, no questions asked. That's character in a nutshell.

Character provides a leader with a moral compass that focuses his efforts on the values we cherish: courage, honesty, selflessness, and respect for our fellow man. Character also allows you to make decisions quickly and correctly. Some may question my decision to disobey a direct order from my commanding officer at Haguenau and to "fake" another patrol as a violation of the very principle that I am advocating. In my heart, however, I could not send men to risk their lives for no apparent reason, when clearly nothing would have been gained that we had not already achieved. Such a course takes a degree of moral courage, which I have found is far rarer than physical courage. Was I correct? In my estimation, I thought so and I have never regretted my decision.

The same holds true for developing leaders of competency. Those entrusted to lead must study their profession to become totally proficient in tactics and technology. Prior to the invasion, I read every tactical manual I could lay my hands on to improve my tactical knowledge and professional competence while the other soldiers were out carousing in the pubs. While they were enjoying the social life of the neighboring towns, I was reading and educating myself, getting ready to lead the men in combat. While I was staying with the Barneses for the nine months that they hosted me, I was studying, developing my own personality, my own personal perspective on command. The intense study paid huge dividends in Normandy. Before the final attack at Noville, I studied the *Infantry Manual for the Attack*. I must have read that manual hundreds of times, but if I could glean one additional insight with another reading, perhaps I might save one more life. The bottom line is that leaders have entrusted to them the most precious commodity this country possesses: the lives of America's sons and daughters. Consequently, they must have a thorough understanding of their profession.

Second, don't waste time attempting to define leadership. No need to go to the dictionary. The Infantry School at Fort Benning, Georgia, has defined leadership in just two words via its motto: "Follow Me!" Never ask your team to do something you wouldn't do yourself. When I hit the ground outside Ste. Mere-Eglise armed only with a trench knife, there was no time to conduct a lengthy estimate of the situation or to find my leg bag. I grabbed the first trooper I could find, and said, "Follow me!" Off we went until other paratroopers joined us as we proceeded to our D-Day objective. At Brecourt Manor, Carentan, and at the crossroads on the dike in Holland on October 5, I made a quick but thorough reconnaissance then developed a plan, and personally led the attack. You cannot make sound decisions unless you are at the point of attack. Leaders should always position themselves where the critical decisions must be made. Precisely where that location should be is a judgment call, but in my experience leaders should be as far forward as possible. Successful leaders must be highly visible, if for no other reason than to share the hardships of their men. I am thinking of General George Patton, who made a habit of always visiting the front lines in his jeep or tank. When he returned to his field headquarters, he normally altered his mode of transportation to an airplane to avoid having his men see him moving back.

Physical fitness is another prerequisite for success. I freely admit that I was blessed with a sound physical constitution, but whenever possible, I took opportunity to improve my physical stamina. Because

I was in such good physical shape, I easily survived Toccoa. While men washed out on a daily basis, the contingent from Easy Company that completed the training and earned their wings at Fort Benning were tough as nails. Not surprisingly, I felt that I was in the best physical shape in my life as Easy Company prepared for the invasion at Aldbourne. This did not happen by accident. Following a rigorous day of training, I would take a run every evening following tea with the Barneses. As they were on their way to bed, I would say, "Well, I'm going to take a walk." I would go out and run for several miles even though blackout conditions were in effect. Then I'd come home and go to bed. Because I was in such good shape, my fatigue level never reached the point of physical exhaustion that contributes to mental exhaustion and, ultimately, to combat fatigue. We all experienced sleep deprivation at times—that is the nature of stress—but a physically exhausted leader routinely makes poor decisions in times of crisis.

A fourth key to Easy Company's success, as well as 2d Battalion's, centered on the development and the nourishment of teamwork. Captain Sobel began the process at Toccoa. He undoubtedly deserves much of the credit for developing such a cohesive team, but the teamwork didn't end there. The noncommissioned officers kept their squads and platoons physically hardened and combat ready. Until casualties removed so many Toccoa men from the ranks, Easy Company was just about the finest rifle company in the European Theater. Because each knew the other's strengths and weaknesses, we could assign the right men to the proper jobs. Burr Smith, who had been a soldier of one kind or another most of his adult life, knew only a handful of great soldiers. One was Bill Guarnere, platoon sergeant of 2d Platoon. The loss of Guarnere, Joe Toye, and Buck Compton absolutely devastated Easy Company at Bastogne, but others immediately stepped into the breach. In this case, 1st Sergeant Carwood Lipton ensured that the company did not disintegrate.

I have always felt that my principal contribution to the success of both Easy Company and 2d Battalion was based on my knowledge of what to expect from each man. It was hardly accidental that I selected Easy's "killers" for the assault on the battery at Brecourt. Nor was it coincidental that I positioned Floyd Talbert on my flank as we destroyed two enemy companies on the dike in Holland. At Haguenau, I knew that Sergeant Ken Mercier would get the job done. Having selected the right men for the right job, I then delegated the authority to my subordinates and allowed them to use their initiative to execute the mission. There is no need to tell someone how to do his job if you have properly trained your team. This is precisely why I respected Brigadier General Tony McAuliffe more than General Maxwell Taylor. Steve Ambrose thought I was unfair to Taylor, but I disagree. McAuliffe allowed us the flexibility and the latitude to do what needed to be done. The same holds true with respect to Colonels Sink and Strayer, who rarely interfered in small unit actions. The only time I can think that I purposely interfered with a mission was when I deliberately imposed safety limits on Harry Welsh for a combat patrol across the Rhine when 2d Battalion was holding the line in order to seal the Ruhr Pocket.

I have also discovered that careful preparation and anticipation of potential problems eliminate many of the obstacles that one encounters on the battlefield. Don't wait until you get to the top of the ridge and then make up your mind as to what course of action you intend to follow. The reconnaissance that I conducted at Brecourt on June 6 and on the dike on October 5 paid huge dividends when Easy Company swung into action. Before Sergeant Mercier led his combat patrol across the Moder River to capture some live prisoners, virtually every possible contingency had been thoroughly anticipated and planned. So, too, was the case of the attack on Foy, where I personally directed the fire support plan. The only thing that I had not anticipated was the mental breakdown of the company commander in the midst of the attack. Fortunately Lieutenant Speirs was on hand to take corrective action and direct the remainder of the assault. Good preparation is always vital to the success of any operation, but leaders must remain flexible once the action commences. Steve Ambrose likes to quote General Eisenhower, who claimed, "Before the battle is joined, plans are everything. Once the battle is joined, however, the plans go out the window."

I would also urge leaders to remain humble. If you don't worry about who gets the credit, you get a lot more done. I was only moderately successful in ensuring my men received the credit for their actions at Brecourt and on the Island. I recommended every man for a battle-field citation for the assault on the German battery on D-Day. Regrettably, many of the citations were downgraded by higher headquarters, but each trooper received some recognition. When I wrote the after-action report for the defense of the Island, I purposely wrote it in the third person. Never once did I use the word *I,* nor was there any reason to do so. Leaders should assume blame when the operation fails; when it succeeds, credit the men and women in your team. They do the lion's share of the work.

Since the release of the HBO miniseries, many of us have been flooded with hundreds, sometimes thousands, of letters from adoring fans across the nation. A surprisingly high number have also originated from Europe, Canada, East Asia, and Australia. In a span of six months, I received one hundred and fifty letters from England alone. It is easy to get one's head "lost in the clouds." The attention is certainly flattering and greatly appreciated, but it remains better to remember Eisenhower's address at Guildhall Hall on June 12, 1945. To an ecstatic British public, which showered the Supreme Commander with a tumultuous parade through the streets of London, Ike reminded them, "Humility must always be the portion of any man who receives acclaim earned in the blood of his followers and the sacrifices of his friends."

Next, I would encourage leaders to take a moment of self-reflection before rushing into an important decision. Many leaders don't take the time to consider carefully their decisions or the implications of their actions. In battle I periodically detached myself mentally from the noises and chaos of battle. I found it useful to separate myself momentarily and to carefully think through what actions I needed to take to accomplish the mission. The opportunity for self-analysis allows you to find your own self-consciousness, which in turn tells you if you are getting off track. Nobody will have to tell you that the course of action that you are contemplating is incorrect or ineffective. If you take advantage of opportunities for personal reflection, and if you honestly examine yourself, you will be a more effective leader. After the squad destroyed the German machine gun position on the dike on October 5, for example, I went off to be alone for a few minutes to think while the remainder of the platoon came forward. In the interim from when I summoned them forward and when they arrived, I determined that the proper course of action was to conduct a bayonet assault. At Bastogne, the ability to sit back and reflect on the next day's action ensured our battalion's success on the attacks on Foy and Noville.

Lastly, "Hang Tough!" Never, ever, give up regardless of the adversity. If you are a leader, a fellow who other fellows look to, you have got to keep going.

How will you know if you have succeeded? True satisfaction comes from getting the job done. The key to successful leadership is to earn respect—not because of rank or position, but because you are a leader of character. In the military, the president of the United States may nominate you as a commissioned officer, but he cannot command for you the loyalty and confidence of your soldiers. Those you must earn by giving loyalty to your soldiers and providing for their welfare. Properly led and treated right, your lowest-ranking soldier is capable of extraordinary acts of valor. Ribbons, medals, and accolades, then, are poor substitutes to the ability to look yourself in the mirror every night and know that you did your best. You can see the look of respect in the eyes of the men who have worked for you. A year before he died, "Burr" Smith sent me a letter in which he wrote, "Dick, you were blessed (some would say rewarded) with the uniform respect and admiration of 120 wartime soldiers, essentially civilians in uniform, who would have followed you to certain death. How many men in all of human history have that knowledge to carry to their grave . . . certainly

no more than a few . . . and you have it. Looking back from this perspective you may well feel that you didn't deserve it, but at the time we
thought you did, and that's all that counted." Burr was right about one
thing—I was extremely blessed to have been the commander of Easy
Company. No single individual "deserved" the privilege of leading such
a remarkable group of warriors into battle. And to this day, I am humbled by that experience.

The shadows are lengthening for those of us who fought World
War II. In the twilight of our lives, our thoughts return to happier days
when we struggled together not as individuals, but as a team—a team
that willingly sacrificed itself to protect its members. Sixty years after
our final victory, these men remain different. Not one man walks
around wearing his wings or medals on his chest to stand out. It is what
each man carries *in* his chest that makes him different. It is the confidence, pride, and character that make the World War II generation
stand out in any crowd. I'm proud to have been a small part of it. I certainly harbor no regrets. And not a day goes by that I don't think of the
men I served with who never had the opportunity to enjoy a world of
peace. Their collective legacy is best summarized in Henry W. Longfellow's "A Psalm of Life." In describing songs of hope and courage,
Longfellow writes:

> *Lives of great men all remind us*
> *We can make our lives sublime,*
> *And, departing, leave behind us*
> *Footprints on the sands of time.*

I wish to convey a final thought—and I hope that it doesn't sound
out of place—but I would like to share something as I look back on the
war. War brings out the worst and the best in people. Wars do not make
men great, but they do bring out the greatness in good men. War is ro-
mantic only to those who are far away from the sounds and turmoil of
battle. For those of us who served in Easy Company and for those who

served their country in other theaters, we came back as better men and women as a result of being in combat, and most would do it again if called upon. But each of us hoped that if we had learned anything from the experience, it is that war is unreal and we earnestly hoped that it would never happen again.

Leadership at the Point of the Bayonet

Ten Principles for Success

1. Strive to be a leader of character, competence, and courage.
2. Lead from the front. Say, "Follow me!" and then lead the way.
3. Stay in top physical shape—physical stamina is the root of mental toughness.
4. Develop your team. If you know your people, are fair in setting realistic goals and expectations, and lead by example, you will develop teamwork.
5. Delegate responsibility to your subordinates and let them do their jobs. You can't do a good job if you don't have a chance to use your imagination or your creativity.
6. Anticipate problems and prepare to overcome obstacles. Don't wait until you get to the top of the ridge and then make up your mind.
7. Remain humble. Don't worry about who receives the credit. Never let power or authority go to your head.
8. Take a moment of self-reflection. Look at yourself in the mirror every night and ask yourself if you did your best.
9. True satisfaction comes from getting the job done. The key to a successful leader is to earn respect—not because of rank or position, but because you are a leader of character.
10. Hang Tough!—Never, ever, give up.

MAJOR DICK WINTERS
EASY COMPANY, 506TH PARACHUTE INFANTRY REGIMENT
101ST AIRBORNE DIVISION
BAND OF BROTHERS

Index